DANCING AT CIRO'S

ALSO BY SHEILA WELLER

*Saint of Circumstance: The Untold Story Behind
the Alex Kelly Case: Growing Up Rich and Out of Control*

*Raging Heart: The Intimate Story of the Tragic Marriage
of O. J. and Nicole Brown Simpson*

*Marrying the Hangman:
A True Story of Privilege, Marriage and Murder*

Hansel & Gretel in Beverly Hills
(a novel)

DANCING AT

Ciro's

A Family's Love, Loss, and Scandal
on the Sunset Strip

SHEILA WELLER

St. Martin's Press
New York

Grateful acknowledgment to Burt Boyar and Farrar, Straus and Giroux for permission
to reprint excerpts of *Yes I Can* by Sammy Davis, Jr. and Jane and Burt Boyar.
Copyright © 1965 by Sammy Davis, Jr., Jane Boyar, and Burt Boyar.
Reprinted by permission of Farrar, Straus and Giroux, LLC.

Photo of Marilyn Monroe and Herman Hover on page 259 courtesy of Reggie Drew.
All other photographs in the text are from the personal collection of the author.

All endpaper photos courtesy of Reggie Drew, except for: photographs of the author's
family, which are from the personal collection of the author; newspaper announcement
of the marriage of Herman D. Hover and Yvonne Ealy courtesy of the Hearst
Corporation; photo of Helen Weller and Mrs. Sonny Tufts reprinted with
permission from Hachette Filipacchi Media U.S., Inc.

Materials from *Screen Life, Screen Book,* and *Motion Picture* magazines reprinted
with permission from Hachette Filipacchi Media U.S., Inc.

www.stmartins.com

ISBN 0-312-24176-3

First Edition: February 2003

10   9   8   7   6   5   4   3   2   1

For Liz, with love.
We got through it, and we got the best from them . . .
which we passed on to our three wonderful children.

CONTENTS

My eye was caught by something shining in the bottom of the ditch. I reached my hand down and picked it up; it made my heart thump for I was certain it was gold. Then I saw another.

—SAWMILL CONSTRUCTION ENGINEER

JAMES MARSHALL, 1848

For we were the luckiest Jews who ever lived. We are even the spoiled brats of Jewish history.

—ESSAYIST AND PUBLIC INTELLECTUAL

LEON WIESELTIER, 2002

DANCING AT CIRO'S

Introduction

BEVERLY HILLS: JANUARY 8, 1958

For the first twelve years of my life my family enjoyed a kind of blessed existence, and yet, for some reason that I could not articulate, and with no external clues, I was consumed with a prescient dread. "Please let it always be like this," I, a nonreligious child, would murmur to God. "Please let our lives always stay this way."

My father, whom I adored, was a charismatic neurosurgeon, one of only about fifteen practicing in Los Angeles County and only about 520 at work in the entire country at the time. He performed the most intense and complex operations, often saving, sometimes losing, lives—neurosurgery was a risky business in those days. On Sunday he was a "Man of the Sea," the proud captain of our seventy-foot sailing sloop, the *Manuiwa*. Trimming main and jib sheets, listing to port and starboard, our family, wet and laughing, rode the choppy blue-black sea off Newport Harbor, and when we came back to shore we compared notes with our slipmates, Roy Rogers and Dale Evans.

My mother was a former newspaperwoman, Hollywood columnist, and magazine writer, never quite meant to be the luncheon-going "doctor's wife" the times required her to be—it was a role she performed ambivalently, and badly. Irreverent, funny, and disdainful of all things smug and stuffy, she was a transplanted New Yorker who divided humanity between the go-getting, sparkly "bright" people and the plodding, pitiable "drab" ones. Her brother's nightclub, Ciro's, was the most glamorous nightclub in the world, a driving force in the lore and evolution of Hollywood. My mother was my uncle's business partner; Ciro's was the air our family breathed, a nightly fount of glittery melodrama that could not help but outsparkle every other aspect of our family's life.

I grew up in that nightclub. When I was four and five and six and seven, my mother picked me up after school and drove me to Ciro's, to wait while she huddled deep in business with my uncle in the office upstairs from the kitchen. I'd suck maraschino cherries in Bobby the bartender's long, cavelike service bar, its floorboards marinated with twenty-five years of libations, as humid and perfumed as a rain forest. Then I'd circle the large main room, its round wooden tables naked until roped bundles of linens, tossed in like hay bales by Mexican busboys, were knifed open and flapped over the dark green leather banquettes. I helped Nancy the photographer fold the cardboard photo holders and line up the Ciro's lipsticks on the Dutch doorsill. Then I'd assist Reggie the cigarette girl in stacking the Old Golds and Camels and (brand-new) Marlboros in the tray attached to the velvet rope that she would later wear above her thigh-high skirt and fishnet stockings. Out on the floor, the long-legged girls in toreador pants, with Grace Kelly scarves over hair rollers, huddled with orchestra leader Dick Stabile while mike cords were whipped and baby spots dimmed: These are the Proust's madeleines of my childhood.

The big, two-tiered nightclub bulged with secrets; you could tell from the almost theatrical circumspection of Johnny the maître d', whose impeccable graciousness and not-quite-sardonic expression told you he'd seen everything and then some. Much later, he told me some of what he'd sealed his lips to: that Walter Winchell consistently came in with Marilyn Monroe, and that the two sat huddled all night at a tiny table. Winchell was so powerful their dates never got into the papers. He told me that Sammy Davis Jr. was indeed forced by Harry Cohn to break up with Kim Novak, and that the entertainer was so upset about Cohn's order that he sobbed backstage, uncontrollably. He also said that Frank Sinatra, melancholic after Ava Gardner left him, used to get drunk at the club and once took a few swings in the lobby at a reporter who dared notice.

The very air of Ciro's was charged with a sensuality that even a child could feel—its booths draped with exotic-smelling people who tossed their heads carelessly, smoked their cigarettes deliberately, and cuddled close together (mink stoles slipping off shoulders), laughing as if at a series of very private jokes. Insinuation, flirtation, irony, and (when Peggy Lee, Billy Eckstine, or Nat King Cole performed) a delicious pathos perfused the room. Ciro's was a place of sublime conceit—a diorama celebrating clever people's ability to restyle themselves according to their passions. It was heady, but also unsettling: Amid those louche patrons, my "normal" family seemed emotionally ingenuous, too naive to withstand the buffeting of a hedonism they could admire and mimic but whose inner rules and secret safety valves they could not fathom. Despite my youth, I sensed that when you live your life in a Hollywood nightclub, whether you're prepared or not, your life is destined to follow the curve of the melodrama. That is why, on the drive home after the first show, I—a sleepy passenger, twisting in the backseat, gazing at the bucket of lights past the undulating ridge of Sunset Boulevard—would intone that strange prayer, "Please let it always stay this way . . ."

January 8, 1958, was an unseasonably warm winter evening, even for Southern California. A record-breaking eighty-degree afternoon had yielded to an evening still warm enough for me to go up the flagstone walk from the car to the house with no sweater over my cap-sleeved cotton shirtwaist. That dress, which I wore collar turned up with a scarf tied around my neck, must have been navy blue or burgundy, because my sister Lizzie and I were going to dinner with our father, a man equally merry and authoritarian, who liked us to dress like East Coast private school girls: tailored, in sharp white and—only solid—dark colors.

As a man of serious accomplishment ensconced, by way of marriage, within a show business family, my father, Daniel Weller, was a picture of ambivalence. He was seduced by that world, but he also stood apart from it, viewing himself, with a cocky and sometimes bitter pride, as the lone representative of worthy pursuit in a swelling pond of frivolity. His clothes policy was one small way he could put his stamp on his progeny and trumpet a sensibility more refined than that of his obtrusively famous brother-in-law, Ciro's owner, Herman Hover.

If there was a secret tension in our family's life, now bubbling up from just below the surface, waiting for a seminal event to spark a family holocaust long in the making, well, everything until this moment did a good job of obscuring it. The childhood years Lizzie and I were leaving behind us—she was ten, I was twelve—could have been plucked from both an *Our Gang* and *Our Town* rerun: The Adohr man left bottles of milk on our back porch every morning; the Wonder Bread bakery sat on Little Santa Monica between Elm and Foothill, just over the railroad tracks, where a freight train toot-tooted as it rumbled through daily. You could buy warm bread straight from the bakery's foreman. Beverly Hills was just waking up from its slumber as a sweet, almost dowdy, small town.

Our neighborhood, the Beverly Hills Flats, spanning twenty-two streets (running the virtual length, but not width, of the city, from

Doheny on the east to Whittier on the west), had a coziness to it. It was a patchwork of friendly and lavish houses, from forties Hollywood ranch to Tudor to Spanish to modern to what we called Early American. (The faux chateaux and other monstrosities that would soon make Beverly Hills a laughingstock had not yet been constructed.) Lizzie and I would walk five blocks to Hawthorne School, an Alhambran Spanish edifice with arched patios and a fountained courtyard, pulling on the bougainvillea vines that grew springy and wild all over our neighbors' stucco garden walls. Sometimes, as night fell, I'd walk the half-mile length of Elm Drive, from Carmelita to Sunset and back, making up stories in my head as the shadows of the canopying leaves thrust witchy handmarks on the sidewalk and the lights snapped on in kitchen after kitchen, where maids and cooks stuffed chafing dishes and put vegetables in pressure cookers.

On these sheltered, unassuming roads and drives, movie stars lived like regular people. Elizabeth Taylor's mother had a forties ranch house a half block from us. On the day Michael Todd was killed in a plane crash, his young widow took to her bed inside, while press photographers clogged the street in their snub-nosed cars. A couple of doors north resided the Robert Youngs; his shiny-haired daughter would bound through their white picket fence in her saddle shoes and Marymount pinafore. Danny Thomas and his family had the southeast corner house on Elm and Elevado; the illuminated Nativity crèche mounted on their lawn every Christmas drew visitors, like pilgrims, from far-off neighborhoods. The Thomas home was ringed by a flagstone ledge where Ralph Edwards's daughter Laurie and I used to sit after school, making up dirty lyrics to "April Love" and "The Purple People Eater." Around the corner, on Maple between Elevado and Lomitas, America's most adorable newlyweds, Debbie Reynolds and Eddie Fisher, dwelled—right under the watchful eyes of neighbor Louella Parsons. A block east, in the 600s of Palm, next door to my best friend Phyllis Perrin, lived the flamboyantly loving couple Esther Williams and Fernando Lamas. "Hello, darling!" "Hahlo, dahlink!" they would trill out to each other throughout the day. (Years later, Williams wrote that Lamas had kept her captive in that house.) At Sunset and Elm was Johnny Mathis's Moorish villa, bought by his manager since Realtors wouldn't sell Negroes houses in Beverly Hills. A few blocks west, up Bedford (Uncle Herman's street), Lana Turner lived with Johnny Stompanato, an untrustworthy beau if ever there was one. When the pair went to Ciro's together, Stompanato would attempt to seduce Uncle Herman's cigarette girl, our family friend Reggie Drew, whenever Turner ducked into the ladies' room.

My mother, father, sister, and I inhabited a big, unhandsome house—520 North Elm—between Santa Monica and Carmelita. It was originally Spanish, but my parents, like everyone else at the time, had squared off all the rounded arches and demolished the back rooms—constructing instead a huge, dramatic, sextagonal "lanai" with sleek, pole-legged furniture on a floor of black and white tiles. In one corner of the room was a wet bar studded with Ciro's highball, gimlet, martini, and champagne glasses and tumblers (nobody ever had wine, except for Mogen David), and—probably a gift from one of my father's patients—a gigantic swiveling vat of Drambuie, which occasioned many a Kodachrome of Lizzie and me extravagantly impersonating drunkards. Thickly impastoed Utrillo knockoffs of Parisian street scenes and artily framed Degas lithographs of preening dancers were grouped on three white-grasscloth-wallpapered walls. The other three walls, all glass, were hugged by a tangled mass of tropical plants, banana fronds, and honeysuckle. Out one glass door, pink flagstone steps led down to the turquoise swimming pool, to the bougainvillea-trellised "monkey house" (a wonderful weathered wood gazebo painted with a faded jungle motif, where we barbecued), and to the fiberglass-roofed patio and dressing rooms, which we'd annointed "the cabanas."

We were a jazzy, happy, upper-middle-class Jewish L.A. family: always entertaining with the record player perennially spinning (a half dozen Decca and RCA Victor 45s piled up around its fat center spool), and Lizzie and I inflicting upon our parents' guests a constant round of musicals, water ballets, and hula hoop competitions. Like most of their peer group, my parents trusted Edward R. Murrow, voted for Adlai Stevenson, and worshipped Jonas Salk. They made cracks about everyone's reliance on Miltown (that formidable grandparent to Prozac and Valium), smiled knowingly at Mort Sahl's "neurotic" humor, and laughed out loud at Mel Brooks's and Carl Reiner's "The Two Thousand-Year-Old-Man." Humor was their most cherished value—after accomplishment.

For all their 1950s sophistication, my parents always had a wistfulness about them. In the case of my father, whose heart had been impaired in childhood, that anger-tinged sorrow may have been caused by his habit of imagining the good days left of a life that he knew would be short. My mother's melancholic irony may have come from the fact that she and her brother—the two middle siblings among four—had somehow walked into halcyon lives while their sister and brother had perished. Then again, perhaps my parents' wistfulness was tribal—a sense that, as Southern California Swimming Pool Jews (as their cohort might be called), they were inhabiting a realm of blithe living of which they had no race memory. Maybe their hearts were uncomfortably light. Maybe they felt lonely with their fortune.

The adults in my family belonged to the progression of East

Coast Jews who bobbed their noses and changed their names and migrated west between the wars, hoping to partake of the dazzle of the burgeoning entertainment industry. Or, like my father, they spearheaded the first generation of American Jews to break through the barricades and win distinction within the elite medical specialties, some of the more cutting-edge of which (my father's, for one) were in their own exciting infancy.

Much has been written about the freighted phenomenon of exodus to California, the promised land of golden possibilities, where fame and wealth awaited the intrepid—a place for starting over. The early homesteaders came for the cheap orchard land; the gold prospectors, in search of riches; the "Okies," to escape the devastation of the Dust Bowl; the moviemakers, from Chicago and New York, for 350 days a year of sunshine—the better to weave their webs of fantasy. The New York Jews, in the 1930s, came there to complete the metamorphosis they had begun in Brooklyn and on Broadway—trading, in the course of a single generation, centuries of one way of living and thinking for a new way.

If New York was a culture and an ocean away from the tragic inevitabilities that brewed in Europe over the ages, from which their own parents had fled, then California seemed *two* cultures away— an ocean plus a continent. To the migrating New York Jews like my parents, California felt like home base. Arriving there symbolized beating the odds and beating the system.

It took several cycles of self-invention for my father, my mother, and my uncle to become who they were in 1958. My mother had metamorphosized from a provincial Brooklyn girl to a Broadway reporter to a chronicler of Hollywood romances, marriages, careers, and scandals—and then to a nightclub coowner. My father had evolved from the severely afflicted son of a ne'er-do-well cavalry bugler–turned–underwear salesman to a prominent member of the elite club of neurosurgery, arguably the most difficult medical specialty. My uncle had transformed himself from a bourgeois Jewish boy to a tap and ballet dancer, Broadway stage manager, and speakeasy choreographer, and then to the owner of a legendary nightclub.

Still, they were innocents. The moxie that catapulted them into this new world was rooted in the old one. The very structures and qualities that enabled their success—the close-knit family's doubling as creative and economic unit, the secret superiority complex, the almost genetically based jumpy vigilance—also contained, in this new setting and time, the seeds of their destruction. Their constant exposure to glamour and hedonism would not immunize them from anxiety, pessimism, and ultimately loss; it only gave them a higher ledge from which to fall. So my parents' wistfulness—which set my mother's voice to cracking as she sang Gershwin songs and had my father squinting meditatively over his ever-present pipe—like my own childhood dread, seems clairvoyant: the trembling of small animals sensing the onset of a natural disaster.

Most days after school, Lizzie and I and our friends would "go into Beverly," as everyone called the process of visiting the shopping streets—Canon and especially Beverly Drive, between Little Santa Monica and Wilshire. Going into Beverly in the 1950s was to enter a world of almost hysterical winsomeness. The streets were full of sweet shops—See's Candies, with its trademark picture of a beatific grandmother adorning its shiny white wall and white boxes; Wil Wright's, with its dainty chairs and tiny marble tables and button-sized macaroons wrapped in their own little waxed-paper envelopes; and Blum's, with its nodding Dutch girls and almondette sundae. We'd stop at the soda fountain of either Gunther's or Whelan's for milk shakes; at Pixie Town and Bobbi Teen we'd try on clothes; at the Gramophone Shop we'd sit in a glass booth and listen to "Heartbreak Hotel" and "Stagger Lee." At the center of our little downtown was the Oriental-domed Beverly Theater, which, on January 8, 1958, featured the two biggest movies in the country, *Peyton Place* and *The Ten Commandments*, their themes—untrammeled passion and religious constraint—echoed the warring sensibilities of the 1950s.

On January 8, Lizzie and I didn't go into Beverly after school but came straight home to go to dinner with our father, at Ah Fong's, a Chinese restaurant that was considered top-rate and served ketchup with its egg rolls. We were closer than preteenaged sisters usually are, even though (or maybe because) we were temperamentally and physically opposite: I was light haired, blue eyed, high strung, talkative, seemingly bratty but secretly earnest, naive, and bereft of self-entitlement; Lizzie was brown haired, brown eyed, shy, self-possessed, seemingly very vulnerable but actually steely, shrewd, and self-preserving. My little sister's bout with polio gave her a saintly glow, and I would huddle near that light, both to assuage my guilt at having somehow deflected the dread disease from myself and bounced it on to her, and to try to cadge some goodness by association.

When our father arrived, he rang the bell rather than use his key: our first intimation of the gathering storm. Our mother, seated straight-backed at the Steinway, didn't turn to greet him. A heartful if not truly gifted pianist, she usually leaned langorously over the keys and half hummed, half sang, as she played with abandon. But today—stiff and taut, ramrodded by some unnameable pain—she kept hammering out "The Morris Dance" over and over and over, in one octave and then another. At the end of each stanza, she would lift her curved fingers an inch from the keys and her feet from the pedals, hold them frozen for excruciating seconds in desperate search of an unmined octave. Then, failing to find one, she would repeat the piece in the same key, crashing the ivories nervously, hitting the wrong chords, her thick breathing and the panicky flutters of her eyelids beating out a Morse code: "I *know* how awkward and tense this is! But ignore it—*please* ignore it!"

I divined from my mother's face, as I had on other occasions, that she was afraid of my father. (Fifties family life, with its separate realms for adults and children, allowed only for guessing what it meant when the air in the marital room changed temperature.) But there was something bigger than fear here now (was that plaguelike force that my mother and her friends sometimes whispered about— the "nervous breakdown"—descending?), and I struggled to comprehend it from its markers. Whatever was happening, as this agonizing prelude to our dinner with Daddy eked out—minute by self-conscious minute—it became clear that my mother's desperation was increasing in inverse proportion to my father's diffidence, and his power.

I dared not shift my gaze to Lizzie, for then she would see we were thinking the same thing. Through the instinctual communication of young siblings, we had understood that the melancholy our father nursed, the hauteur he appropriated, were signs of disaffection. Deep down we feared we could not hold him, so we stiffened and avoided each other's eyes like little English bobbies.

At Ah Fong's our father was distant and angry. Vague anger was a card that he kept at the top of his deck; my mother, sister, and I were given to understand it was an offshoot of his hard work, bad heart, recent heart attack, and bleeding ulcers attack, so we accepted it uncomplainingly. I sat there, in my little navy or burgundy "tailored" dress with a scarf around my neck, talking too much, too fast, vainly trying to inject some light into the void of his preoccupied silence. As we labored over the spare ribs and won tons and ketchuped egg rolls, the owner came to our table, and the opportunity to charm changed my father's mood. The owner, putty in Daddy's practiced hand, sat down and laughed with him. People often did that. He had a mischievous smile and bright blue eyes, a roguish streak and a Talmudic sorrow: He drew people to him with a lazy confidence. Yet to me he was growing unreachable; it was seemingly impossible for me to make him love me.

I sat in the backseat on the way home, as Lizzie took her turn in front. As she talked to our father quietly, easing from him a gentleness and interest that I could not inspire, I contemplated the interior of the Chrysler Imperial: the tufted upholstery, the silver knobs and ashtrays, my father's bald spot, his weary, steely eyes in the rearview mirror. *Is this how you lose your father?* I thought. *Without being told, without knowing why?* Too soon he pulled up in front of the house, idling the car as we got out, impassively receiving our anxious kisses.

Shaken by his indifference, I didn't notice the other car—the hidden car—parked in the shadows across the street. I made my way up our flagstone path, some fifty feet long, with Lizzie limping behind me. The house was dark; our mother had gone out. Our housekeeper, Jenny, was in her room, near the kitchen.

I walked inside, but some impulse compelled Lizzie to turn around and look back. She saw our father outside his car, flapping his arms wildly—he was *struggling* with someone! Lizzie scurried back down the path toward him. Seeing her approach, my father called out, "Lizzie! Come here! Open the glove compartment! *I have a gun in the glove compartment!*"

Terrified, my sister hurried toward our grunting father. He was heaving off the hulking man, who was scrambling for his throat and tearing at his clothing. Lizzie managed to wrench open the passenger-side door and click the latch of the glove compartment. Our father hurtled over with the attacker on top of him, yanked out the gun, and shoved it in the man's face, kicking him down to the ground by the car's back tire. "Don't! Don't!" my sister screamed to the attacker. "He's a *wonderful* man! *Don't hurt him!*" Impervious to my sister's admonition and the gun, the assailant kept coming, pulling my father down and pummeling him.

Roused by my sister's screams and the war yelps of our frightened cats, I ran outside just in time to see the jettisoned gun fly low across the curved asphalt, then smash with a harsh clink against where curb met gutter. My father and the other man were fighting, rolling, tumbling, grunting—like bears—before my horrified eyes. Rolling, grunting man-bears whose disjointed moving body parts were bizarrely strobed by the heavenly flecked white from the beveled-glass street lamps.

I ran, with my heart stilled.

By the time I got close, my father was flat on his back in the street, not moving. His eyes were half rolled up in his head, which was bibbed by his vomited blood. I leaned over him, blubbering tears and mucus onto his still face, unable to believe that this was *him* now—unable to believe this was happening. His lashes grazed my cheeks like baby bird's wings. I sobbed hysterically.

"Call an ambulance," he whispered. Then he commanded hoarsely, "Call the police. That *sonuvabitch*."

Neighbors were inching out of their front doors, pools of light behind them, hugging themselves as if it were cold. I ran back into the house and called the police, even as I heard, in the distance, the wail of a siren already coming to the rescue. All of a sudden Jenny the housekeeper ran out of the house as well, improbably shouting, in her Slavic accent, "I am in love with the doctor!" The strange confession of this homely woman had nothing to do with events, except it told me, with a kind of slap on the face of my mind, how attractive my father was to women.

Several neighbors had interceded. Two held the assailant in place, another bent over my father and tried to revive him, but the assailant broke free and went after my father again. Then the police came and slapped him into handcuffs.

The assailant was my uncle.

Later that night my mother would learn how her world had been torn in two as cleanly as a melon whacked by a cleaver. Two days later the rest of Los Angeles would get the news, under a headline on the *Times*'s front page, "Ciro's Owner Arrested Wrestling with His Brother-in-Law on Lawn."

The newspaper recounted:

The two girls . . . summoned police.

When Officer W. F. Franklin arrived he saw the pair wrestling on the ground. The doctor's face, he said, was covered with blood and Hover was choking him. Hover was taken into custody and Dr. Weller, who suffered a heart attack, was . . . transferred to Cedars of Lebanon Hospital. . . .

Later the nightclub owner was released on $250 bail supplied by Capt. Horace Brown, husband of Marion Davies.

If his attack on my father had been gross and public, the reason for it was a secret that Uncle Herman seemed determined to guard. The newspaper story continued:

Hover refused to discuss the incident when he appeared in Beverly Hills Municipal Court yesterday, explaining only it would "make things worse by talking about it."

The next day Lizzie and I visited our father. He was under an oxygen tent in the Cedars of Lebanon intensive care unit. Rabbit pale, he lay as tautly sealed as long-stemmed roses in a florist's box. "I love you," I said, the moistness of my face clouding the clear plastic between us. The tubes in him kept him from saying those same words back, but I felt them when he nodded.

I was still nursing that warmth when I got home and saw my mother, sitting stuporous by the telephone. The nervous breakdown she had been trying to keep at bay was about to come trampling through her mind. She was shaking her head, as if helplessly denying a charge (which she was), but her overwide mouth and eyes suggested that what she had learned was a truth even worse than the lie she was combating. When I found out what it was, I wanted to die. In terms of my relationship with my father, it would, indeed, turn out to be fatal.

I'm now older than my parents were when their world blew up. From the distance of a few decades I can squint and see our lives, and our cascade of calamities, as true to a type, representative of an almost hidden category of American family. I've crossed paths with many New York-to-Hollywood early midcentury Jewish families with similar brio—and similar casualties. Different in so many outward ways, these people seem to pop into my life at odd angles and moments, and, however haphazard and casual the connection, I understand immediately (and often they do, too) what we have in common: my sister's childhood best friend, whose actress mother grandiosely killed herself—and whose screenwriter father followed suit, albeit more quietly, a year later; my mother's chums, with their clanking bracelets, showbiz pasts, and stints in sanitariums; the composer ex-husband of my close friend who bridged his parents' histrionic divorce with coast-to-coast train rides; and the woman I met twelve years ago in the West Village playground where our young sons played. Her Brooklyn-born musician father had been my mother's first beau's brother. There had been dazzling accomplishment in her family, too, then destruction, and finally her mother's suicide.

This archetypal family has, I've come to see, certain hazy stock characters. There's the Abrahamic figure, the Glamorizer—the man who, through his talent and fortune, moved the family west and pushed them all out past their timorous parameters, their hereditary plainness and bookishness. There's the Perfectionist, the Tortured Soul: At once tempted and insulted by the new values, he is alienated and wounded and superior. There's also the Female Partner, thrilled by the promise of the new life—until she realizes her nervous system and her program is overmatched by the milieu. Having grown up absorbing the lessons of a sensible, domineering woman who controlled her husband as her mother had controlled *her* husband, she is lost now that the mold has been broken. She is at once too controlling and too vulnerable, and she is of genetic stock that can compete in almost every arena, except the one that is overrepresented in her new surroundings: physical beauty. She becomes the Hysteric.

All it takes to wreak havoc in these lives is a trigger: a malady, physical or emotional, or a character flaw—vanity, jealousy, womanizing. If womanizing is the trigger, chances are that for this group the woman will be another stereotypical character: the beautiful, cold-hearted shiksa.

"Please let our lives always stay this way," I had prayed as a child, intuiting even then that things could not stay as they were. I wonder now: Did I understand the contours of my parents' journey? Did I sense the archetypes they were inhabiting?

So many people of my parents' generation fashioned lives for themselves through joyously radical self-invention. Change, for whatever it cost them, was their wellspring. They were supreme romantics: believing, literally, in the power of love and romance (my mother), the power of aspiring to mastery of the noblest, most difficult, and perhaps the craziest, work (my father), the power of creating a place—a space, a dreamlike world—that transported and entertained others (my uncle).

The adults in my family had migrated to the golden land on the warm, young coast and remade themselves as dashing, bright new people, but they could never escape their heavy, responsible, Old World souls. They would die in those old souls, finally.

This book is an investigation of my father's, mother's, and uncle's voyage to the new world, a personal look at that unique subculture of Southern California Jews near and at midcentury. It was a world built on verve, through leaps of faith, but with big gaps between hubris, spirit, and work ethic, on the one hand, and the subversive laws unto themselves of temptation, mystique, and beauty on the other. It was a world that was triumphantly glittering but ultimately brittle.

For some, that world was durable. For others, like my family, it proved to be a way station between gorgeous opportunity and almost biblical calamity. I always told myself that when I was old enough to take these grown-ups who'd held my childhood world aloft (and then let it crash into a million pieces) and view them as if they were my own younger siblings, I would go back through what records and memories existed and examine what happened to them, as much journalist as daughter.

This is my love letter to them.

Part I

Chapter One

Though my mother and father would not cross paths until they moved to Hollywood as young adults, they grew up a mile from each other in and near Brownsville and East New York. The neighborhood was a launching pad from which the sons and daughters (American-born, unaccented, regular Yankee Doodle Dandies) of immigrants from the shtetls and ghettos of Europe were expected to shoot like rockets from the shoulders of their peddler, tailor, and shopkeeper fathers and pierce the professional stratosphere.

My mother's parents, the Zlotchovers, law student–turned businessman Isidore and his artistic wife Celia, both from Austria, were more prosperous than many. When Isidore left insurance for the field he eventually prospered in—real estate—the family purchased a lovely Georgian house on Arlington Avenue in the elite, near-pastoral Brooklyn neighborhood called Highland Park. They moved their brood in: Shirley (born in 1903), Herman (in 1905), my mother, Helen (in 1911), and Leonard (in 1913). The house's parlor was walled in floor-to-ceiling mirrors, installed during the room's former life as a ballroom, giving the family area a theatrical cast. Celia and Isidore rented its upstairs apartment to local clergyman Rabbi Sachs. The Hovers moved there in 1916. Woodrow

Wilson was president. The Great War was under way. My mother was five.

I am named for Shirley Hover. Shirley, Sheila, and our mutual Hebrew name, Shelka: the three *shhh* sounds, so rich in appeasement, warning, and secrecy, neatly lined up. Shirley is the only name by which I ever heard mention of my mother's sister when I was young, yet in the last ten years of my mother's and uncle's lives—when, aswim in the soupy timelessness of old age, they would banter about events that had occurred seventy-five years earlier—I'd hear them call her Sadie, the name they'd called her by when they were all children. She had been "Shirley" in their dealings with the assimilated world, the aspired-to world, but Sadie was her ethnic name, her "home name." When, in their twilight years, long after the uniquely simultaneous failure of both of their marriages, my uncle and mother spoke of "Sadie," I heard the name as a poignant marker for the integrity of their original family—a symbol of the innocent, original Brooklyn selves they had so imperfectly grown beyond.

My mother worshipped her older sister. They even looked alike, with their father's relatively light coloring and sharply peaked eyebrows, like upside-down Vs, set unusually high over their sleepy, sloe eyes. (Herman and Leonard—square jawed, swarthy, with eyes like wet, black olives—resembled their mother.) On Friday night, Helen would study Sadie standing at the head of the table, next to their mother, swirling and swirling her open-fingered hands in front of her tightly closed eyes, reciting prayers over the candles. Soon enough my mother would benignly reject those Jewish rituals that Sadie's earnest Shabbas incantation embodied, yet she never lost her superstitious nature, and I think those memories of Sadie's prayers were her soul's collateral: a keepsake faith, stored in an imaginary drawer in the heart for Helen's emergency use.

On Saturday night, the mirrored parlor would fill with boys in newsboy caps and knee-banded trousers and girls in middy blouses over petticoated skirts. From her upstairs bedroom, Helen would thrill to the catchy sounds of "Hindustan" issuing tinnily from the megaphone speaker of the talking machine, directing the *clip! clip! clip!* of a dozen young feet.

Celia, an emotional and domineering woman, used her self-appointed role as the family's seamstress to control her progeny. She was always sitting at her magisterial sewing machine. Her insistence on making nearly all her daughters' garments was a corraling gesture by which she literally took the measure of her brood. With eight-years-older Sadie, Helen could break free.

Sadie took Helen on after-school forays to procure exotic items—

a corset with waist stays, filmy envelope chemises, shiny, grooved, orchestra recordings of fox-trot tunes. At the pharmacy Sadie bought violet talcum, which she later dabbed on her little sister when she stepped out of the claw-footed bathtub. Helen was very self-conscious about a light streak of pigmentation that zigzagged down one leg from thigh to knee. (As a result of her shame at exposing it, she never learned to swim.) Celia had wrung her hands and taken Helen to doctors while her mother, Rose, who lived with the family, bewailed the birthmark as an ill omen by the Dybbuk. Sadie made Celia and Rose leave Helen alone; she swabbed her sister's stain with concealing lotion, then combed the tangles out of Helen's wet hair. The yanking was a small price to pay for closeness.

In retrospect, I can see so many vestiges of Sadie in my mother's life. It was Sadie who taught my mother to read music. The budding star in the family, Sadie was taking piano lessons with Edward Morris at the Brooklyn Conservatory of Music; she seemed on her way to becoming a concert artist. Dignified and feminine (in contrast to her impatient, aggressive younger sister), the young teenage Sadie would sit on the piano stool, playing Mendelssohn, Grieg, and Chopin for one hour each morning before school and two hours again at night. Then Sadie would reset the metronome for her sister. As it ticked, she'd place her hands over Helen's smaller ones, whispering, "Andante," "Rondo," "Pianissimo."

All her life, my mother's moments at the piano seemed regenerative and transporting. Leaning her whole body over those keys, attacking the sweeping chords of Gershwin and Brahms, and even Gilbert and Sullivan, she'd become another person—stately, meditative, almost somber. That change in her used to puzzle me, but now I understand. She was channeling her sister.

It would be popular, not classical, music that would set the Zlotchovers' future course. Isidore sang popular songs—"straight from the heart, beating time with his hands," my uncle Herman recalled in his unpublished memoir. " 'Any Little Girl That's a Nice Little Girl Is the Right Little Girl for Me,' 'I Tore Up Your Picture When You Said Good-bye but I Put It All Together Again,' and 'Who Put the Overalls in Mrs. Murphy's Chowder?' He would finish them with an 'Off to Buffalo' shuffle, his face agleam as he stuck out his hand like a typical vaudevillian."

Vaudeville had sprung up in the 1890s and was in its heydey during the late nineteen-teens. It was a form of popular theatrical revue consisting of eight to fourteen carefully integrated "turns," often featuring acrobats and animals as well as dancers, singers, comics, and musicians. Vaudeville's reigning impresario was Benjamin Franklin Keith, who owned three theaters in Brooklyn alone: the Orpheum, Bushwick, and Prospect. The most popular acts appeared on B. F. Keith's stages: the Avon Comedy Four, Julian Eltinge, Blackstone the Magician, and such soon-to-be stars as child actress Helen Hayes and the teenaged Jimmy Durante. Salami sandwiches tucked in their pockets, Sadie, Herman, Helen, and Lenny—fourteen, twelve, six, and four—would stream down the Orpheum's aisles for the Saturday "Four-a-Day." After the last act of the first show (an intentional dud called "playing to the haircuts," because it caused people to turn and leave), the kids clambered down from the mezzanine. "We watched the second show," continues Herman's remembrance, "smack up against the orchestra pit." To his siblings, these afternoons were amusement, but to Herman they were a summons to his true vocation. He was expected to embrace the legal profession his father had spurned, yet he had fallen madly in love with the musical theater.

"No one could understand how fascinated I was with vaudeville," my uncle wrote. He'd memorize the dance steps and, once home, face the parlor mirror for hours, perfecting his heel-and-toe alternation, his cane- and hat-handling. Then came floor back bends and acrobatics. "I trained myself to stand on my head and swing by my knees from a trapeze. I juggled apples, oranges, rolled-up sox, knives, and forks, until I could juggle four objects at once." At night he'd place his "lucky" tap shoes—worn at the sides, ribbons frayed, heavy as barbells—by his bedroom door, far from the window so the cold wouldn't crack them.

Herman often shared his routines with the family, inviting their participation. My mother remembered that he would perform the trademark "waltz clog" of the elegant Pat Rooney, the Fred Astaire of his day, while she, Sadie, and Lenny sang "She's the Daughter of Rosie O'Grady." These were among her happiest moments. During these collaborations, the idea of the family as an entertainment-producing community took root in her heart.

While Herman was laboring to become an entertainer, the rest of the Zlotchover family underwent a more subtle transformation that more firmly staked their claim on the New World. On my mother's seventh birthday—January 10, 1918—in front of the justice of the Kings County Supreme Court, Isidore stood, "praying," as the court papers put it, "for leave to change his name from that of Isidore Zlotchover to Isidore Hover." The request was granted. The family felt exonerated from their "Hun" name, cleansed of its unpronounceability, liberated from their thick ethnicity. With this move, they shed the remnants of their immigrant status. Now they were a wholly *American* family.

On the heels of this good feeling came unsettling events. Spanish influenza had begun rolling down the Eastern seaboard after having been carried ashore by returning soldiers. The disease could be low-grade, or it could be quickly lethal, often by way of its side effect—pneumonia. It was this latter strain that had caused Army Surgeon General Victor Vaughan to note, of one fort, "Every bed is full yet others crowd in. In the morning the dead bodies are stacked about the morgue like cordwood." It was this strain that hit New York in the late summer of 1918.

Thousands of people fell ill and died around the city during September. Along with lists of local boys killed or missing in action, the newspapers published daily front-page articles about the rapacious advance of Spanish influenza. The city's health commissioner, Dr. Royal Copeland, attempted to stave off panic with frequent announcements that the epidemic had crested. He issued daily edicts and advisories such as: suggesting that women wear veils to shield themselves against the bacteria; threatening to close movie theaters whose owners disobeyed the new sanitation codes; and conducting a "war against spitting" by taking offenders to court.

Even though influenza cases took a sharp jump in the city on October 4, the health commissioner decreed that the situation had not yet reached the point where schools, churches, and theaters had to be shuttered. Any adult could voluntarily refrain from attending a movie palace or house of worship, but children had to go to school. They were the epidemic's captives.

On the afternoon of October 7, 1918, Sadie came home from school sick. She took to her bed. The family physician was summoned. He, Celia, and Isidore entered Sadie's bedroom—and stayed there. My mother, seven years old, went to bed in her room, across the hall from Sadie's. It was hard to sleep, she recalled, with her parents talking so emotionally and light from Sadie's room beaming across the landing. At intervals she opened her eyes and the light was still there—a stern yellow shaft, aggressively spilling under the door and creeping out over Helen's floor.

Herman, six years older, was much more aware of the nature of the crisis. "I had been sent to bed but I could see through the open door of my bedroom three specialists in the parlor," he wrote in his memoir. "They were talking in whispers. Mama walked in. A breeze blew in through the open window. It felt as though there was somebody in the room I couldn't see. I fell asleep but soon awakened. The breath in my sister's chest sounded as if it was choking her. Then there was subdued sobbing."

Herman knew Sadie was dead. He went to Helen's room, woke her, and told her. They fell upon each other and cried, their grief and incomprehension forging a bond that would never be broken.

That early tragedy informed my mother's life. The sudden loss of the nourishing intimacy she had with Sadie would leave her with a hunger for a continuation of that truncated relationship—a hunger she couldn't fill through my father but tried to fill through me, and I through her. It was a hunger that led her periodically to announce, out of the blue (as if the thought seized her very being), with the hard-sell brio of a toastmaster but also with a stinging sadness, "There is *nothing* like a sister!"

The overnight death of her sister left its handprint on my mother's heart in another way, too: in the form of a terror of middle-distant light. For the rest of her life—when she was twenty-five, thirty-five, fifty, sixty, seventy, when she was *eighty-one* years old—my mother would walk around her house, turning off lights. When I'd come home from college and, later, when I'd visit from New York, I would walk into the house—and the only illumination would be the police-interrogation-harsh cone of light from my mother's gooseneck office lamp. Under it, hunched over her Selectric, she (now, in her dotage, a senior L.A. stringer for the *National Enquirer*) would be pecking out a story, that orb of brightness in the grotto-dark room backlighting her preposterously, like a gold-leaf halo behind the Virgin Mary. Defiantly, I would flick on the lights. She would rise and turn them off again.

Lights across halls were too freighted for my mother to bear—too mocking. It had shocked her to the core that light—world-renewing light—had been the very thing to augur and usher in death. The connection of Sadie's death to light may have also announced a grimmer irony. In the Hovers' elegiac shedding of the frightened shtetl world for a life of assimilation, opportunity, gaiety, and even glamour, this light was the hand that yanked the trespasser back. To my mother, light was like a semaphore, a warning—and an accurate one, borne out by the events of the rest of her life—that sorrow slunk behind the most euphoric times, that life was fraught with treachery.

For me, as well—a girl in L.A., the great-granddaughter of that shtetl world—jarringly persistent light would also feel sadistic, four decades later. This time it wasn't lamplight under doors but sunlight through windows, asking: If your life is so blessed, then why are you so anxious? Then why is there such illness, rejection, and tragedy around you?

Around the same time that my mother was experiencing the seminal event that triggered her melancholy, two blocks south and eight déclassé avenues west of where the Hovers lived, on the tumbledown corner of Bradford Street and Blake Avenue, my father was undergoing the defining experience of his young life: the rheumatic fever he contracted at age nine. He'd had a twin brother who died at birth, so his whole family already regarded him, the youngest child, as the fragile, chosen survivor, worthy of special indulgence, even before he fell ill with the infection that damaged his heart.

When my father talked to me of the symptom-by-symptom advent of his rheumatic fever, he always imbued it with suspense, like an unfolding drama. He spoke of how the skin on his arms, legs, back, and stomach had itched as if he had been bitten by a hundred mosquitoes. Then came the joint aches, as if some invisible culprit had wrenched his elbows and fingers and knees with pliers. During a game of horseshoe tossing on Bradford Street, he had picked up the metal U, but the act of closing his fingers around it proved so excruciating that he dropped it. Amid razzes from the other boys, he collapsed on the stoop, fighting back tears, stiffening his throbbing arms and legs like a tin man.

The most frightening development occurred that evening. His mother, Lena, had drawn a hot bath and left him alone to soak in it. His heart had pounded, seemingly out of control. He had covered his ears to muffle the pounding sound, but, of course, that had only increased the sensation. Loath to call out for his mother, he stepped out of the bath, shrouded himself in the cheesecloth tub curtains, and flopped onto his brother Milton's bed, not waking until the next morning.

That's when the fever spiked. He awoke, the next day, as if afire. He flailed, whimpered, and eventually broke down and screamed. Indomitable Lena ran down the street to the iceman's cart. She ferried back blocks of ice in her apron, chopped them into shards, wrapped them in her good napkins, and laid them on her Daniel's chest, wrists, and forehead. When the ice failed to bring relief, Lena dressed her pained boy and trundled him off to the charity doctor at the settlement house.

When the physician pressed his cold stethoscope to Danny's chest, he detected two murmurs, as well as arterial "pistol shots." An X ray of his heart showed enlargment. The doctor declared that he had a very good chance of contracting chorea.

"And what does this mean?" Lena had asked.

"It is fatal," the doctor had said, within Daniel's earshot.

My father's cool, deliberate style grew in part from his furious resistance to the destiny to which that tactless physician had so bluntly consigned him.

The threat of chorea passed. My father's chore, like that of other children with rheumatic fever at the time, was to pass through the course of the fever's symptoms and then, once recovered, to enjoy his youth and plan his life while waiting for the sentence. It would take ten or twelve years to determine whether the fever had implanted rheumatic disease in a child's heart valves and arteries. If there was no rheumatic disease, the young person had a normal life expectancy. If there *was* rheumatic disease, heart function was crippled and life span was shortened.

By his teens, because of relapses that frequently drove him to bed, Danny Weller would know he was one of the unlucky ones. Back home, Lena Weller administered the "aspirin cure"—large doses of aspirin and a tonic—oil of wintergreen. Danny Weller chugged it down while hating it. "Stay in bed!" Lena ordered.

Like Celia Hover, Lena Rosenbloom Weller was not to be defied. She was unquestionably the roost ruler, staunchly possessive of her four sons. Under her determined ministrations, three of them (Alex, Milton, and Daniel) would turn out to be doctors (the oldest, Harry, became a businessman; daughter Rosie, a schoolteacher)—no thanks at all to their ne'er-do-well father, she would tell you in a stage whisper. Louis Weller, a slight, hawk-nosed, piercing-blue-eyed cantor's son, was, in her view, a kibbitzing slacker. His death certificate eventually listed his profession as "underwear salesman" at Namm's, the department store that Lena's wealthy relatives owned in Brooklyn. But that inglorious end belied his dramatic, romantic past.

When I was a child, my father told me snippets of the tales he'd been told as a child by Louis, tales that, almost unbelievably, cast this slightly built Jewish man, this accented immigrant, as a Wild West horseman. I always assumed they were considerably less fact than fiction, but the tales were so appealing, and my father, despite his sardonic facade, was so enormously invested in them—they were clearly his life's inspiration and the core of his personal mythology—that when I started this book I hesitated to subject them to the scrutiny of research. I knew I would be too uncomfortable to discover they were gross exaggerations.

I needn't have worried. The stories, it turns out, are true.

In 1887, when he was about eighteen, Louis Weller emigrated from the village of Kaidan, Germany (now Lithuania), along with his father, the cantor Toderes Weller (renamed Theodore at Ellis Island), his mother, Miriam (who became Mary), and his three younger siblings. New York City was reeling from the incoming tide of huddled masses; 301,000 steerage passengers had landed the year before. The Lower East Side saw four dozen new cases of smallpox, thirty-two of typhoid, and two hundred of scarlet fever in the month the Wellers arrived. Death from measles and diptheria reached six hundred.

Theodore sang at the pulpit of Congregation B'nai Israel Anshei Kaidan at 87 East Broadway, and the family moved into a crowded old-law tenement around the corner, at 108 Henry Street. To escape the squalor, young men fresh off the boat often worked as servants in the Beaux Arts limestone mansions of the wealthy. In February 1887, the *New York Times* was full of advertisements placed by "respectable" young immigrant males seeking positions as grooms, footmen, valets, waiters, butlers, "useful men," "second men," gardeners, and "man cooks": makers of breads and pastry. Louis Weller worked as a man cook. Then, after two months of kneading dough all day and coming home to an airless room packed with his entire family, he left New York for Baltimore, where, on April 14, he became a private in Troop G of the U.S. Fifth Cavalry and was shipped off to Fort Reno, just west of Oklahoma City.

The plains of Oklahoma were being readied for controlled settlement by would-be homesteaders, but some armed and aggressive "Sooners," their lives still unreconstructed after the Great Depression of 1875, were attempting grabs of the Indian land before the territories were opened. My grandfather would spend five years evicting these Sooners, becoming, in effect, a "good" version of the Cossacks he had fled, protecting the minority population of the plains from the marauding white majority.

Louis became one of his troop's two trumpeters. The other was one Victor Goyer of Detroit. It was Weller's and Goyer's alternating duty to sound the trumpet in the morning, play reveille at sundown and taps at burials, issue a "Charge!" when the unit had to rush across the plains, and another call to signal retreat. Both men rode close by the unit's commander, Captain Edward Hayes, near the front of the three-hundred-yard line of cavalrymen. In a battle or altercation, a soldier 250 yards back might not hear the captain's command, but he could always hear the trumpet.

On April 22, 1889, the territory was officially opened to the homesteaders. On that landmark day, Captain Hayes noted in his logbook, the troop "accompan[ied] a large body of intending settlers on the march through the Cherokee Strip to keep good order and protect property." Or, as my father would put it, relishing the use of cornpone patois, "Your grandpappy opened the gates to Oklahoma."

Adding up all the "Total Distance Marched" columns in the muster rolls that list his name, I compute that my grandfather rode a grand total of 1,244 miles on horseback across the Oklahoma plains. After his honorable discharge, Louis embarked on one last, great adventure: He briefly joined Buffalo Bill's Wild West Show, in which he rode around the ring off-saddle, clinging to the side of a horse, and, during one revolution, bent down and plucked a handkerchief off the ground with his teeth.

He finally returned to conventional life. He went back to Brooklyn and married a girl from the Old Country, Lena Viola Rosenbloom, a pretty, fat-cheeked woman as shrewd and ambitious as he was irresponsible. Louis and Lena then left New York and opened dry goods stores in several mill towns. She paid the bills, signed the leases, bought the stock (while popping out babies). He was the clerk. Their last stop was Vandergrift, Pennsylvania, a couple of cantering-horse hours northeast of Andrew Carnegie's Pittsburgh. Vandergrift was an unexpectedly elegant town laid out by Frederick Law Olmstead under the sponsorship of a wealthy mill owner who sought to use aesthetics to stoke his workers' productivity. Foremen dropped dollars to see Evelyn Nesbit–wanna-bes at the Casino Theater, and the town's boilermakers, shearmen, roughers, cranemen, pipefitters, bricklayers, and molders bought their knickers, caps, waists, and suspenders at Weller Clothing on the town's cobblestoned main street, a half mile from where three huge foundry chimneys were poised like siloed missiles.

It was deep in this bosom of the industrial working class that my father was born, along with his stillborn brother. With Daniel's birth, Lena had too many children to mind to supervise adequately her extra child—her lackadaisical yet increasingly restless husband. Louis missed the adventure of the plains. A notation in the National Archives reveals that he had secretly written to his old commander, Edward Hayes, seeking reassignment, but at that point he was too old, and so the request was denied. Abandoning his hopes for a heroic life, he returned with Lena to Brooklyn and, with help from Lena's relatives, rented a house at 421 Bradford Street. Lena pushed him into the underwear sales job at her family's department store and turned her attention to the more promising males of the family. Bedridden Danny—thirsty to be distracted from his anger and fear and to be transported from his illness—was the willing captive audi-

ence to whom Louis relived his glorious cavalry days at the end of
each soul-numbing day selling union suits.

Those stories saved young Danny from despondency. Delivered
as they were, in the interstices of lucidity between my father's fever,
they probably formed a golden vision of a glamorous rebel life that
he himself could attain. Yet his fascination with his father's past
may have even predated his illness. I have a photograph of him
when he was about two—an adorable child, the Campbell's Soup
child reincarnate, with the roundest face on record. He is standing
on a chair, his right elbow on a table, his right fist propping up his
dreamy face. He's wearing side-laced ankle boots and bandage-thick
leggings, topped by an odd garment. It's an oversize jacket, huge
torsoed and coat length on him, the hem engulfing his knees, the
rolled-back cuffs swallowing his fingers, the wide belt drooping over
his hips.

For years I never knew what that garment was—so comically ill
fitting in an era when portraitists went to pains to supply their
clients with dress-up clothes meant to be taken for their own. But
now, matching the garment against the grainy 1886 photo of the
unsmiling, mustachioed men in their caps and with their rifles, I
recognize it, and I'm tempted to chew on the symbolism: It's the
jacket of his father's dress cavalry uniform.

Chapter Two

NEW YORK: 1919–1932

After Sadie died, melancholy was embedded in the Hover house like dust in the cushions and carpet. Celia was inconsolable, visiting her daughter's grave every day, keening and chanting, "Why did it have to happen?"—seemingly regressed from a passably modern American to her Dybbuk-haunted mother. It was Rabbi Sachs, the Hovers' tenant, who restored Celia's composure. He sat with her hours a day, as much horse whisperer as pastor. His homily that my mother remembered best was a simple one, "When one door closes, another door opens."

The door did appear: Isidore bought Celia a candy store; managing it would distract her from her grief. Away all day, her grip on her children loosened. Helen baby-sat Lenny (often at the Orpheum), reveling in her independence. Herman, freed to refashion himself away from convention, threw himself into dance. He took twice-a-week lessons at Michael's School of Acrobatics and weekly ballet classes with Madame La Sylph, where he proudly mastered the ultimate *entrechat quatre*, crossing and uncrossing his ankles four times in one elevation. One of two males in the class, he would enter and exit the studio as furtively as (as he put it) "a guy making a deal with a narcotics peddler."

In 1923 he entered Columbia College, but his heart remained off campus. He studied voice with John Hutchins, sharing the teacher with a "tall, good-looking but rather somber" young Cockney-accented former Coney Island stilt walker named Archie Leach (later reincarnated as Cary Grant). Twice a week he subwayed to Forty-second Street for lessons with tap-dance king Johnny Boyle. He mastered *wings, pull-backs, trenches* and *falling-off-a-log*; his forte was something called the *twelve-tap pull-back*. He worked out every night. "I never deviated," he wrote, "from my determination to become one of the most versatile dancers in the theatrical profession."

Herman was cast in the ballet of the college's all-male varsity show, Rodgers and Hart's *Half Moon Inn*, which toured over Christmas, playing small cities like Erie and Buffalo. With Prohibition in force, the student cast would sneak out to local speakeasies after showtime, hammering on the doors to wake the watchmen, the experience forging in their minds a lifetime link between nightlife and risk, exclusivity, and secrecy.

The varsity show's final performance was held at the glamorous Waldorf-Astoria Hotel. Isidore, Celia, Helen, and Lenny drove to Manhattan in their Chrysler 70, my sixteen-year-old mother resplendent in her Celia-made version of the Patou "New Pourpre" flapper frock, which she wore with a matching cloche. Herman was a solo principal dancer. Although he wore his lucky tap shoes, he had stage fright. "Onstage, and bathed in the powerful spotlight I felt naked," he wrote. "Only the reflex brought about by the strenuous rehearsing propelled me through to the last bar. After my final back flip, I staggered off the stage and flopped on the floor like a sack of potatoes."

Performing the show in Manhattan was thrilling. The city had become a destination of born cosmopolites from the hinterlands

(Dorothy Parker and Cole Porter) and of songwriters lured by the opportunities afforded by the revolutionary new medium, radio. Stage producers of popular fare were now left to capitalize on the only component of entertainment uncapturable by radio: visual beauty, specifically, female beauty. In this arena one man, the elegant Florenz Ziegfeld, had long been without peer.

The son of a Chicago physician and classical-music-college founder, Ziegfeld had studied music in Europe. During his four years in Paris in the Gay Nineties he fell in love with the *Folies Bergère*, the lavish stage show that featured ribald comedy acts and bejeweled, befeathered, long-legged girls, nude but for mesh and stripes of satin. Returning stateside, he opened his own version, the *Ziegfeld Follies*, on Broadway in 1907. Over time the *Follies* grew more ornate, with Ziegfeld soon spending $200,000 per show at his own theater at Fifty-fourth Street and Sixth Avenue.

In the late nineteen-teens, Ziegfeld acquired a fierce competitor. An ambitious young showman named Earl Carroll, who'd arrived in New York penniless from Pittsburgh in 1913 and had worked for a music publisher, was determined to steal Ziegfeld's thunder. Carroll named his rival spectacle the *Vanities*. (A third contender, George White, made a bid with his *Scandals*.) Carroll, too, had his own theater built—at Fiftieth Street and Seventh Avenue—and flamboyantly overpaid to secure the most beautiful girls ($500 a month to Ziegfeld's $65). Ziegfeld's girls walked spaced apart and essentially nude. Carroll did him one better; he presented a "living curtain" of actually nude beauties.

In June 1926, three months before he was to start Columbia Law School, Herman auditioned for the *Vanities* male chorus line. He'd heard about the casting call from his singing-lesson mate Archie Leach, who was dating one of the chorus girls, Doreen Glover. Herman made the cut. Rehearsals started immediately. It was supposed to be merely a summer job, but it turned out to be the means by which my uncle finally and truly reinvented himself—and irrevocably altered the family's destiny.

The showgirl revues still relied on vaudeville's rhythm and humor as glue and spark; the *Vanities* star was drawling comic Ted Healy, Carroll's answer to Ziegfeld superstar Will Rogers. Healy was foiled by three stooges, bumbling flunkies forever rushing onstage too fast and sacrificing themselves to Healy's comic Houdini stunts. One was a Brillo-haired boy Herman's age, a fellow Brooklynite named Dave Chasen. "Ted worked easylike," Herman recalled. "I associated him with the motto: It is senseless to do anything standing up that can be done sitting or anything sitting that can be done lying down."

Healy fancied himself a yachtsman. When he invited chorus boy Hover and stooge Chasen to sail with him, they thought they had died and gone to heaven. But past the safety of Sheepshead Bay and out in the gusting Atlantic, it became clear that, as Herman put it, "Healy was not Popeye the Sailor Man." The schooner capsized. Healy and his mates clung to the keel, and when it tore away, my uncle dog-paddled in the icy water, terrified.

A Coast Guard cutter rescued them, and by the time they reached shore, "the press agent of our show," Herman wrote, "with miraculous prescience, was at the pier with a gaggle of newspapermen and photographers. They gave us a hearty if puzzled welcome. Ted puffed up like a blowfish. The distress pictures of the crew were posed, Ted looking for all the world like a big-game hunter after the kill." The next day, both Herman and Chasen shared "a feeling," in Herman's words, that occurs "the first time one's picture appears in a newspaper in conjunction with celebrity. It creates an illusion of accomplishment even though the photo is hardly recognizable. I carried the clipping with me for some time in my coat pocket, pulling it out, folding and unfolding it."

Healy would soon leave the *Vanities* for Hollywood and an MGM contract. Twelve years later, Chasen and Hover would be there, too—the stooge as the town's premier restauranteur, the chorus boy as its top nightclub owner. Both men were now masters of the press agentry they'd learned from Healy, who had faded into oblivion.

The 1926 *Vanities* opened on Broadway with a gimmick. The patrons walked into a theater whose rows of seats had been replaced by cafe tables. "The showgirls acted as usherettes," Herman recalled. "They were dressed in see-through material which alternately billowed and clung to the bare body. Promptly at 8:30 the girls ran up on the stage and into the opening number. 'Let's see your checks, please. Seats on the left, please. Yes, you're right, sir. Warm tonight, sir. Now that you're seated I guess we'll beat it." The girls did a high-stepping dance while chorus boys dressed as waiters (Herman among them) rushed the stage.

Canada Dry paid Earl Carroll to have the chorus girls serve the patrons bottles of its ginger ale during intermission. One of Herman's tasks was to keep the beverage company's representative from ogling the servers. It also fell to him to prepare the understudies, popping them into the show when the main girls were called home to the family farm or were out having abortions. Stage manager Russell Markert made Herman his assistant and let him stage the opening scene, in which the girls paraded onstage, faced the audience behind a torso-wide strip of velvet, and recited:

> *Yes, you guessed it, we are the showgirls*
> *My, but we are intellectual;*

But it isn't what is in our head that counts
For that is ineffectual
So promise not to make a fuss
And we'll show you more of us
More and more and more and more and more

They did a half turn in unison, walked two steps upstage—then revealed themselves completely naked from neck to ankles. (The thin gauze that clothed them was virtually invisible.)

A few weeks later, Herman was summoned to Earl Carroll's office. Russell Markert, it turned out, was leaving for another job. "Measuring his words carefully, Mr. Carroll offered me the opportunity to be Russell's replacement. I stared at him incredulously; never was a person less prepared to take over a task." Carroll cautioned the twenty-year-old not to panic. "Then he grinned sinisterly and offered a cautionary note: 'I hope you have a lot of friends outside the theater. When you're stage managing, you might not have any in it.' He leaned back in his chair, like a cobra who had just feasted on a mongoose."

Herman left Carroll's office, dizzy. "Never in my wildest dreams could I have foreseen what a temporary summer employment would lead to in September," he wrote. "I was barely out of my teens, in show business three months, and being made stage manager of Broadway's biggest hit and largest musical comedy."

I am startled to envision my uncle as this abashed, reverent manchild. Picturing him this way is like having one of those dreams in which a deeply familiar person appears in a different body. All my life Uncle Herman was, in various ways, the Heavy. In the last thirty years of his life he was a big, obtuse, blinking bird, a perennial hasbeen, so broke he took to typing his memoir on the back of Ralph's Market flyers. In my childhood he was the gruff, intimidating Family Star and Benefactor. In between he'd achieved a dastardly incarnation: as the man who tried to murder my adored father. The Herman who bursts whole from his memoir, however, is a different soul, not merely in age and physique but in temperament: vulnerable, grateful, his heart trilling. Was this girded, emotionless man really, the whole time, a poet? Despite all the ways in which he affected my life, his profoundest feat turns out to be this end-run whisper from the grave, reminding me of the piety from which self-invention springs, warning me not to know him—or *anyone*—so easily.

Suddenly Herman was in charge of forty dancers. Most were working-class girls with guttersnipe cadences. (The talkies had made a refined voice a criterion for film work, glutting the nonverbal end of the market with locutionary rejects.) But to Herman they were "beautiful, tempestuous, spoiled, patronizing, and argumentative. Backstage had an *Alice in Wonderland* quality: the Red Queen taking Alice by the hand, 'Faster! Faster!' "

Mounting fourteen ensemble numbers a night, suspending eight naked girls on a bar at audience level during the famous Gate of Roses sequence (a rose clenched in each girl's teeth), presiding over weekly nude weigh-ins ("There is something poignant about a girl who is putting on weight," Herman noted), disguising stretch marks and blemishes with makeup, rejecting girls with ragged appendix scars, relegating "satchel-assed" girls to loose-bottomed costumes and exempting girls who were "hung low" from high-kicking numbers, Herman quickly "got to know every dimple, crack, and freckle on a girl's body." He dispensed pain pills to menstrual sufferers, taught newcomers dance routines, and rang down the curtain on unbidden inebriates, such as the beauty-contest winner who "waddled up to the center of the platform, took the microphone and hissed, 'Miss California, *my aaaass!*' "

One night, Herman, sitting on the stage with notepad and pen, was doodling around with introductory patter. The stentorian master of ceremonies of the Hippodrome—B. F. Keith's Manhattan vaudeville megatheater—rang through his memory. "Through these portals pass the most beautiful girls in the world," Herman wrote. Carroll liked how the phrase rolled off monologist Julius Tannen's tongue. Sure beats Ziegfeld's "Glorifying the American Girl," Carroll thought, turning Herman's phrase into his advertising tag line.

Backstage was a mélange of the proprietary and the predatory. Both costume mistresses were, as was the custom, called Mother; they could recite any stage-door Johnnie's shit-heel credentials through a mouth full of straight pins while cinching a waist, begauzing a derriere, and plumping a bosom. The starchy set carpenter, Mr. Parker (no one addressed him otherwise), approached his task of lifting the unclothed girls onto the swinging gate with pompous rectitude, and then, once the show began, slipped out of sight and, as Herman recalled, discreetly "mounted a rigging he'd put up in such a way that he got a full gander at the girls' underneath parts." Paymaster Jimmy Cody once carried on a perfectly banal conversation with Herman while running his hands up and down a chorus girl's nude body under her kimono.

At home Celia and Isidore made a show of fretting that Herman wouldn't return to law school. Musical theater was not something to make a life of, they insisted. My mother told me, however, that they were secretly thrilled by their older son's movement into this dream of a world so beyond their own grasp, and beyond their own propriety. Herman's lucky tap shoes still stood on the floor by the door of his Arlington Avenue bedroom, a reassuring sign to the elder Hovers that his heart remained in that house, and that the magic those shoes had purchased was brought home to the family.

During that halcyon summer he had vaulted beyond his parents' reach and, in large part, stayed there. He'd rented a twelve-dollar-a-week furnished room with kitchenette in an "irreverant theatrical hotel" next door to Schaeffer's Delicatessan. "Pub downstairs, rooms above, the walls reeking of atmosphere, it was already in an advanced state of degeneration, but I felt I had to live there," he wrote. "On my own and earning my own way gave me a glorious feeling of living dangerously."

He seems to have been an abashed naïf, shirking from the homosexual advances of Nick Van Lowe, the *Vanities* star juvenile dancer who dabbled in Eastern mysticism, and waxing incredulous the first time he walked into one of (Loew's Theater front man) Nils Granlund's Sunday salons at the Hotel Des Artistes's swimming pool. What a scene unfolded there! It was dreamlike. There was Dorothy Parker, F. Scott Fitzgerald, Clara Bow, George S. Kaufman, Lupe Velez, and Helen Morgan. Herman plucked hors d'oeuvres off a waiter's tray, trying to keep the room from spinning. "Cries of merriment approached fierceness," he wrote, "as luscious creatures in provocative dresses were being chased and gotten hold of with unexpected ease and no opposition."

In time, Herman set up housekeeping with one of the showgirls, an English blonde named Phyllis Lofthouse. Phyllis couldn't cook. No matter—they sent out for meals from Schaeffer's like all the other tenants. Each afternoon, Phyllis twisted her hair around wooden spools with rags, painted her bad teeth with white paste, slapped a mud pack on her face, and lay down for her three-hour "beauty nap" in a creamy negligee and satin eye mask. When Herman came home from the orchestra tune-up and the light check, he changed into his tuxedo and high hat, she flung a cape over her nude body suit, and, hand in hand—"happy as clams," he wrote—they strolled the one block to the theater.

One day Herman came home to find the flat filled with dozens of bouquets of flowers. Phyllis said she was keeping them for her fellow showgirl Connie, whose husband "Dandy Phil" Kastel, a New Orleans–based racketeer and associate of Frank Costello, had just been released from the federal penitentiary. Herman asked why were they keeping the flowers Connie got from her husband? The flowers to Connie weren't from *Phil*, Phyllis explained. They were from Don, the manager of the Essex House, with whom Connie had been having a fling during her husband's incarceration.

In this and myriad other ways, showgirls and mobsters were bound together. Prohibition was in full swing, and the suppliers of illegal alcohol, from the lowest to highest level, permeated the world of big-city American night life. A number of the girls in the *Vanities* were dating fellows "on the circuit." One night, four months after he started, one of them coolly informed my uncle, "The boys at the Slipper want to see you."

The Silver Slipper was the most glamorous speakeasy in America. The Broadway theater was one thing; it was controlled by unions; it was "legit." But the speaks were a mysterious alternate kingdom ruled by a lawless power structure. That structure was a pyramid, at the bottom of which were "cornermen" (lookouts), "functionaries" (young actor George Raft among them) who retrieved newspaper-wrapped bundles of cash from the bread pantry and ferried them over to the local precincts, and "henchmen," including bodyguards who referred to their machine guns as their "equalizers." It was the task of all of these "bottom drawer" men to get the liquor in and make sure things ran smoothly—smoothly for the bosses, that is, and decidedly bumpily for distributors who got too greedy or missed a meeting because they dinghied up too late to the offshore carrier.

Above them were the front men, chief among whom was Harry Block, the nightclub's "paper" owner and beard to the legitimate world. The beards answered to the real owners: five key bosses in the Italian, Jewish, and Irish underworld. These were "the boys at the Slipper" the *Vanities* showgirl was referring to.

My uncle's job interview with "the Boys" was a thing of wonder. He was Dorothy, and they were the Wizards of Oz. "I was ushered into a storeroom," he recalled. "It was small, with a low ceiling and a tart kitcheny odor, and so dark I banged my shin on a serving cart." He walked past a clot of stacked chairs and glanced at the walls, adorned with pictures of prizefighters. In the place of honor was a portrait of newly elected Jimmy Walker, who had finally unseated longtime Republican mayor John Hylan. Walker's championing of the legalization of prizefighting and Sunday baseball while he was state senate leader, and his congenially corrupt fledgling administration, made him kinlike to the Boys. In fact, it was an open secret that Walker himself owned speakeasies. The young man who helped the mayor operate them was a young, stylish, fresh-up-from-Nashville beverage company owner's son possessed of a million ideas for striking it big in the entertainment world and a gambler's sense of creative recklessness. His name was Billy Wilkerson, and though Herman knew nothing of him then, their paths would cross—significantly—later.

Sitting with their backs to the wall were three of the five men who had called Herman there: Owney Madden, Frankie Marlowe, and Arnold Rothstein. Madden, the head of the cabal, nonetheless looked to my uncle like a neighborly grocer; Marlowe was deceptively phlegmatic even though he had a legendarily fast trigger finger; and suave Rothstein had gained notoriety by coming in on the deal to fix the 1919 World Series. (The two other owners—bland, thin-lipped Lucky Luciano, who controlled New York's prostitution, and skinny, choleric, exceptionally treacherous Jack "Legs" Diamond—were absent.)

"Mr. Madden pumped my hand with unexpected hardiness [sic] and spoke affably," Herman recalled, of the estimable gangster who would later serve a stint in Sing Sing. As he accepted a cigar, "I felt like a cornered mouse confronted by a big purring cat."

"We want you to do the girls here, the hoofers," Madden said, in a genial mumble that radiated the luxury of power.

Like it or not, Herman now had two jobs.

Herman had to scramble every night at curtain from the Earl Carroll Theater over to the Silver Slipper, to preside over the after-hours scene. But it was worth it. Just to be in that fabulous atmosphere—why, *he* would have paid *them*, he often said. Intrigue was shot through the place; walking inside made Herman's heart quicken. The backstage life of a theater had its sensual and risqué moments, but they were filled with a kind of wholesome camaraderie. A speakeasy, on the other hand, was "masked." It attracted staff and talent who either had a duplicitous streak, or were hungry to attain one.

No one at the Slipper was quite what he or she seemed to be. Headwaiter Charlie Aronson lived in a rented room with a toilet down the hall and owned but a single high hat and tuxedo, yet his demeanor was patrician, and he was the club's unforgiving etiquette arbiter. Fourteen-year-old ingenue Imogene Coca was the picture of vulnerability, yet she drove such a hard bargain that at contract time a cornered Madden finally ordered, "Just give the little girl what she asks for!" Ruby Keeler, the club's star tap dancer, was the nice Brooklyn girl forever talking to the press about buying a home for her mother and putting her sisters through college. Yet she was romancing the Boys' protégé Johnny Irish, "a hot-tempered young hood with the wholesome look of a fraternity man," as Herman recalls—as well as sneaking off on the side with Al Jolson.

One of the most intriguing Slipper employees was a man who remained anonymous in my uncle's memoir (and in the recollections of others I interviewed): the brooding, curly haired, tombstone-faced men's room attendant, a born-too-soon hipster who spoke in rhyming slang and wielded a deadly carnal power despite his lowly station. Herman often glimpsed him at the stage door, one of the girls (who could easily have had a wealthy lover) gazing at him with abject beseechment. Was he a pimp? An artiste? An exceptional lover? A plyer of some arcane narcotic? No one knew, and that tantalizing mystery was interest compounded on the principal of the young man's unaccountable self-possession.

Then there were the customers. Babe Ruth was a regular. Charles Lindbergh dated Slipper showgirl Blanche Satchell. Damon Runyon had a fling with Patrice Gridier, who specialized in a suggestive flamenco. A young sportswriter named Ed Sullivan started stopping by, and through his nights there grew intrigued with the world of entertainment. Debs slummed with mobsters, and the men of "the 400" consorted with showgirls, among them Arline Judge, whose eventual seven husbands included brothers Dan and Bob Topping (the former was the owner of the New York Yankees). Judge's reputation for pluralism was later outdone by Lucky Luciano's girlfriend Gay Orlova, who, during World War II, years later, had simultaneous affairs with both French and German generals.

Parked at the cramped employees' table between shows, Herman would watch the svelte, slightly sinister men and the louche women, gay and feline, through the tendrils of exhaled Chesterfield and Lucky Strike haze. Their permed and pomaded heads bobbed in bas-relief against the room's mesmerizing silver-and-black-striped wallpaper; their hands and eyes beckoned in code. These people had invented a social—a sexual—persona. They had slipped into theatrical versions of their most heightened selves. "They were players," he wrote in his memoir, "in their own play, and I was drunk from the sheer sight of it."

One night Helen Hover and her friend Lucy Neufield—their hair worked into Claudette Colbert spit curls—drove Isidore's Chrysler into Manhattan late at night and waited outside the Slipper stage door. Then, at a propitious moment, they shot inside like deer across a highway. As for what she saw, my mother recalled, "It was like taking a drug. It was magic." Herman came upon his jail-bait kid sister and her friend, pulled a twenty-dollar bill out of his pocket and sent them off for dinner at the Hollywood Restaurant, which (as my mother would later write in *Radio Guide*) "enjoys a unique position in the life of Manhattan's stay-out-lates; anyone who's anything on Broadway manages to wind up there."

"Herman wasn't mad" when they barged into the speakeasy, my mother said. "He knew what we saw; he was living it, and he couldn't blame us for wanting some part of it." She felt she had run after her brother down a hill; found, and ducked beneath, the same secret pasture fence he had found and opened. Seeing him in that world gave her permission to go there, too—to transform herself as he had. If the night of Sadie's death had occasioned their first bond—a shared vulnerability, a strong, sudden dose of tragedy— this evening was their second: the ticket to a dream made real, a blueprint for self-reinvention.

If the *Vanities* was Herman's education in managing the nuts and bolts of a stage show, and the Slipper was his education in creating the chemistry of an electrifying nightclub, then the third leg of his education—building the girls' dance routines—was inspired by Dave Bennett, the dance director of the show *Rose Marie,* who created formations rather than discrete steps, and whose "rippling line of girls" became the gold standard of chorus choreography. Herman bought small dolls at the five-and-dime and used them to work out formations. "If you had walked into my room at the hotel," he wrote, "you would have seen a cardboard model of a stage with proscenium and several stage settings."

The Slipper productions all had an Arabian Nights theme—that's the way the Boys wanted it. The show was variously called "Oriental Fantasy," "Paradise in Persia," and "The Rajah's Harem." Doubling as the orchestra to back the high-kicking girls, the Slipper's musicians—jazzmen in their preferred, authentic life—indifferently tooted out "Scheherezade" and "Song of India," getting that hokey part of the evening over with so they could move on to the scatting they'd picked up in Chicago's colored clubs from horn-man Louis Armstrong. They puffed on hand-rolled "mezz" cigarettes while tooting and shouting, until the orchestra leader bopped them on the backs of their necks with his baton, steering them back to the mandated Arabiana.

To make up for the unimaginative theme and orchestration, Herman became creative with the dances. Improvising on the waning Charleston craze, he was working on a triple-tap version of the dance when two songwriters who'd sold several compositions to the Cotton Club stopped by and played him one of their compositions, "Florida Lowdown." Herman fitted his triple-tap Charleston to its off-beat tempo and staged it for the girls. They performed it; the patrons loved it. Then, according to Herman, "six months later, a Broadway musical came out with the same dance, set to an original song written especially for the show—and my dance swept the country under its new name: the Black Bottom." Who knows if he was exaggerating?

When Herman wasn't working at the *Vanities* or at the Slipper, he was helping showgirl Tex Guinan choreograph the girls in her own club on Fifty-eighth Street. Guinan was a Roaring Twenties cross between *Gunsmoke*'s Miss Kitty and Phyllis Diller. In the dark club, a spotlight with an amber gel (to pick up the gold of her chemise, cloche, and cigarette holder) would escort her through the parted curtains, while the snare drum punctuated her stage strut. Twirling her strand of pearls around her fingers, she'd survey the room and then drawl her trademark "Hello, Suckers!" The amber light would land on the face of a society girl at a ringside table. "That's a lovely fur coat, honey," Guinan would say. The drum's thump underscored the society girl's "Why, thank you!" expression. Guinan continued, "Did you get it for being good, or being quiet?"

"There was a spirit to that harsh age that was wholesomeness itself," my uncle noted.

Typifying that spirit was the evening of February 22, 1926, at the Carroll Theater. Carroll was throwing a "joint birthday party" for his backer William Edrington—and George Washington. Herman oversaw the placement of a huge cast-iron bathtub on the stage; it had to be centered so that the mirrors behind and above it would capture and throw off the scene within—faithfully. The tub was filled with sherry and Canada Dry.

When showgirl Joyce Hawley arrived at the stage door she was set upon by wardrobe mistress "Mother" Mary Pratt, who shaved and scrubbed her torso to a fare-thee-well. After Carroll's three hundred male guests were seated, Hawley was lowered by Mr. Parker, via overhead wire, into the tub. She frolicked in the bubbles while silently cursing the clamminess. ("Jesus, Mary, and Joseph," she told Herman, "it was like takin' a swim in cold chicken soup!") Waiters passed around cups; each guest stepped up, dipped a cup in the bath, and partook of the uniquely spiced beverage.

Carroll, a publicity hound to the core, invited the press but forbade them to write about the entertainment, which seemed to Herman like being asked to recline next to a beautiful woman but not touch her. When Herman began disinviting the press, Carroll almost tore the phone out. The impressario thundered that that was a surefire way to turn valuable friends into enemies. Besides, if the press wanted a story, they got it. When Walter Winchell was barred from the Schuberts' theaters, he simply put the Schuberts' security men on his own payroll.

It wasn't Walter Winchell who did Carroll in; he sat on the story. Phil Payne, editor of the *New York Mirror*, broke it. Even before corner newsboys chanted the *Mirror*'s scoop, word had gotten out. "Did you *hear* what happened at Earl Carroll's last night?" was whispered on cane el and trolley seats and into telephone mouthpieces across the city. Carroll's party was lambasted in newspaper editorials and excoriated from church pulpits as the high-water mark in Jazz Age decadence.

Federal authorities arrested Carroll for violating Prohibition. The showman fought the charge, stood trial, was convicted of perjury, and was hauled off to prison in Atlanta for a one-year sentence.

By then Herman had enrolled in Columbia Law School. The transition from show life back to student life was profoundly anticlimactic. He told his father that he would stick it out and get his law degree but that he would not become a lawyer. He said, "I looked at my dad's fine face, etched with lines of fatigue, and I felt a pang of guilt. He wanted the best for me, but the world I lived in never existed for him." Isidore did not counter his son; he chose to trust Herman's instincts. At that moment in America, there was such a mixing up of the rules of status and prosperity, who was to say that Herman's course would be improvident?

From his Georgia penitentiary cell, Earl Carroll was planning to launch a new, traveling version of *Vanities*. He designated Herman his proxy. It was the summer of 1927, and Herman was back at work at the Slipper. He reluctantly resigned from that job to throw himself into the new show and take it to Springfield, Providence,

Rochester, and Newark. The show was a hit; Carroll raked in $20,000 a week behind bars. He paid star showgirl Dorothy Knapp the unheard-of sum of $1,000 a week, and he was twice as generous with Moran and Mack, the comic tramps who, in blackface as "The Two Black Crows," were his show stealers.

When Carroll was freed from prison four months later, he signed torch singer Lillian Roth and low-muttering comic W. C. Fields for the next year's *Vanities*, upping the ante in his escalating duel with Ziegfeld (who, as Herman put it, still "bestrode Broadway like a colossus"). Fields was hugely disliked by the *Vanities* players and crew, embodying, as he did, his motto, "Never give a sucker an even break." He maneuvered himself so his fellow players had to recite their lines with their backs to the audience. He was also cruel: When a college humor magazine writer who'd repeatedly tried to sell him sketches asked, "Isn't there any way I can get some of my sketches on the stage?" Fields replied, "Yes. Tear 'em up and we'll use them as snowflakes."

"There was continual conflict between Bill Fields and everyone else," Herman recalled. Yet he learned from those conflicts that a shrewd impresario sacrifices his pride to the star's ego. "Anyone who wins an argument with an actor has only himself to blame," he said. "For a star only two things count: One is for him to think he is having his way; two is for him to have it."

After his evenings at the Carroll Theater and the Slipper, Herman, like all Broadway players and crews, would repair to the Cotton Club, an upstairs room at the corner of 142nd Street and Lenox Avenue. The club was owned by the Slipper owners, also under front man Harry Block—Madden had wanted a Harlem location from which he could sell his Madden's #1 beer, so he and his cabal had taken over heavyweight boxer Jack Johnson's bankrupt Club Deluxe.

The best talent in the city (sepia talent, it was billed) was concentrated on the Cotton Club's stage, and the higher paid pros went there to learn from their poorly paid betters. Sunday night was its big night. The Broadway theaters were dark, and all the stars in town showed up and were happily coaxed onto the stage for impromptu performances. Sophie Tucker belted out "Some of These Days." Ted Lewis crooned "When My Baby Smiles at Me." Clayton, Jackson, and Durante hoofed, and then were put to shame by the Cotton Club's Step, Berry, and Nicholas Brothers. But the whites were just the wanna-bes, the appreciators. What carried the club were the phenomenal orchestra leaders—first Duke Ellington, then Cab Calloway—and the chorus line, including two standouts, Pearl Bailey and Lena Horne. Herman dreamed of having his own nightclub where he could book these acts.

Toward dawn, Herman would return to his rented room. I picture him—swarthy, lean, his tux open, its bowtie askew, pausing under the lamplight on the deserted sidewalk, doing a double-time tap step. The fingers of one hand go to the opposite sole and repeat and repeat and repeat and repeat: *clickety clickety clickety CLICKety/ clackety clackety clackety CLACK.* I picture him upstairs in his room, looking out the window as the dawn slowly putties the cracks of black sky between the gray stone and limestone and red brick. I see my young uncle standing in his undershirt, slack suspenders, and beltless pants, staring out like a figure in a Hopper painting. He is lonely, but contentedly so, kept company by the romance of the life he's claimed, as simply and purely as if it has been destined. He has refashioned himself into his dream of himself. He knows the best has not yet begun.

The magical world that Herman had entered was one of the few spheres of society relatively untouched by the crash of 1929. If anything, people *needed* escape during the Depression. The *Vanities* was a hit show year after year; Herman's writing for W. C. Fields earned him a theatrical award. As Isidore's fortune shrank over the last three years of the twenties, he and Celia developed a respect for the prescient design of their son's life, and were proud that he'd picked a field through which the family could avoid not merely catastrophe but also dreariness. Celia clipped the reviews of the *Vanities* openings and spoke of her older child as the family avatar. When Herman interrupted his glittery life long enough to drive over the Brooklyn Bridge and come home for dinner, everyone lapped up his insider's nuggets about the shooting death of his old boss Arnold Rothstein at the Park Central Hotel, Lillian Roth's elopement with society scion William Scott, and Al Capone's incarceration in Leavenworth.

No family member felt the transformation that Herman had bestowed upon them more deeply than Helen. "I was enamored by my brother's life," she told me. "I basked in his reflected glory. I was known in the neighborhood as Herman Hover's kid sister. We'd come home from school and there was *my* brother pictured in the paper, demonstrating the Lindy Hop. Herman's best friend at the time was William Leeds, a handsome playboy, an aluminum heir. The Tin Plate King, they called him. Herman would pick me up from school in Leeds's car—oh, it was marvelous!"

Inspired by her brother, Helen was striking out herself. She had graduated from high school in 1928 and was now attending New York University, making the long daily commute to the University Heights campus, pulling away from Celia's nosiness, control, and melancholy with each subway stop. "Helen was very aggressive," her cousin Hilda Stone told me. "In temperament, more aggressive than Herman. And she always wanted to be a newspaperwoman."

Her goals dovetailed well with the times. Female role models in the media and the arts abounded. Margaret Bourke-White had become an esteemed photographer; former Associated Press reporter Willa Cather was a respected novelist; Clare Boothe Brokaw, a glamorous journalist. Pearl Buck won the Nobel prize for literature for *The Good Earth*, and Jane Addams won it for peace (decrying, in her acceptance speech, the practice of women giving up their careers after marriage). Every day the newspapers flashed the image of another smiling young leather-capped "aviatrix" climbing into a pilot's seat, or a jaunty fox-stoled woman flying to Nevada to obtain a divorce. My mother often rhapsodized, "It was a wonderful time to be a young woman."

Or a young man. Other Jewish boys and girls from Brooklyn— young songwriters, directors, producers, managers, show business journalists, actors, and comics—were proving that the dreamed-of life lay right on the other side of the door of the prosaic one. Helen's antic childhood friend Irvie Mandelbaum was now Broadway's "boy genius" publicist. Borrowing a page from John Garfield (né Garfinckle) and Ethel Merman (née Zimmerman), Irvie had renamed himself Irving Mansfield, and he was living, like Herman, in a Broadway hotel, boulevardiering with all-the-rage bandleader Richard Himber and stopping in at Leo Lindy's with Walter Winchell and Dave's Blue Room to jostle the showgirls, many of whom Herman directed. Eventually he would meet and marry a young Jewish actress from a good Philadelphia family and guide her career as a writer. Her name was Jacqueline Susann.

Then there was the Cinderella fate of Helen's friend Gertie Finkelstein, the astonishingly beautiful ragpicker's daughter for whom Celia used to charitably cook hot meals and sew a wardrobe. Gertie's mother had developed the tactic of combing the society pages and ferrying her daughter (whom she'd somehow managed to send to some version of afternoon finishing school) to the proper hotel lobbies on the nights of the debutante parties. A Park Avenue

Yale boy had fallen in love with her. Now, despite the Depression, Gertie was living in a Locust Valley mansion, "a regular 'Lipstick Girl,' " said Celia, referring to the popular women's page serial about romantic social climbing.

Eventually Broadway's fortunes fell. By the summer of 1931, many theaters were dark and Earl Carroll's launching of Fanny Brice in an operetta was a very expensive disaster. Across the continent, Hollywood was unaffected; its moviemaking duchies (titaned by Jack and Harry Warner, Adolf Zukor, Louis B. Mayer, and William Fox) seemed a separate country. Helen and her friend Lucy Neufield went to the Loew's every Saturday to watch the handsome talkie stars—Ramon Navarro in *Daybreak*, Gary Cooper in *City Streets*, and Douglas Fairbanks in *Chances*—whose personal lives they followed by way of Eileen Percy's syndicated column. The movie gossip and the Lindbergh kidnapping addicted the girls to newspapers. In February 1932, in the middle of their third year at New York University, Helen Hover and Lucy Neufield went to the recently merged *Brooklyn Daily Times Standard-Union* and, pencils behind their ears, presented themselves as a pair of reporters.

The bemused city editor sent them to the women's section. Along with food and fashion, the page featured comics—"Sally's Sallies" and "Etta Kett" depicted slouchy debs, and the "Just Between Us Girls" cartoon often showed savvy women manipulating the weaker sex ("A kiss seems to have turned out to be a labor-saving device to help a wife run her husband," read one caption).

"It was a flirtatious, gamey, *tough* time," my mother said, approvingly. In March, Helen and Lucy were given a column. They were to bottom-feed on the paper's advertising market, convincing small businesses to pay a few dollars a month to have their products plugged in a breezy advice-fest. The twice-weekly effort was named "Nancy Goes Shopping." Its logo was the sketch of a gal in a swingy skirt and Isadora Duncan neck scarf, rushing a toppling pile of store boxes to her client.

Helen and Lucy inherited a mélange of piddling accounts—a Flatbush typewriter store, a Swedish masseuse, a Fifth Avenue druggist, and several clothiers. They added an electrolysist, a chiropodist, a beautician who made house calls, a reducing expert, an upholsterer, an orthopedist, a laundromat, a handwriting analyst, a dentist, a baldness specialist, a Chinese facialist, and a milliner. Their task? To spin a golden web of style advice out of this sad-sack lot of services ("The wrinkle-removing Chinese cream Won Sue Fun now has a companion cream which takes off dead tissue in a jiffy!").

As they rode the subways and buses, notebooks in hand, they mused over their namesake. Was Nancy a pouty secret roundheel, like *Lady with a Past*'s Constance Bennett? Or a tough operator, like *The Purchase Price*'s Barbara Stanwyck? Sometimes Helen and Lucy turned their alter ego into a pert working-class sister. ("The Depression shouldn't take away your smartness. I can tell you where to get smart dresses for $3 to $6.") Other times she morphed into the snooty fiancée of a Princeton aviator. ("A mannish navy coat or black jacket—chic, n'est-ce pas? I saw the same style on Gwen Whitney as she strolled down Park Avenue.") Their Nancy was fond of aphorisms, whether soothing ("There's no companionship a girl appreciates more than that given by the modern mother"), scolding ("Remember, haphazard buying makes haphazard outfits"), or nonsensical ("Nothing ages a woman as quickly as a lowly corn. Nothing adds crow's-feet like a bunion").

"Lucy and I laughed the whole time we were Nancy," my mother often said. "We laughed in the stores, on the street, at the office, on the subway." Giddily, the girls hatched a contest; the reader who wrote the best one hundred-words-or-less letter praising her favorite Nancy tip would win a gift pack of Won Sue Fun facial cream and Remov-All depilatory. In the April 7 column, Nancy proclaimed, "The winnah, ladies and gentlemen, is Miss Rose Kronstein, of 2728 W. Third Street! Here is her letter. 'The topic I like best in your department is Beauty Hints. In my opinion Beauty Hints take into consideration everything needed to bring out the attractiveness in a person.' Thank you, Miss Kronstein!"

On July 6, a celebrity crime story broke that made my mother wonder: What am I doing writing a shopping column when there are stories like this to cover? Smith Reynolds, the twenty-year-old heir to Reynolds Tobacco and the husband of torch singer Libby Holman, had been shot to death during a party at the couple's Winston-Salem mansion, and Libby, who had been drinking heavily, was found leaning over his body. Initial reports held that he had been cleaning his gun. Then the story changed: He'd killed himself because Libby was leaving him. Finally, Libby was a suspect. She was grilled by the local police, this Jew and fallen woman. Shrouded in a bedsheet, Libby was hustled out of Winston-Salem and taken by her father to her hometown, Cincinnati.

With Herman's connections, Helen found stagehands and musicians who'd worked with Holman, and they gave her an earful. Holman had had affairs with women; Smith Reynolds had thrown himself at her, had proposed twenty times, and finally had threatened to kill himself if she didn't marry him.

My mother wrote the story on spec and took it to Curtis Mitchell, editor of the new *Radio Stars*. The magazine, like its rival *Radio Guide* (the brainchild of upstart publishers Walter and Moses Annenberg), was aimed at Americans on farms and in small towns, sitting in front of their consoles, listening to *Helen Trent*, the orginal (white) *Amos and Andy*, Irving Berlin's composed-for-NBC-radio hits, like "Say It Isn't So," as well as the sermons of the eventually ravingly anti-Semitic Father Coughlin.

Mitchell published a toned-down version of the piece as "Libby As They Knew Her" and started giving twenty-one-year-old Helen Hover assignments, which she juggled with "Nancy," and then offered her a job as the magazine's principal reporter. My ecstatic mother dropped out of New York University, quit the *Standard-Union*, and embarked on her real life: transforming herself from a naive Brooklyn girl into her image of a knowing young newspaperwoman.

Chapter Three

NEW YORK: 1932–1936

A photo of my father during this era—on May 6, 1932, to be exact—shows him bent over a metal bar two steps up in an operating theater at the Peter Bent Brigham Hospital, in Boston. He is one of fifteen young men crowded together, stooped over intently on three steep levels of cantilevered flooring, with folded arms bearing down on the thin metal railings. They are wearing identical long-sleeved, high-necked, back-tied surgical greens. Every mouth and nose is covered by the same white antiseptically treated muslin sash, like a bandit's mask, knotted behind the head. All eyes are fixed on the careful excision of a malignant brain tumor by the man in the pit of the theater: the then sixty-four-year-old Dr. Harvey Cushing. To these neurosurgeons in training (and my father, an awed undergraduate smuggled in by his brother Alex's neurosurgical intern friend Mandy Fuchs), seeing Cushing remove a glioma was equivalent to novice composers watching Beethoven structure a symphony.

I remember walking with my father through the parking lot of L. A.'s Queen of Angels Hospital one Saturday morning when I was about nine. He was going to check up on a Mexican woman he'd saved from paralysis. The surgery had taken hours the day before, and the ivory rosary the patient's husband had bestowed upon our family lay in a heap in my father's tobacco-flecked night-table drawer. My father's calling was very different from my mother's and my uncle's. Its setting was not flashy and dashing—show business! Hollywood!—but substantive and quiet (the hushed hospital, the operating room) and its symbols (the rosary), odd and pious and ordinary.

I could tell that my father was tired and preoccupied that morning (though, with his gold-braided sea captain's cap on his head and corncob pipe jutting out of his mouth, he must have appeared jaunty to others), and I was walking fast to keep up with him. I yearned to get the attention of this almost theatrically wry and proud and wistful man, who drew people to him wherever we went, with his irresistibly twinned mischievousness and sorrow.

I asked him a question I'd snatched from Dorothy Kilgallen and Bennett Cerf. "Daddy, how'd you pick this . . . line of work?"

He usually didn't like it when I tried to be cute, and he would dismiss my clumsy attempts at ingratiation. But the answer to this particular question was clearly too long-held and important for him not to stop, turn, and smile. "I was privileged enough," he answered, with exaggerated ceremony, "to watch Harvey Cushing perform an operation."

Neurosurgery was still wildcatter's work in 1932. It had only been a surgical specialty since 1919, and it was yet to be either recognized by the American Medical Association (that would not come until 1937) or regulated by its own board (that would have to wait until 1940). Yet it already had a hero.

Stories abounded about the passionate and glamorous Cushing: He smoked every minute of the time he wasn't in surgery. He was so self-controlled, he'd performed a four-hour operation right after he learned that his adored oldest son had been killed in a car accident.

He dressed like an aristocrat and tossed his head like a screen actor. (His daughters inherited his glamour. The Fabulous Cushing Sisters—as Minnie, Betsey, and Barbara, or Babe, were called—married, respectively, Vincent Astor; FDR's son James Roosevelt and then Jock Whitney; and CBS chairman William Paley.) None of this trivia would have meant anything but for one fact: Harvey Cushing *created* modern neurosurgery.

Before 1890, brain surgery had barely come any distance since primitive forms of it were practiced around the world. It was an option of extreme last resort at a time when *any* surgery was a death-defying proposition. Prior to the 1870s the germ theory of disease had not been widely accepted; Lister's antibacterial carbolic acid spray was not in routine use in operating theaters; and general anesthesia was in its infancy. Consequently, a high percentage of all American surgical patients' wounds became infected, and many operations ended in death. *Brain* surgery, which required not only a patient's unconsciousness but also great manual dexterity on the part of the surgeon, had much higher fatality rates. Except for superficial kinds, it was not practiced.

It was Cushing's forebear, the distinguished British neurological investigator Dr. Victor Horsley, who, in the 1890s, undertook the task of making brain surgery modern. Horsley knew that drilling a burr hole in the skull and making an incision in the dura (the first layer of tissue under the skull) of a tumor patient would relieve the patient's severe headaches and preserve his eyesight. Yet, ironically, Horsley could not perform his own operation; there was no safe technique. Despite the boost afforded by Wilhelm Conrad Roentgen's 1895 discovery of X rays, treating tumor-ridden patients was intensely frustrating for surgeons at the end of the nineteenth century.

It took Harvey Cushing to ease that frustration by closing the gap between knowledge and technique. Cushing discovered how blood pressure rises from cerebral compression, and he refined cauterization. He devised the silver clips that are a staple of hemorrhage prevention. Cushing found a way to remove the pituitary gland through the nasal cavity, pioneered brain surgery on newborns, and changed incision sites to give access to formerly inoperable tumors. He wrote the primer for performing cranial operations, from the timing of the shaving of the head, to the improved positioning on the table, to the method of anesthesia. His closure of wounds was so meticulous that, in 350 craniotomies by 1908, he never produced an infection, a feat his followers, even twenty-five years later, were hard put to duplicate. When Cushing entered the profession, using the techniques bequeathed to him, 90 percent of his patients died; when he left, two thousand brain surgeries later, using the techniques he devised, only 8 percent succumbed.

To the outside world, Harvey Cushing was a minor notable whose achievements were arcane, but to young Daniel Weller of Brooklyn, New York, Cushing was the North Star. The polished, dashing man, whose work was both intellectually demanding and fundamentally risky and physical, represented everything Daniel Weller wanted to be—and decided that day that he *would* be.

It took vanity to harbor such a goal, and my father was vain. He was vain about his work, about his person, but he was vainer yet—and much more defensively so—about his manliness. He wanted no one to see his vulnerability. Once, according to his sister, Rosie, when he and two friends, Marty Lasoff and Danny Kaufman, were in their twenties, they ran out of gas on a trip to the Delaware Water Gap. My father set out to walk to a gas pump. The walk, in the sun, was longer than he had figured. He rolled up his sleeves, took off his hat, sat down by the empty road while his heart thumped as it had in that Bradford Street bathtub. An hour passed. He walked, stopped, walked, furiously suppressing his panic.

Finally, a car was heard approaching. Too relieved to stay vigilant with his image, he stood in the center of the road and waved his hands like a shipwrecked man to a distant ship. The car bore Lasoff, the smoothie of the trio, who had set out hitchhiking after Weller had gone off, and who had persuaded the driver of a car going the other way to pick him up, turn around, and go find Weller.

Lasoff and my father kibbitzed with the driver all the way to the gas station and then back to their own car, where Kaufman was waiting. Then my father, forgoing the benefit his heart had accrued by sitting in the cool automobile for the hour, reeled back and pummeled his slick friend's face with a series of punches.

That story always made great sense to me. It reminded me of the time I confessed to my father that my new pet turtle (which he despised) had somehow escaped its tiny plastic palm-treed pen and was somewhere in his bedroom. He turned me over his knee and spanked the dickens out of me. Even at ten I understood that he was punishing me not for my irresponsibility, but for having forced him to reveal his cowardice, just as Lasoff knew that Weller was striking him not for showing him up by arriving by car, but for witnessing his terror and weakness on the roadside.

My father, Marty, and Danny Kaufman were all intent on proving themselves in the world beyond Brooklyn. They fancied themselves Scotty Fitzgerald–like. They would dress up and drive around in Lasoff's vintage Pierce Arrow to Asbury Park and the North Shore of Long Island, flirting with all the pretty girls. Danny Kaufman's widow, Esther, recalls her young husband's characterization of my young father: "Danny Weller always said he knew he was going to die young, and he lived as if every day was his last, 'and whatever comes up, I'm going to do it and face it.'" She was charmed when she met him: "He was a very sweet person, and he had a mischievous smile, and his eyes just twinkled." Well into his adulthood—all his life—that smile and those twinkling eyes were assets he knew how to brandish winningly.

The three friends had gone to Thomas Jefferson High School together before dispersing to separate colleges—my father went to Long Island University and then the University of Louisville. They aspired to medicine, not an accessible field for young Jewish men. Although the dean of Yale Medical School, Milton Winternitz, was a Jew, and although the secretary of the Harvey Cushing Society, Ernest Sachs, was a Jew, and the premier medical educator Abraham Flexner was a Jew, such men were rarities, and they generally kept their heads down. (Flexner commented to Winternitz, during an anti-Semitic incident at Yale in the 1920s, "I am a Jew myself and have been for years making my way among Christians and working with them. . . . Prejudice need not be stirred.")

The elite echelons of medicine and, especially, of surgery were gate-kept by men who had ideas about the "appropriate" background of medical students. A renowned Austrian surgeon named Christian Billroth had even written a tract stating that Jews should be excluded from medical school because of their lack of cultural background and poor manners. "In the 1930s," said Dr. Gert Brieger, addressing the 1993 annual session of the American College of Phyisicians, "restrictive practices [against Jewish applicants to medical school] began in earnest."

Quotas were devised for boys "of Hebrew descent," to use the term of the day. Even brilliant Jewish boys had to wait their turn, and the more ordinary Jewish students, such as my father and his friends, had to scramble to find out-of-the-way, second- or third-rate medical schools. Dan Kaufman was off to the University of

Arkansas. Marty Lasoff had just enrolled in some other obscure college. My father was trying the overseas route, because he was rejected by Long Island College of Medicine. Fearful that it would take years of reapplication to burst through, he had applied for admission to the University of Heidelberg (he had studied German at Louisville) and had been accepted. How bizarre that, in the fall of 1932, as Hitler consolidated his power, it was to the University of Heidelberg that my father was sailing to circumvent Jewish quotas!

He sent Danny Kaufman a postcard from the ship *Deutschland* in October 1932. In his fat-vowelled, sideways-angled hand, he wrote:

Dear Dan,
    Well, am on my way.
    Heard you were ill. How are you. Boy what beer on board. And old tub sure can rock. Will write later.

                                                        Regards,
                                                        Dan Weller

Events in Heidelberg belied that first sentence's ceremony and optimism. Danger was in the air; the prim, gleaming ugliness of the Reich made itself apparent. My father got a boat back within half a year. Then, from Bradford Street, he wrote a new round of letters to medical schools, deleting mention of his heart condition. Finally one school, the University of Missouri at Columbia, accepted him—though not into its medical school (that, too, had a waiting list) but rather for a master's of science program in anatomy. He accepted immediately.

At Missouri my father was mentored by a professor of anatomy and neurology, and he displayed enough talent to become principal author of a paper, "The Effect of Estrin on the Prostate Gland of the Albino Rat and Mouse," to be published in the May 1936 issue of the *Anatomical Record*. But the master's degree took an extra semester because he got sick and had to come home to Brooklyn.

Alex and Milton were practicing medicine by then, living as bachelor doctors with their indomitable mother, who vetted their girlfriends sternly. (The oldest brother, Harry, had essentially evaporated—becoming a prosperous businessman outside the city and, according to the disdainful reports of various relatives, passing as a gentile.) Rosie, the expendable female in the hothouse that Lena maintained, had married and moved to nearby Sackett Street. Daniel convalesced in her extra bedroom. An imperious busybody cut in the mold of her mother, Rosie doted on her favorite brother even more possessively than Lena had, fortifying his resolve not to give up the plan of medical school despite the setbacks. Soon Rosie divorced, having perhaps learned that she was a better sister of three men than a wife to one man.

My father was twenty-five. It was late to be applying to medical school, and the Jewish-quota situation was worsening. Alex and Milton tried to talk Danny into dentistry. Medical school took four years; then came two years of grueling internship and residency. As for neurosurgery, Daniel's brothers considered it preposterous. The specialty had the longest post–M.D. apprenticeship in all of medicine—five to seven years. Danny wouldn't start practicing until he was thirty-six or thirty-seven. Would he *live* that long?

Even if he crossed all those hurdles, there was another consideration. Neurosurgical operations took ten to twelve hours. Did their sickly, indulged brother possess the stamina, brilliance, or discipline for it? "Alex and Milton knew he would never make it," Rosie said. "They knew he wouldn't outpace them."

They were wrong. They didn't recognize his stubbornness and steeliness. That same rock-ribbedness that made him pursue his dream despite its lack of likelihood and its sheer impracticality let him slam the door on me, his daughter, when I was thirteen—and not look back. I asked Esther Kaufman if my father spoke of me during the last year of his life. After the family disaster, my father had returned to New York with his new wife and settled in Great Neck, where Esther and her husband saw them almost daily. Surely he mused about his oldest daughter. Surely something made him occasionally recall me, I silently hoped—and expected.

"No," she answered, her calm words a knife to my heart. "He never mentioned your name."

It was the required physical examination—and the Jewish-quota system—that almost kept my father out of the Long Island College of Medicine not only the first time he'd applied, but also the second time, in 1935. At least that's what I'd always thought. He had told me he had "hidden" his bad heart on both applications. Later, when I finally saw his application, there it was in black-and-white: *Have you any physical handicaps?* "No," he had scrawled, the *o* running off in a defiant long line. On the two lines that followed *If so, specify:* he'd made two long slashes: no, and no again. As for the quota system, clearly the medical schools cared about one's bloodlines. The application queried: *Racial Antecedents.* My father had answered, "Hebrew."

"Oh, he wanted to be a doctor so badly," my mother would say, admiring him deeply for that even after all that had come between them. "But there were quotas. And his heart—"

His heart: It was the root of his poignancy and his selfishness; it became, in my hagiography of the man, the scapegoat for the flaws in his character. More, it became one of the totems by which I am left, years later, to reconstruct his image. I had so few real years with my father, and fewer hours within the days of those years. For all his ego and self-possession, he left a scanty, haphazard record that would indicate a humbler, less-accomplished man (or a frantic, angry one). Thus, touchstones—the medical career documents, the few photographs of him in his youth, the lore of his father's Oklahoma years—are the precious evidence of the self he created. Of these totems, the greatest one is his damaged heart—and his romanticization of it.

Was it really his bad heart and the quota system that had made getting into medical school so difficult? When I obtained my father's undergraduate records, from both Long Island University and then the University of Louisville, I realized that he had actually been a very mediocre undergraduate. His overall average was C+. No wonder he had not gotten into medical school when he had first applied—he was too poor a student. And no wonder he had gone to the University of Missouri to obtain a master's of science first. He *needed* to.

Yet, warring with this apparent laziness and disregard was a steeliness, a stubbornness—a passion. As I began to study his life, I saw that this oscillation (so inexpressably poignant to me, and eventually fatal for him) between, on the one hand, casual self-destructiveness and balmy nihilism and, on the other, an almost desperately earnest pursuit of his serious goals was a leitmotiv of his life. Was it a duel, inside his character, between the slackerly Louis Weller and the gleaming Harvey Cushing? Or was it, instead, a conflict pitting the angry, fatalistic boy who knew he would die against the prematurely wise young man who refused to see his physical weakness as a barrier? It was that latter man whom people fell in love with—whom I loved, utterly and helplessly. It was the former man who ultimately prevailed, though never quite fooling his conscience.

In his medical school essay, despite his undistinguished grades, my father is virtually begging to be admitted. At one point he makes an almost poetic plea. "The stimulating factors" leading him to medicine "have been so many, so penetrating and influential that the desire to study medicine has become a part of me." At another, he sets off a one-sentence vow in a paragraph of its own to underscore his seriousness. "Fully aware of the duties, I am willing to forsake an easier life for the one of a physician."

In the summer of 1935 my father was accepted into the Long Island College of Medicine's class of 1939. According to a story my father told, he had a congratulatory evening with his buddies. "So, blow my plumbin', you wore 'em down!" Lasoff and Kaufman had said, when, twirling imported cigars, they picked my father up in the Pierce Arrow. Both were then in their second year of medical school; Danny would be two years behind them.

In-his-cups Danny had bought himself a trumpet. He had been fascinated with the instrument, not just because of the love of jazz he shared with his chums, but because of the instrument's centrality to his father's romantic years in Oklahoma. "Rosie and Ma were bellyachin', my ticker couldn't handle it," he complained, gingerly easing the horn into the back of the sedan. On the way out to Coney Island for clams, Lasoff and Kaufman had to suffer through Weller's poor imitation of Dixieland Eddie Edwards and his tales of having purchased a clandestinely made recording by the great colored trumpeter Freddie Kepper from a hobo's cart on Pitkin Avenue.

When my father stumbled into his bedroom that night, he saw a spill of blond hair fanned out on his pillow. Turning back the bedsheets, he beheld a bewigged anatomy-lab cadaver dressed in a Kings County Hospital nurse's uniform. "Christawmighty! Lasoff! Kaufman . . . !" He ran outside, but they'd driven off already.

Milton and Alex paid Danny's tuition, $550-a-year and, with

savings from a summer job, my father paid for his own registration, activities, admission, laboratory, and student health fees: another $65. On his twenty-sixth birthday, a week after school started, Lena bought her youngest son a Bausch & Lomb microscope. (He sentimentally held on to the instrument long after it was outdated, keeping it in the closet with his trumpet.)

He took the standard freshman course load: anatomy (he got a grade of 90), neuroanatomy (he received a 77, just two points above passing), biochemistry (78), physiology (76), and medicine (he passed the pass/fail course). The grades for his heavier workloads in the second and third years (bacteriology, clinical lab methods, psychology, neurology, obstetrics, opthalmology, pediatrics, urology, psychiatry, and otolaryngology) were in the B range.

Despite the undistinguished marks, he was assertive, even a bit pompous. "To be sure, Danny is voluble," his entry in the 1939 *Lichonian* begins. "His loud stentorian tones have a ring of authority and sincerity, which inspires utter credence in anything (well, almost anything) he says." He had started medical school an earnest supplicant, but had ended supremely confident. The charisma I knew him to have was developing. "Where will Danny go in medicine?" the yearbook asked, and then answered:

Why, Danny might become Health Commissioner or Surgeon General. There are practically no limits to the places into which he can talk himself. Of one thing we are positive, and that is Danny's success as a physician. God, what a bedside manner!

In my father's fourth year he worked in the wards of Long Island College Hospital and then applied for internships at fifteen hospitals. The only thing in his medical school file (other than a picture, in which he looks as sensual as the young Paul Newman) is a scrap of paper with the notes of one interviewer. His entire school record is reduced to one extraneous detail:

IMPRESSION

1. Has cardiac lesion
2. Nice chap—? No mention of cardiac lesion in application
3. Should live a carefully regulated life

On Thursday night, June 8, 1939, at 8 P.M., my father marched down the aisle of the Brooklyn Academy of Music, with his classmates, to the strains of Verdi's *Aida*. He took a seat on the risers on the stage. Lena and Rosie sat facing him in their auditorium seats, corsages bobbing on their breasts, cheeks wide with pleasure. Milton and Alex flanked them; everyone was proud of Danny.

After a minister's invocation, the welcoming address by the president of the college, and the commencement address by another clergyman, the academy orchestra played a medley of Stephen Foster's folk songs. Then the graduates rose. Their satin gowns rustling like rain, they jacked their right hands up at their elbows and, led by a professor of clinical medicine, they repeated the Hippocratic Oath:

I swear by Apollo, the Physician . . . To reckon him who taught me this art equally dear to me as my parents, to share my substance with him and relieve his necessities if required; to regard his offspring as on the same footing with my own brothers and to teach them this art if they should wish to learn it. . . . I will follow that method of treatment which, according to my ability and judgment, I consider for the benefit of my patients and abstain from what is deleterious and mischievous. . . . With Purity and with Holiness I will pass my life and practice my art. . . .

Almost all the class would be interning in New York or New Jersey, but my father was bound for Cedars of Lebanon Hospital in Los Angeles. The old Kaspare Cohn Hospital had been transformed and enlarged, renamed for the biblical site, and was now serving the burgeoning L.A. population. The city, having grown faster in the last ten years than the planners had imagined, desperately needed medical professionals. Cedars welcomed this intern despite his bad heart. In fact, Cedars was the only hospital that would take a chance on Danny Weller.

So my father traveled west to seize his only chance to shed the skin of sickly Mama's boy and become, at last, the Doctor. His mission was—comfortably—ironic: In this land of ease he would "forsake" that "easier life for the one of a physician."

Chapter Four

NEW YORK AND CALIFORNIA: 1935–1939

While my father was embarking on medical school life, my mother was interviewing entertainers, hustlers, outcasts, and convicts, and spending her evenings in nightclubs. The theme of his created life was seriousness, of hers, human melodrama.

At *Radio Stars*, my mother interviewed Beatrice Lilly and Fanny Brice, analyzed the wild appeal of Rudy Vallee, filed reportage from Harlem and Sing Sing, and was one of the first reporters to find, and interview, the mythic Jackson Whites: the maligned, birth-defect-laden New Jersey tribe of part-black, part-Indian, and part-Hessian hill folk who had virtually made themselves into a race of their own through 225 years of intermarriage.

"So where did you go? What did you do?" Celia would excitedly ask whenever Helen got home from such an outing. Though her mother's nosiness was oppressive, it never occurred to Helen to move out of the Arlington Avenue house. For one thing, she couldn't bear to be separated from her dreamy, homely, trusting little brother Lenny; she felt like his protector. For another, it wouldn't feel right. As often as she shouted, "Ma! *Ma!* I can't *breathe!*" (a lament she shrieked regularly until the day Celia died), she hewed to the common assumption that a family traveled as one, and rose and fell together. Living alone, or with a roommate? Only odd, unhappy, or stridently bohemian girls did that.

She managed to have her share of racy romances right under her overbearing mother's nose. Her dates would sit with her at the piano in the Arlington Avenue house parlor as she played "Thou Swell, Thou Witty, Thou Great, Thou Grand," "Willow, Weep for Me," "You Ought to Be in Pictures," and her old favorite, "I Can't Give You Anything but Love, Baby." *Dream a while, scheme a while, you're sure to find . . . Happiness, and I guess all those things you've always pined for. . . .* She loved its sneaky sadness. One beau was a jazz pianist at the Village Nut Club, on Grove near Bleecker; another, a *Daily Mirror* sportswriter. In time, these boyfriends' lack of earnestness bothered her; they exhibited character flaws—drinking, gambling, insufficient innocence and substance—that made her bourgeois Jewish soul recoil. Yet she preferred these offbeat sorts to the "husband material" boys who took her friends dancing to Eddie Duchin's orchestra at the Central Park Casino. She disdained boys who were "stuffy," pitied boys who were "dreary," and despised boys who were "smug."

She was then twenty-three, the age at which she was supposed to be getting engaged. But that fate, to which her friends Lucy Neufield, Charlotte Simensky, and Gertie Finkelstein were happily acceding, seemed, to my mother, too commonplace—and too fast a foreclosure. "It was wonderful to be young and single in those days in New York," she would often recall. "You'd ride the Third Avenue el and you'd start talking to the boy sitting across from you. You'd walk down Fifth Avenue and men would *notice* you." Not that my mother ever felt beautiful, or even very pretty. Her nose was too coarse, and she desperately wished she was taller than five-two. But she had a distinctive look. Her long-lidded sloe eyes, and the extremely sharp-peaked eyebrows that jumped high above them like upside-down Vs gave her long face a soulful languor.

My mother avoided her romantic confusion by throwing herself into the reporter's life. (Escape through work would become her lifetime salvation.) In early 1934, when Curtis Mitchell was named the executive editor of *Radio Star*'s front-running rival *Radio Guide*, my mother went along as star writer, earning $40 a week, a handsome sum in the Depression. She subwayed daily to the magazine's office at Fifth Avenue and Forty-second Street, and while Mitchell penned his weekly editor's note (praising FDR's latest fireside chat or commenting on the just-born Dionne quintuplets), she ghostwrote "Confessions of a Bandmaster" for heartthrob maestro Abe Lyman and "think pieces" such as "Why We Must Dress for Radio," lambasting the notion that radio stars could wear any old thing and still convey a certain mood in their voices.

It was in her cover profiles, written as high-tabloid sagas with scenes and dialogue, that my mother defined her sensibility and her morality. Through these pieces she invented herself. Her radio stars had to *earn* their stardom, their satisfaction, and their fans' respect by winning some significant character challenge. Grit, empathy, earthiness, vision, and a quality I call scuffed integrity (ethics weathered, by imperfect options in a nonpristine profession, so that they *appear* sullied but are really humbled and thus enhanced) were the qualities rewarded in her stories, and in her value system.

Each piece was a Depression-era morality tale in which family loyalty, friendship, true romance, or personal enterprise is threatened by meretricious values. For example, she opened her piece on rebel bandleader Kenny Sargent by asking the readers to:

Imagine yourself in your first good job, after years spent in the search for one. Imagine yourself deeply in love, after years of hidden loneliness. Then imagine hearing your boss threaten to fire you—if you refused to turn away that love!

That's the predicament Kenny Sargent found himself in six years ago.

The boss was a famous Southern maestro who, for purposes of this story, we'll call Bob Smith. The girl was Dorothy Morelock, who sold cigarettes, and the place was Memphis, Tennessee—where you could have the Beale Street Blues on Beale Street itself. Kenny had them—plenty.

Svengali-like, Maestro Smith had turned former nobody Kenny into a dreamboat to the Memphis debs. Smith refused to let Kenny romance the lowly cigarette girl, but Kenny saw through the shallow planters' daughters. It was Dot, "small, blue-eyed and frank— musicians failed to dazzle her," who inspired him to stand up to the maestro's snobbery and manipulation and quit the cotillion circuit, unearthing deeper levels of talent in the process. The moral? Kenny restored his authenticity and earned his success by standing tall against domination, falsity, and smugness.

My mother loved finding what she called "*marv*elous stories, of love and sex and hardship!" These included feisty-child-actor tales, which had been tabloid staples since the early days of vaudeville. Her take on fifteen-year-old Sally Breen's championing of her brother Bobby opened thusly:

They looked so out of place in that office. She, a half-frightened little thing with spindly legs that barely reached the floor. He, a ruddy sort of boy in an immaculate sailor suit. . . . The secretary glanced at the two children and decided to do something. Forty-eight hours they had been sitting on that hard bench waiting patiently and sweetly until it hurt you to look at them. She marched into the Broadway producer's private office.

"For the love of Mike"—the producer's voice floated into the outer office. "Why don't they beat it. Tell them to scram—"

He broke off. There were two pairs of gray eyes, at an elevation of five feet and three feet respectively, focused on him. The kindergarten conquerers had managed to slip in.

The boy—skinny little thing—wanted to sing.

"Who's your manager?"

"I am." It was the girl.

He eyed her skeptically. Couldn't be more than fifteen. Mmm, not bad looking, if only she had some decent clothes on her back.

"Whose idea was it to come here?"

"Mine." That girl again.

"Who's taking care of the boy?"

"I am."

Couldn't your heart break for the Breens' tender chutzpah? Don't you just know Bobby will step in and save his sister's honor when that lecherous producer makes Sis's putting out for him a condition of Bobby's stardom? And that Bobby will become a star despite it all, because, with a devoted manager like Sally, and with the moxie unleashed in his honor duel with the producer, he's demonstrated to himself he's got the *stuff* for it?

My favorite of my mother's *Radio Guide* pieces is about has-been "radio sensation" Benny Fields and his wife, star Blossom Seeley. Helen turned the trusty whore-with-the-heart-of-gold plot into a lesson of inventive marital sacrifice.

"For better or worse. Til death do us part." Blossom meant it
when she whispered those words to Benny fifteen years ago.
She has had only too many occasions to prove it. During the
past few years Benny became a down-and-outer, and Blossom walked out of Hollywood stardom to stick by him. . . .
When they first met, he was a young squirt who had just
graduated from singing in a saloon to vaudeville. Shy and
self-conscious, he was scared to death of the haze of faces on
the other side of the footlights. She was the glamorous Star, a
successful blues singer who got first billing. The Star plucked
Young Squirt out of obscurity and put him in her act. Two
years later, they were married.

Wife overshadowing husband was a big theme in Hollywood stories of that era. So, too, the theme of the showbiz couple facing "the
grim fact that there was no more vaudeville. Blame it on the Depression, on the talkies, on radio." Whatever the source:

Blossom and Benny tried to crash the talkies as a team. But the
producers wanted Blossom alone. They saw her as a type, a
sort of combination Lilyan Tashman–Mae West–Texas Guinan. As for Benny: he wasn't young and handsome, and outside of that vague smile, he looked distressingly average, too
darned average for Hollywood.

A lesser fellow would start drinking after this stream of indignities, but stand-up Benny took it. Finally, "his last shred of pride
torn to bits," he accepted an engagement at a sleazy Chicago cabaret
and then learned (by reading the newspaper, no less) that the club
had been shut down in a gambling raid before he could collect his

paycheck. What a blow to absorb while you're having 2 P.M. breakfast coffee with your negligeed missus:

> Blossom dropped the paper. Benny stared, bewildered. This
> final irony capped two years of bad breaks. Blossom rose and
> disappeared into the bedroom. In a few minutes she came out
> in a black rhinestone evening gown. "Be right back, baby,"
> she said.
>
> She walked—evening gown and all—until she reached the
> Chez Paree, one of Chicago's leading nightclubs. She swept
> past the doorman who stared at the wild-eyed woman coming
> in unescorted. She went straight to one of the owners, Mike
> Fritzel, whom she had known in her palmier days.
>
> "Mike," she cried. "You've got to give my Benny a
> break! . . ."

Mike delivered the break: He let Benny perform. (My mother's
narrative waxes tactfully ambiguous about how Blossom might have
repaid Fritzel.) The performance led to his comeback. Blossom had
saved Benny's ego and his career.

The milieux my mother chronicled (the world of nightclubs and
nightclub personnel, of press agents, managers, cigarette girls, and
bandleaders) and the fraught bonds she assayed (the deep closeness
of a brother and a sister; a woman's love for a difficult man; the nav-
igation of a wife's career around her husband's ego) would fore-
shadow the setting and themes of her own future. Her favorite
moral—that humanity glistens all the brighter for having been
muddied by compromise and indignation—would emerge as her
gift to herself; to us, her daughters; and, later, to the wacky band of
confidantes and mentees she acquired after she hit bottom. In time,

she would become one of the people she loved to write about, those knocked-around heroes and heroines who grabbed life rafts in ingenious ways and cobbled together their own cockeyed silver linings. "Sure, I'm playing the piano in the whorehouse, but I'm tickled to death to be working at all at my age," my mother said when, in her late seventies, she became a *National Enquirer* reporter. When I waxed disdainful of her new career turn, she merely whispered, "I know the work I do is dishonorable, but it has saved me. Let your *better* work save *you*." She had learned how to locate the crevice of open-mindedness in a snob's wall of scorn and plant wise advice therein—forgivingly.

In 1936, Helen joined the brand-new *Click* magazine, Annenberg's answer to Fawcett's *Life* and Cowles's *Look*. Two months after she was hired, the editor of the New York office (the publication was headquartered in Philadelphia) was fired. Helen ascended to the job, for which her soft-touch personality was ill suited. "There were always a row of hungry photographers at the door," she often told me. "I couldn't bring myself to turn them away. I bought more photos than we needed."

Helen was still struggling with her new authority when, one day in 1937, Herman, who'd been biding his time at a law firm, called his sister at *Click* and invited her to lunch at Leo Lindy's. There, over corned beef sandwiches, Herman pulled a telegram from his vest pocket and handed it to Helen. Jerkily typed on the two strips of paper pasted on the yellow Western Union form were the words:

AM BUILDING DINNER THEATER ON SUNSET BLVD STOP
YOU'LL BE MANAGER STOP FIRST-CLASS BILLET AT
ACCOUNTANT'S OFFICE STOP EXPECT YOU FORTHWITH
STOP CARROLL

The suddenness of it shocked my mother, but the opportunity thrilled her. Walking back to work, Helen fixed Herman in the role he assumed in her mind ever after: that of the pathbreaker, off to do the family's advance work in that halcyon place shimmering across the continent. It was now all a matter of waiting to join her brother.

When Herman alighted at Union Station in Los Angeles in the spring of 1938 and walked through the sweet-smelling air looking for Earl Carroll's chauffeur a block from the century-old marketplace on Olvera Street, he was struck by the place's exoticism—the veined adobe walls, the primitive tiles, the eucalypti that draped overhead like the fringed shawls of grieving duennas. He hadn't expected, as he told my mother, the place to be so romantic, so old, and so Mexican. More than that, it was hot, bare, biblical, and golden. The low-buildinged, sparely built basin of a city offered no defense from the sun, which, having cooked over the ocean twenty miles west, now poured in at all angles.

Twenty years earlier, the city had commissioned a chamber of commerce brochure entitled "LOS ANGELES, CALIFORNIA, City and County, To-day." An artist had rendered a Pickfordesque maiden standing at a weathered adobe arch in a patch of sage, a wildflower bouquet in one arm, lifting the other high in welcome. Beyond, the artist had depicted the fledgling urbanscape—Union Station, the L.A. River, City Hall—giving way to rainbowlike bands of farmland, then brown-capped mountains, and finally snow-peaked mountains. Here was a different Lady Liberty than the one in New York Harbor: flowers instead of torch, diaphanous frock rather than the smelted gown. In place of roiling ocean was this curious, evocative vista. My mother said, "Herman wasn't sure if it was beautiful or strange, but he fell in love with it in that way you can fall in love with something you don't understand, someplace that has a pull over you."

There was still an unfinished quality to the place. The whole Los Angeles basin, from San Bernadino to Santa Monica, had, two centuries earlier, been a swamp-pocked plain where antelope and wild cattle grazed on patchy grass amid alder, willow, and sycamore; where cacti, manzanita, and buckthorn sprouted, giving the ground a scrubby aspect. Into this abyss, several leather-jacketed Spaniards—members of a company led by Captain Don Gaspar de Portola (the Spanish governor of the Californias)—and a gray-robed Franciscan friar named Juan Crespi had stumbled in August 1769. They encountered stocky aboriginals who "began to howl like wolves as they drew near to us," their diary reads, but they eventually agreed to barter. The explorers christened their new friends the Gabrieleno Indians.

Priests, soldiers, and colonists made their way up from Mexico over the next fifty years. The city passed from Spanish to Mexican rule in 1822, and the 1841 Pre-Emption Act allowed settlers to homestead for $1.25 an acre. After a trio of events—the Gold Rush of 1848, the cession of California to the United States that same year, and statehood in 1850—Hollywood and West Los Angeles attracted migrants who, over the next thirty years, built citrus orchards on acreage that would later become Melrose, Fairfax, and Fountain Avenues and miles of Wilshire, Santa Monica, and Sunset Boulevards.

Danish sailor Christian Duen homesteaded 160 acres that squared Santa Monica, Normandie, Melrose, and Western. Kentucky miner John Bower worked a plot between Franklin and Sunset. A 1870s roster of Hollywood fruit farmers includes "a German cripple, a French sailor, a Basque sheep raiser, a Mexican war veteran, a Prussian cavalry officer." Eventually, this ragtag lot would disappear, to be replaced by a civic culture so bland, it would lead H. L. Mencken to dismiss L.A. as "double Dubuque." Yet something of this haphaz-

ard diversity lingered, making for a class system that upturned eastern caste rules. The Irish, scorned in Boston, became L.A.'s elite; the
Mulhollands and Dohenys were the young city's Astors and Rocke-
fellers. In Los Angeles, Jews didn't try to "pass." People *wanted* to be
Jews; many who weren't born Jews later converted.

Perhaps the most beautiful acreage was that of Danish farmer
Ivar Weid (for whom Ivar Street was named)—it rose up into the
hills by way of its own canyon. As seen from its crown, Cahuenga
Peak, "the rolling valley waved its heavy heads of barley and oats,"
wrote a picnicker in 1901. "To the west each succeeding canyon presented its own shade of blue deepening with the distance. Like a
squirming centipede, the Santa Monica coastal range, rich in chap-
arral, extended to the west and north where to the east it dipped its
feet into the winding Los Angeles River bed."

Hollywood was much of this sleepy area's name, even back then,
at the turn of the twentieth century. One day in January 1907, when
bad weather closed down his operation, William Selig, a Chicago
producer of silent movies, opened a Los Angeles Chamber of Commerce brochure promising 350 days of sunshine each year. By 1909,
D. W. Griffith had established Biograph Studios, and soon six other
New York and Chicago studios—the New York Motion Picture
Company, the Kalem, the Rex, the Power, the Bison, and, most significantly, German refugee–turned–Oshkosh Clothing owner Carl
Laemmle's Independent Motion Pictures (I.M.P.), which would
become Universal Studios—moved west. By 1926, motion pictures
were the country's sixth-largest industry, and 90 percent of motion
pictures were made in Hollywood.

The growing new film colony needed night spots and, between
1915 and 1930, it got them. Speakeasies and gambling haunts flourished under the helpfully closed eyes (and outstretched hands) of
L.A.'s corrupt police department. Hollywood Boulevard's Mont-

martre was the hot wartime venue, followed by the New Yorker Club down the avenue near Highland, and the Hollywood Ballroom on Vine Street. To the southwest, near Goldwyn's MGM in Culver City, were the Cotton Club and Fatty Arbuckle's Plantation. The former hoped to invoke the cachet of its New York counterpart; the latter's owner allegedly raped and killed a young woman.

On January 1, 1921, the self-consciously Versailles-like Ambassador Hotel opened its doors on Wilshire Boulevard and Seventh Street, on the site of an old dairy farm. The Coconut Grove was the hotel's nightclub. Props from Valentino's *The Sheik* became the decor of the club, which featured chorus girls and stage shows as well as dining and dancing. The hotel was ground zero for Hollywood bonhomie. Marion Davies rode a horse through the lobby. Rudolph Valentino trysted there with Pola Negri and Norma Talmadge. However, it also had a dark side: The Grove's band singer Russ Colombo was shot dead by his best friend, and Jean Harlow's assignations in the cabanas with William Powell preceded her fiancé Paul Bern's suicide.

It was the Grove that Earl Carroll had come west to battle. It was large (one thousand seats), self-aggrandizing, and a bit cheesy: his taste precisely. Yet just as Carroll had started out trying to beat Ziegfeld at Ziegfeld's game and had ended up trumped by the movies, Carroll had planned his L.A. dinner theater to target the Grove, only to find that the real competition was coming from another source—the young man who had started out in New York, running Mayor Jimmy Walker's speakeasies, and who was now the publisher of the *Hollywood Reporter*: Billy Wilkerson.

A smartly dressed raconteur with a square face, slick, center-parted hair, and a pencil-thin mustache, Wilkerson had come to the West Coast via New York. He was originally from Nashville, the son of a gambler (an affliction that would prove to travel from father to son) who had won widespread Coca-Cola distribution rights in a poker game. Wilkerson was a clever, restless young man who had picked up and dropped two callings—the priesthood and medicine (plus, of course, saloon running)—before settling on newspaper publishing. In 1930, new to L.A., he had borrowed $5,000 to start Hollywood's first trade paper—an idea whose time might have come but which was met with great opposition from the ever controlling studio moguls.

It is difficult to overstate how important the punchy, chockablock, shiny-sheet *Hollywood Reporter* immediately became—and never stopped being. In "items"-ese (a language that, if it didn't quite invent, it perfected), it took the sparkling but amorphous city-within-a-city—the movie industry—and thematically packaged it and presented it daily to its far-flung denizens and residents, from beefy sound technicians to erudite novelist-screenwriters, from Realtors to soda-machine and vending-machine renters, from gossipy socialites to contract lawyers, and from movie stars to hatcheck girls. If you grew up in L.A. even tangentially related to "the Industry," all of your family's passages (weddings, births, first jobs, promotions) were likely half-sentence-itemed between ellipses in the *Reporter*. (In September 1993, I knew my mother knew she was dying when she ruefully flicked from her hospital bed the *Reporter* resubscription form—she'd been getting the paper daily for fifty years.)

Wilkerson's *Hollywood Reporter* editorials were wonders of vendetta. F. Scott Fitzgerald once became so enraged at the *Reporter's* criticism of his paramour, actress (later, gossip columnist) Sheilah Graham that he waited outside the *Reporter's* Sunset Boulevard office to challenge Wilkerson to a duel. Wilkerson never showed; the spectacle of the prince of American fiction biding his time on a street corner waiting to engage in a medieval joust must have amused the publisher.

Wilkerson's subtle readings of the film community's psyche had turned him into the town's new nightlife baron. His four-year-old Club Trocadero was farther west, for one thing—in the middle of the twisting part of Sunset Boulevard called the Strip. It was also much more intimate. Lodged in a former roadhouse that had had a second incarnation as Club La Boheme, "the Troc" was the first true Hollywood nightclub: elite and mystique-drenched. He had gotten the idea for it after Norma Shearer came up to him at a party and said, "Billy, it's a pity there isn't a good place we can go at night where we won't be hounded by autograph seekers."

The Troc was elegant and exclusive, with nooks and crannies for favored patrons. A small bar and a fireplace sat in one corner of the cavernous cellar (which housed Wilkerson's estimable cache of spirits); a back room hosted gambling; a mural of the Parisian sky graced the dining room. Wilkerson had heralded its 1934 opening in his paper as a "huge and glorious party" hosted by Myron Selznick, Hollywood's first superagent. Guests, some arriving in white horse-drawn coaches, included Dorothy Parker; the "Freddy" Astaires, Bing Crosbys, Sam Goldwyns; William Powell; and Jean Harlow. Sonja Henie, Robert Taylor, Tyrone Power, Clark Gable, Harlow, Astaire, and Crosby all came to Club Trocadero.

Aside from merely being the town's in-spot, Wilkerson's Troc also pioneered certain uses and powers of a nightclub in Hollywood. The occupational fusion of club owner–as–trade paper publisher led to economical synergy; studios teamed players up for Troc dates—and *Reporter* romance items. In the manner of the Cotton Club, the Troc also screened and showcased talent. Newcomers competed in the Troc's Sunday night amateur hours; one winner was Jackie Gleason; another, Judy Garland.

The Troc was a kind of smoky Harvard or Century Club of the movie industry. The backroom poker games of Irving Thalberg,

Darryl Zanuck, Joseph Schenck, Goldwyn, and Laemmle were as pure a concentration of competitive studio-head power as ever existed in any twenty-foot-by-thirty-foot room on any Saturday night, then or in the future—yet they were only the tip of the iceberg of Wilkerson's gaming fetish. He loved craps, the racetrack, and poker. Evenings found him at Goldwyn's or Schenck's house, playing poker with twenty-thousand-dollar chips (a staggering amount for 1940), often dropping thousands in a visit. Not surprisingly, Wilkerson had a close friendship with racketeer Johnny Roselli and, later, a very close friendship with Bugsy Siegel. Thus, gangsters and their lieutenants became Club Trocadero regulars, mixing a soupçon of Silver Slipper danger into the stew. By 1937, the Troc had become *the* place. Then, with a shrug and the snap of his fingers, Wilkerson sold it.

Herman was astonished when Earl Carroll's chauffeur pulled the car up to a small bungalow at 6230 Sunset Boulevard, on the corner of Argyle. Smack up against the tiny shack was a large, recently denuded lot with a few leftover lemon trees—a vestige of Ivar Weid's old farmland. Herman had been led to believe that Carroll had already built his theater, but in fact his old boss had just purchased the land; he had lured his trusty assistant out to start the operation from scratch. The bungalow consisted of two rooms of rented desks and file cabinets. Tacked on the office wall was the intended façade logo: THE EARL CARROLL THEATER in rounded, high-hat print, and an evocative cameo line drawing of a glamorous woman's face with a border of indecipherable script encircling her hair like a halo. Carroll greeted Herman with a hail, "Don't look so confused; we're going to be busy!" Then he bid his protégé into his town car.

"This is the city!" Carroll bellowed, as the chauffeur drove west.

No more ridiculous arrests for putting girls in bathtubs! No more excoriations from idiot bluenoses! Even at their starchiest, Carroll told Herman, L.A. cops knew what side the city's bread was buttered on. "Entertainment is what *made* this town," he declaimed. "The economy *depends* on people being fascinated with movie actors. The city's *got* to keep that public appetite whetted. This whole boulevard's a stage! Everything we had to push against in New York, it's *gone* here. The man who builds the biggest pleasure palace doesn't go to prison. He wins the jackpot!"

As the car moved west, my uncle noticed that Sunset Boulevard took on a more picaresque aspect. The dry hills closed in around Club Seville, as if only that lonely boîte would stanch a landslide. At alleylike King's Road, the hills shot up north at a ninety-degree angle and, just as precipitously, plunged south to T-square the Santa Monica Boulevard trolley tracks. *This* Sunset Boulevard was a cliff's edge: a patch of San Remo or Monte Carlo.

There seemed a subterranean intimacy there—a whiff of danger. Carroll's elucidation of the neighborhood bore out Herman's hunch. Up King's Road, architect Rudolph Schindler's Japanese house was a commune where arty residents performed Balinese dances in the nude and guests made love to one another's spouses. Back down on Sunset, next to the Club Seville, bulked a French chateau-style apartment house with an elegant double staircase. Wealthy men kept secret suites there; mistresses fled down the left stairs while angry wives stormed up the right one. A few blocks west, at Doheny, sat Maxim's. Inebriated patrons who exited after the 2 A.M. last call would careen down the steep street, feather boas twisting around lampposts.

The Strip, a 1.7-mile, twelve-block stretch of Sunset Boulevard was no-man's land: unincorporated territory between L.A. itself (of which Hollywood was part) and Beverly Hills, the now-separate city to the west. The Strip was originally known as Sherman, and it was governed by an opportunistic and libertine sheriff; its lure to club owners was its largely tax-exempt status.

A family named Montgomery owned most of the Strip; they'd bought it in the 1880s, taking a chance that the mountain would not crash in on the boulevard. The Montgomerys lived in a mansion just above their holdings; they leased their lots out carefully, strictly controlling building design. The heart of the Montgomerys' duchy, between Sunset Plaza and La Cienega, had the look of an elegant village. A cluster of shops were French Regency, while pillars gave a neoclassical cast to the bank and office buildings.

The clubs on the Strip were inflammatory, both literally and figuratively. Carroll pointed to the site of the old Russian Eagle, which had flourished in the twenties. Opium had been smoked in the back room. John Barrymore, Ramon Novarro, and Russian femme fatale Alla Nazimova had hidden out in the club from photographers. The Eagle's owners were Russian émigrés with raging tempers. One night, the pair fought noisily—one was romancing the other's wife. The cuckolded partner came back in the dead of night and set fire to the club. Flames shot up against the mountain, loosening a wooden footbridge, threatening an avalanche, and reducing the club to embers. (Nazimova kept memories of that night close to her vest; she had turned her nearby mansion into a hotel—the Garden of Allah bungalows. There she played hostess to the likes of John O'Hara, Robert Benchley, and William Faulkner, when movie work brought those writers westward.) More recently, the Clover Club, the Strip's reigning gambling joint, had also mysteriously burned down, but not before it, too, hosted its share of storied fistfights, including that of talent agent Pat DiCicco (eventually the first husband of the much younger "Little Gloria" Vanderbilt) and New York Yankees owner Dan Topping.

At the legendary and just-sold Troc, Carroll and Herman got out of the car, as if to pay their respects to the one place that had captured the unique and elusive spirit of the boulevard. With its black-and-white awning under its pillared porte cochere, and its more stylish version of the high, rounded art deco script that Carroll was using, the Troc was *soignée*. What could Billy Wilkerson have had in mind when he abandoned it at the height of its glory? Another nightclub? Where? Who was putting up the money? Roselli? Carroll confessed to Herman that he had been obsessing about his aggravating Midas-touch rival.

It was getting dark by the time Carroll and Herman returned to the bungalow office on Argyle, but Carroll had one more thing to show Herman before delivering the weary traveler and his valises to his lodging. "Look at this," he said, pulling the tacked logo design down from the wall and pointing to the words encircling the woman's tilted head. Herman read:

Through These Portals Pass the
Most Beautiful Girls in the World

There were his words, in the embryonic nightclub's motto.

"I should charge you royalties," my uncle quipped.

"I, *you*," Carroll replied, "for all you've learned from me."

"These portals": his innocent phrase, meant to refer to the Broadway stage door. Yet suddenly the portals now harkened to something else: the weathered adobe arch next to which the Pickfordesque maiden stood in the field of sage flowers, welcoming all to this place, this land, this opportunity.

The next morning Herman awoke at 4 A.M.—7 A.M. East Coast time. Then, as he often recounted, to stretch his train-cramped legs he walked for three hours. He struggled to superimpose the intensity of Manhattan upon the miles of telephone wire looping from pole to pole over yawning lots, the low-slung shops, and tidy rows of Monopoly-board stucco houses, their rectitude contradicted by the heady scent of the jacaranda, hibiscus, and bougainvillea buds, whose vines curled around windows and porches and roofs, all sappy and dewy at that hour. This sleepy, prim, erotic place was home now, and he was transforming himself once again—from impresario's aide-de-camp to impresario-in-waiting. He was thirty-three; Carroll was forty-six. Creating the ultimate Hollywood nightclub was not Earl Carroll's job, my uncle Herman understood, during this predawn walk. It would become his own destiny.

Herman's phone calls from the West Coast were full of bulletins:

- He was running into a different friend or colleague, from Broadway or Brooklyn, every day, sometimes every hour.
- His old *Vanities* pal Dave Chasen had opened a restaurant on Doheny Drive and Beverly Boulevard. Frank Capra named it Chasen's Southern Barbecue Pit. Dave served spareribs for thirty-four cents and chili for a quarter.
- He was scouring the "race rooms"—the Last Word and Club Alabam, next to Hotel Dunbar on Central Avenue; the Swanee Inn; the Paradise Cafe—for the best talent: a pianist, Earl "Gatemouth" Hines; another, Nat Cole; a third, Billy Daniels.
- Carroll and Herman had hired Gordon Kaufman as the architect, Frank Don Riha as the interior designer, and Ford Twaits as the construction engineer. The floor show would be three solid hours.
- Carroll wanted snob appeal. Tables would be arranged in six rising tiers; the arc of closest-in tables was named the Inner Circle, the seats reserved for a thousand dollars a year apiece

by stars and socialites. Darryl Zanuck, Bing Crosby, and Walter Wanger were the Earl Carroll Theater's board of governors.

Over the summer of 1938, Herman spoke of the four-bedroom house he had purchased on DeLongpre, off Franklin. In September he sent a ceremonial Western Union telegram:

GROUNDBREAKING OCTOBER 18. OPENING NIGHT DECEMBER 26. I AM COMING TO GET YOU.

By the autumn of 1938, the Arlington Avenue house was sold. Helen quit *Click*. Lenny left the sales job he had at a sheet music company. Celia said good-bye to the neighbors and her temple sisterhood, and boxed up every thimble, scrap, and bobbin.

Closing the door behind them for the last time, they drove the short distance to the cemetery. Sadie had died twenty years earlier, almost to the day. I don't know if my mother, in all her journeys back to New York, ever returned to that grave. I would not be surprised if she didn't. Sadie loomed large but too fragile in her heart to risk loosening that tender hold through the awkwardly dutiful, anticlimactic act of standing there. No, that was most likely the last farewell—that day alone, that moment. Leaving New York meant that a stage of the family's life had snapped shut, like the lid meeting the rim of a steamer trunk.

One by one, everyone bent down and laid a stone on Sadie's marker. Then they got into the Packard and drove to California.

Part II

Chapter Five

HOLLYWOOD: 1939–1941

W hen I think about the five Hovers lumbering across the country on the dusty roads and two-lane blacktops, I picture their Packard as a covered wagon—a covered wagon in which the elder pioneers spoke Yiddish. As for so many immigrants, that maiden lugubrious pilgrimage, that initial claim-staking on the place, would take on an increasingly romantic coloration over the years.

They pulled into L.A. at dusk—the young city's few-and-far-between lights shimmering, my mother would recall, like a fistful of diamonds thrown on an old army blanket. Herman dropped Celia and Isidore at the DeLongpre house, where a live-in maid waited to turn down their beds. Then, after a stop at the nightclub's construction site, he drove Helen and Lenny straight to the action—the Hollywood Brown Derby.

This was where the filmland media congregated. In one booth was Hedda Hopper's star writer Spec McClure, who was recently a Laurel Canyon vagabond. (He'd arrived at his first day of work at the Hatted One's office with leaves stuck to his clothing.) He was talking with Warners publicist Irving Fein, who had dubbed Ann Sheridan "the Oomph Girl" and Lana Turner "the Sweater Girl," and who was then naming half of desultory Burbank's newly paved streets after John Garfield's and Clark Gable's leading ladies. With them was young Paramount publicist A. C. Lyles, whose strikingly handsome face and quick-study charm had earned him dates with Joan Crawford and Ginger Rogers. Just two years earlier, Lyles had been an eighteen-year-old movie usher in Jacksonville, Florida. He had jumped on a train for L.A. with two loaves of bread and two jars of peanut butter, and, at Union Station, had hitchhiked straight to Paramount and implored Adolf Zukor for a job as an office boy.

Sleek and queenly in the number one booth, already wearing the new "stemline" silhouette that was all the rage in Paris, picking at the restaurant's famous Cobb salad, was the Derby's publicist, Maggie Ettinger. Besides being Greta Garbo's confidante, Irving Thalberg's chum, and Louella Parsons's double cousin (their parents married each other's sister and brother), Ettinger was Hollywood's first female studio publicist. After leaving Metro, Ettinger had signed up a workmanly film-processing company as her first private client; she told them she would turn them into a household word synonymous with Hollywood. She renamed the company Technicolor.

A dapper man stopped at Maggie's booth and lifted her hand, clad in a fingerless silk-glove, to his lips. Ettinger pretended not to be amused. In his memoir, Herman would describe the man as "Gaylord Ravenal right off the showboat: charming, polished, sartorial, and completely ruthless." Irving Fein, at the Hovers' booth, said, "He's the one who discovered Lana. She was Judy Turner then, pudgy little shiksa, playing hookey and sipping a malted."

"Well, she sure paid him back, with all those nights at the Troc," Helen quipped. (She had been doing her homework.)

The man in question slid into a booth and was soon flanked by scotch-clutching newsmen in snap brims.

"Who *is* he?" Lenny asked.

"That," Herman answered, "is Billy Wilkerson."

The next day Helen bought an open-top car for fifty dollars and, with Isidore, paid a visit to the Annenberg offices, which were smack in the middle of the Strip's media row; they abutted the *Hollywood Reporter*, which was across the boulevard from Dell (it published *Modern Screen*) and catty-corner from both Fawcett (*Screen Book*) and McFadden (*Photoplay*). The offices were equidistant from the Troc and Maxim's, everyone's lunch spots. Agents' and publicists' offices filled out the row. Red and white poinsettias bloomed between the buildings. The pulsing little swath seemed like a snippet of midtown Broadway plunked down beneath the hulking Hollywood hills.

Isidore waited in the car while Helen rushed in, pocketbook under arm, Andrews Sister skirt pleating out over her kneecaps.

"Helen! Well, I'll be damned, You've made the move!" Carl Schrader, Annenberg's West Coast boss, exclaimed. He got right on the telephone to Tom Fisdale, who ran the top radio publicity shop in town. (The top movie publicity house was run by Helen Ferguson.) "Guess who's here? Helen Hover!" Fisdale offered her a job. The industry was growing faster than the talent; any decent pro was put to work immediately. My mother said she'd take it only if she could freelance on the side. Fisdale consented.

My mother sashayed out to the car and drove her captive father to Bullock's Wilshire, where, in an act of celebratory defiance, she bought a wardrobe. She informed Isidore that things had changed: She might continue to live in the same house as her mother, but she would never again be a slave to Celia's sewing machine, her taste, or her domination. With every shirt, suit, and pair of creamy pleated slacks she purchased, she felt more independent.

Still, this gesture was canceled out by the sheer act of Isidore sitting there, and by the fact that the family was re-creating Arlington Avenue on DeLongpre. My poor, clueless mother was overripe for love and marriage, piling up her smart new duds, unaware that she was setting up a half-ancient, half-cutting-edge life for herself, in which she'd be inviting any man who wished a place in her life to compete with the family's star, her brother.

The magazines and publicity firms on Sunset Boulevard were full of women. At Fisdale, Helen was taken under wing by the glamorous Pauline Swanson, a chic, sinewy creature whose successful screenwriter husband, Leo Townsend, would eventually be a victim of the blacklist. Edith Weiss, another young New York girl who joined the office later, remembers "Helen as someone who knew the ropes" and Pauline as "stunning, elegant—the person we both aspired to be." Pauline freelanced on the side—for *Photoplay*, of which Maggie Ettinger had once been editor, and for *Modern Screen*, where wry Sylvia Kahn was the new West Coast chief. Kahn, who later married Irving Wallace, a fellow *Modern Screen* writer who became one of the fifties most successful popular novelists, had survived one baptism by fire just by getting hired. (Dell had almost no Jewish employees, and when president George Delacorte asked the Bronx-accented Sylvia her religion, Sylvia fixed him with a glare and answered with a nonsensical Hindi-sounding word to let him know she resented the hell out of the implication.) At about the time my mother arrived on the scene, Sylvia was about to face another challenge: Erroll Flynn and Cary Grant threatened lawsuits over stories. Those actions augured the long era of star-coddling movie magazines, continued today by every glossy magazine that uses celebrities on its cover.

I once asked my mother, "Did movie stars ever sue the old movie magazines?" She was an *Enquirer* stringer by then; at seventy-six she was the first reporter to name the woman who'd given John Belushi his final speedball. She'd been boot-camped, late in life, to every form of humiliation, deception, and stealth maneuver. ("If," she'd opined in September 1991, "the Communist leaders had prepared for revolt like the *Enquirer* prepared for Liz Taylor's wedding to Larry Fortensky, there would still be a Soviet Union.") So she had snorted, "Sue? There was nothing to sue *over!*"

Through a combination of shrewdness and luck, my mother scored a coup her second week in town: She became the first U.S. reporter to whom Vivien Leigh granted an interview after having been picked to play Scarlett O'Hara. Picking up interviews as well with David and Myron Selznick and Margaret Mitchell, she whipped out "Why Vivien Leigh for the Scarlett O'Hara Role?" for *Screen Guide, Radio Guide,* and five other Annenberg publications.

My mother's lifelong penchant for setting the noncognoscenti straight began with this piece. "The routine story of how Miss Leigh came to David Selznick's attention is that his agent brother Myron brought her to the lot on December 12 to watch the shooting of the burning of Atlanta," she reminded readers. However:

> Actually it goes back a little further. Vivien had come to Hol-
> lywood in December for a short vacation. . . . During her sec-
> ond week, she and Laurence Olivier, a good friend and
> rumored romance [here the libel lawyers made her backpedal]
> (a slightly exaggerated observation since Vivien has a hus-
> band, and a daughter, Suzanne) went to a party at Paulette
> Goddard's house. Up until that moment the role seemed to be
> in the bag for Paulette. But Vivien made an appearance.
> Selznick was at the party. He saw her.

My mother wrote fast, typed fast, and worked the phones prodigiously. A hand-painted cigarette case that MGM made for her as a gift a few years later shows the young Helen Hover as captured by a sketch artist: swiveling in her chair from typewriter stand to desk; her fingers double-jointedly attacking the keys; her ear pressed to one phone, a second phone jangling; papers issuing forth from the Underwood's roller and fluttering over her desk like oversized confetti. That sixty-year-old caricature perfectly captures her. (The only things missing are the balled-up Kleenex she reflexively stuffed under her sweater sleeve and the three daily newspapers' ink-blackened rubber bands she addledly turned into bracelets.) Frantic yet in control, never finishing sentences—that is how anyone who knew my mother remembers her.

She knew she wanted a column, and for that she would have to be opinionated, as she had been in her *Radio Stars* melodramas and for her "Nancy Goes Shopping" persona. So for *Screen Book* she wrote a piece about stars' effects on fashion, called "The Hollywood Dictator." In her trademark style she assayed:

> What the dream girls of Hollywood wear and don't wear immediately becomes the yardstick for millions of adoring fans all around the country. That's why you see ordinary girls wearing their hair swooshed up on their heads like a mop, and hats as large as an eye patch bobbing on top of many a sensible noggin. But if this sounds like so much Einstein, here is the straight of it:
>
> A few years ago a languorous lady by the name of Garbo popped on the movie scene with cornflower hair that hung uncurled and limp, down to her shoulders. Before this, we had been marcelling our hair like the scallops of a fancy doily. Soon, by gad, Crawford combed out the ringlets and let her

mane wave long and carelessly in the California sun. And before you could say 'Schiaparelli,' Loretta Young, Bette Davis, Carole Lombard and all the other movie pets were doing the same. Just between you and me, dearie, it made you look as young as your prom-trotting kid sister. . . .

Impressed by her young protégé, Pauline Swanson asked Helen to help her with a piece she was doing for *Photoplay* on the Jack Haleys' adoption of a child who'd been shuttled around in foster care. According to my mother, when Pauline read her first sentence—"The battered little suitcase finally has a home"—Swanson turned the entire story, and fee, over to her.

Within a month, my mother's dream came true: She was made a Fawcett columnist. She would have a five-to-eight-page monthly section in *Screen Book*, complete with its own logo: a strip of celluloid with "Filmland Whispers by Helen Hover" in tall, thin print, upon which was superimposed a sketch of a hand cupped to an ear. She had gone from being a beat journalist to a personage in the Hollywood food chain. No longer was she merely serving up the occasional new star to the masses. The life of this mythical town was hers to intepret and help shape, as an insider.

With a mock-up of the logo in hand, she drove her coupe down Sunset Boulevard to Argyle. The Earl Carroll Theater was almost shipshape—its hundreds of yards of tufted patent leather, on the banquettes and the ceiling, so spanking-new that it smelled to my mother as if she had just walked into a nail polish factory. Headwaiter Marcel Lamaze (a "portly pixie," in Herman's words) uncorked a bottle of champagne, and in a corner of the cavernous arena he and Herman toasted the new columnist. Carroll strode through the darkened room to offer his congratulations. Then my

mother drove to the nearby Western Union and wired Lucy
Neustein, her "Nancy" partner:

FILMLAND WHISPERS BY HELEN HOVER STOP WELL
SMACK ME SILLY WHO'DA THUNK IT?

She began to make the rounds of the studios, stopping by production bungalows and scoping out the commissaries with a gaze
that would ripen over the years into what her friend, preeminent
Hollywood publicist Frank Lieberman, called "that all-knowing
look of hers." While in Darryl Zanuck's waiting room at 20th Century–Fox one day, she fell into conversation with Zanuck's private
secretary, Beatrice Einstein. With her mess of blond curls, her
squinty, cockeyed smile, and her distracted air, Beadie (as everyone
called her) seemed much more comedienne than poised appointment scheduler. Like Helen, Beadie was twenty-eight. The sarcastic
asides she muttered after she clicked off the intercom to Zanuck's
suite reminded Helen of her own wisecracks. "We became friends
right away," my mother said. "For twenty years, Beadie and I never
stopped laughing."

Helen started dating Beadie's almost-divorced brother, *Los Angeles Times* adman Louie Einstein. "He was bright, funny; he had a
great personality. We had a marvelous romance," she told me. They
often visited the third Einstein sibling in Benedict Canyon. Comic
Harry Einstein had become successful once he'd changed his name
to Parkya Carcass. Everyone called him Parky. (Apparently fond of
punnish names, Parky—who eventually died in Milton Berle's arms
in the middle of his own Friars Club Roast—later named his own
son Albert—Albert Einstein. When Albert Einstein launched a
comedy writing and acting career of his own, he changed his name
to the more buttoned-down Albert Brooks.)

. . .

The Earl Carroll Theater was finally ready. December 26, 1938, was opening night—and a risky time it was to be launching a Hollywood nightclub. Business was unaccountably off all up and down the Strip. The entertainment columnist of the *Herald Express* had recently sneered that "owners of Hollywood nightspots are already snow-blind from the glare of empty white table-tops [*sic*] in their joints." Either Earl Carroll "would hit a new high in bankruptcy figures," the writer continued, "or West Coast cafe society will find itself bumping into itself in the only hot spot able to stay open in town." The pressure on Herman was enormous.

The theater was insuperably luxurious. Outside, the neon ten-foot-radius woman's head beamed elegantly, haloed by Herman's "Through these portals . . ." legend. Inside, sculptor Martin Deutsch transformed the likeness of *Vanities* star Beryl Wallace into a fifteen-foot-tall gold statute for the lobby. Ten thousand neon tubes were suspended from the patent leather ceiling—interior designers Don Riha and Twaits had created the largest assemblage of vertical lighting anywhere—and glowing glass columns striped the bar. A revolving stage faced an arc of six ascending tiers of flooring—bearing tables and booths for 1,160 patrons—160 more than the Grove seated.

Five hundred invited guests turned out, including Marlene Dietrich, Dolores Del Rio, Tyrone Power, Gable and Lombard, Errol Flynn, Robert Taylor, and *Vanities* alumnus W. C. Fields. When everyone was seated, the orchestra started up; after a few bars, the music softened and the wattage in the banks of neon tubes diminished by subtle increments. In the quietly intensifying darkness and stillness, the scattered sounds—a clink of glass, a swish of crepe and taffeta, the random cough, the snap of flint to striker—were portentous and percussive.

Herman strode from stage left to the microphone, his tuxedo slick as sealskin. "Ladies and gentlemen, welcome to the Earl Carroll Theater, the largest, the most elaborate nightclub theater in the world," he announced to the hushed room. "And now, it gives me great pride to present the man behind it all: Mr. Earl Carroll!"

The proscenium curtains parted and, baby spot following him, Carroll walked forward. In quick succession, layer after layer of rear curtains slashed open behind the impresario, and thirty-four feathered, rhinestoned, baton-wielding, nearly nude girls cakewalked down a dozen sun-ray-spaced spokes of rampway. Herman had sweated every single selection, and he could recite their names— Yolande Donlan, Frances Brunson, Vivian Coe, Mary Daniels, Harriet Benney, Virginia Maples, Bonnie Otacar, Patsy Bedell, Gwynne Norys, Betty Ghear, Marna Stansell, and so on—for years afterward. In a routine shaped by Busby Berkeley (to whom Carroll had paid premium price to serve as guest choreographer), the girls walked up to Carroll, one by one, and each, stretching out her baton arm, took her place in one of two facing lines on curved risers. The rearmost curtain crinkled upward, and the arbored row of batons were raised, two by two, like the muskets of cadets at a West Point wedding. The reigning Miss America, Pat Lee, paraded down the center, with her head ringed by an Aztec sun god headpiece and her torso sheathed in a gem-encrusted nude body stocking. The audience applauded heartily.

"Everyone crowded around Herman," my mother said years later. "The press. The studio heads. Ma was in heaven. We *all* were."

Still, there were gaffes ("unintentional comedy reminiscent of Mack Sennett," as *Click* put it), which eluded my mother's recollection. "Revolving stages ran amuck," the magazine continued.

"Mikes went dead. Waiters dropped dishes and curtains stuck. Despite it all, Hollywood liked it and kept coming for more."

Carroll's ambition made for good copy. In its January 23, 1939, issue, *Time* magazine's "People" column ran this item:

Dance Director *LeRoy Prinze* complained bitterly to the Screen Actors' Guild that Producer *Earl Carroll*, who a fortnight ago opened the most elaborate cabaret-theater-restaurant on the West Coast (*Time*, Jan. 9), was violating the Wagner Labor Relations Act. Said he: "Carroll is trying to corner all the legs in Hollywood—the legs that we have trained."

In search of column items, Helen, with Louie and Beadie and Beadie's actor beau, would go to Herman's club—pictures show them sitting between Edgar Bergen and the Ken Murrays—and then to the Troc and Maxim's. She saw for herself, through the lens of her beat, how essential truly wild-hearted creatures were to Hollywood's aura. The fascination they generated lifted the ships of press agent, nightclub, columnist, movie magazine, trade paper, agent, manager, leading man, picture, and studio. They also were becoming rare commodities. Since diction and wit were de rigueur in the all-the-rage "screwball" comedies, the new female stars—Katherine Hepburn, Bette Davis, Olivia de Havilland—were taut and controlled; not so, Lana Turner. Sighting Lana at a club, my mother would rush outside and arrange to phone the car attendants on their home party lines later that evening for details about who escorted Turner home.

"Lana Turner is back with Greg Bautzer again, but not before several dramatic run-ins with other escorts," her first column confided. (Bautzer was the extremely handsome attorney for Howard Hughes and quite the lady's man.)

108 SHEILA WELLER

We saw her at a night spot with Randolph Scott, and the strangest bit of pantomine took place. Lana was laughing and dancing with Randy, looking as though she were enjoying herself tremendously. Then she suddenly fled the table, leaving Randy embarrassed. She ran outside, hailed a cab and jumped in, but not before she had scribbled a note and given it to the waiter to hand to Scott. Randy still doesn't know what it's all about.

My mother started separating people into two camps: the "drab" and the "exciting." Everyone who worked in Hollywood wanted "exciting," and, drenched in that world as they were, they began to emulate the quality. My mother lost weight, had her hair dyed blond, and visited the showgirls' doctor to see about a nose bob.

After their forays at the clubs, my mother and Louie and Beadie and her date would end up at Beadie's apartment, which was in the chateaulike Strip building that housed the married bigwigs' trophy mistresses. Next door, at 8433 Sunset Boulevard, a new building was rising on the lot of the just-razed Club Seville, smack against the King's Road mountain. A rumor percolated up and down the Strip: This was to be Billy Wilkerson's ultimate creation.

"Would Herman ever leave Carroll for Billy?" Beadie asked.

"Oh, I think Herman would *love* to work for Billy," my mother said. "So would I, for that matter."

Beadie blew smoke rings out the window while Helen brushed out her hair at Beadie's night table. The fellows were gone; Helen was spending the night on her friend's Murphy bed. The studio secretary with her own flat; the nightclub-crawling gossip columnist: two nice Jewish girls tiptoing away from the convention that still tethered them.

· · ·

Fawcett gave my mother an office; she was always on the phone, deftly switching personae as circumstance demanded—from crisp professional, to awed and grateful confidante, to tough, wisecracking colleague. Much later, when she worked from home, I'd fall asleep at night and awake in the morning to that shrewd alternation of affect and her landmark exclamations—"Well, I'll be damned!" "You don't say!" "Son of a gun!"—wafting from her office to Lizzie's and my adjacent bedroom.

Often, too, I heard her dispensing advice and heartfelt encouragement to out-of-work actors, desperate starlets, and aggressive but threadbare press agents. She really *liked* these people, and her irony and compassion (both of which grew exponentially after she'd survived her nervous breakdown) led several wildly funny, deeply tormented men—including the brilliant young comedian Freddie Prinze, who, in the early seventies called her his "second mother"— to cleave to her suggestions.

In 1960, when she became the West Coast editor of Dell Publications, other only-in-Hollywood types like James Mason's decadently witty ex-wife Pamela (who allowed her son Morgan to smoke when he was seven) and Fabian's shot-out-of-Philly manager Bob Marcucci became her friends. During the early sixties, porcine art photographer Larry Schiller (who has been known for the last twenty years as "investigative reporter Lawrence Schiller") lived for the work she threw his way, and Raquel Welch (then a Mexican starlet) got her start when my mother selected her for a "Don't Let Them Call *You* Skinny!" *Modern Screen* Wate-On ad.

In the last fifteen years of her life, when she morphed from *Modern Screen* West Coast editor to *Enquirer* sleuth, she acquired confidants with more extreme idiosyncracies. Her best male friend was Don Monte, a riotously funny, ghetto-Italian, beefy gay gossip columnist, who drove a Guido-bowed Cadillac and lived with his mother. Her other friends included a super-wholesome TV star–turned–public official who lost both her socially prominent husband and her famous novelist beau because of her nymphomania, and the rich hippie child-bride of an Old Guard agent, who would sit in our living room, displaying the spoils of her latest shoplifting expedition.

There was also the onetime Elvis girlfriend whose son was paralyzed in a car accident and who herself needed a kidney transplant, but whose best friend's husband, America's top movie hero and good guy, wouldn't loan her money toward either health emergency. Not to mention the pubic-hair stylist to the town's top call girls, and the unusually well-endowed wife of the B-movie mogul, who drove to our house in tears: In midtryst with Evel Knievel, he had ejected her, nude, into the Beverly Hills Hotel lobby. There were dozens of others, terrified their just-diagnosed diseases and just-disclosed addictions would make them unemployable. My mother comforted them, rallied their spirits, and kept their secrets.

Throughout her reporting career my mother also cultivated nightclub and restaurant staffers—the parking lot boys, bouncers, waiters, and cigarette girls. Clear-eyed, rendered invisible by way of their servitude, they watched their "betters" display insecurity, pettiness, and loathsomeness every evening. "They're smarter than half the people they serve," my mother once laughed. "And if you were condescending to any of them, they knew it in a minute." It was from such sources that she was able to report, in February 1939:

Wow—the whispers that went up because Wally Beery bought Mae Murray's lunch four times in a row at the Brown Derby!

Romance? Well, it would make a mighty fine story to have these two old-timers drawn together by li'l Cupid. But it isn't so. Wally, for all his bluff ways, is a big softy. Mae hasn't been having too easy a time, what with no work and all lawsuits. Wally has been lending her his hefty shoulder to rest her troubles on.

In her "When They Weren't Looking" section, she wrote:

Deanna Durbin and Vaughn Paul skipping lunch at the studio cafe to sit and hold hands in his automobile . . . Janet Gaynor weighed down with a 50 carat topaz while her friends ask, 'Where's that big ring taking the little girl? . . . the Beverly Hills Brown Derby a Sunday dinner rendezvous for Hollywood's married couples: the Clark Gables, the Fred MacMurrays, the Jimmy Cagneys.

But business, not social life, was her main beat:

Wha's this? Is Dolores Del Rio's return to the screen a slap on the wrist for Hedy Lamarr? That's what they're saying along Hollywood and Vine. Hedy's tiff for higher pay at M-G-M is keeping her inactive; and bringing in Del Rio, who is the same dark, exotic type, may serve as a club over her head.

Soon Fawcett gave her a second five-page column, "Intimate Gossip by Helen Hover," in its new monthly, *Screen Life*. Now she was always working, a not-unhappy turn of events for her (my mother always thrived on work, despite its trivial content). Celia worried: Would Helen *ever* marry? Or would she be like Olivia De Havilland, of whom my mother wrote:

Speaking of Olivia, they're now calling her "The Mary Brian of 1939." Time was when Miss Brian was the most dated girl in Hollywood. Remember? Then all her beaux went off to marry other girls. Buddy Rogers, Dick Powell, Cary Grant, et al. History seems to be repeating itself. Brunette, demure and petite, she packs the same charms for the stag line that Mary had. But the romances don't last. The boys march to the altar with others.

All of Helen's old friends from Brooklyn were married in this last year of the 1930s. She alone had stayed the career course into her late twenties. Romantically, she encountered a rocky road. She had broken up with Louie Einstein because his divorce was not coming through fast enough, and she had embarked upon a romance with rising-star bandleader Harry Warnow. (Eventually, under the name Raymond Scott, Warnow would headline on TV's *Your Hit Parade*.) But Warnow was hard to snag; he wanted to play the field—and he did, leaving her dismayed and vulnerable. Hollywood men were challenging, even for stars, as she told her readers:

All the girls want Jimmy Stewart to date them now that his *Mr. Smith* seems headed for the Oscar. But he's cagey. He caused a ripple of excitement in this town by having dinner with Marlene Dietrich . . . [and] he dates Loretta Young when she has a free night. How that boy manages to steer clear of the tie that binds!

Yet she was a striking, vibrant woman. My favorite picture of my mother from those days shows her standing over Groucho Marx, who is reclining on a divan in his dressing room, looking up at her anxiously. In a pinstripe-plaid suit with pointy white pocket hankies, she is Hepburn-chic, and, wielding a palm frond, half smiling down on Groucho, she's as cool as one of Carroll's showgirls. Her hair spills down her long neck; her skin is creamy; her eyebrows are arched provocatively high; her newly bobbed nose makes her almost beautiful.

Lenny, who had a job at the Carroll, told his sister about a friend who had a friend for her: a medical intern at Cedars. Helen declined. "Doctors," she said, "are conceited and boring."

Lenny persisted. This fellow wasn't boring, his friend conveyed. Helen continued to balk at her younger brother's offer.

One of my best sources of intelligence on my father's life during those years was his Cedar's internship roommate, Dr. Irving Newman, with whom I had several conversations twenty-five years ago. Newman said:

> Your father used to lie awake at night, keeping me up laughing with re-creations of the old Fibber McGee and Molly shows and the old Monroe Gold monologues. Radio, Victrola, whatever he heard—he had them memorized. He spent so much time in bed as a boy, what else could he do but memorize them? He would stare at the ceiling and do the characters—the farmer with his problems with his cow, the old Jewish man with the *tsuris* with his wife: McGee, Monroe, McGee, Monroe—sometimes he had them talking to each other! Then he'd pick up that damn trumpet . . .

Of their interning days, Dr. Newman had marveled:

> I never knew how Danny, with that heart of his, could take those fourteen-hours-a-day rotations. We'd fall asleep standing

up. We used amphetamines to stay awake. Joy pills, we called them. I'd say, "Danny, what the heck are you doing, taking those things, with your bum ticker?" He said Cedars was the only hospital that took him, that didn't have concerns about his health, his stamina—well, dammit, he was going to rise to the occasion. He used to say, "If you see me turning blue, throw me a hose [an oxygen mask]—but *don't* let anyone see it."

And he always had that pipe in his mouth. No one thought of tobacco and the heart back then. Even if he suspected, he wouldn't care. He was jovial *and* bitter about his health. He felt he got a raw deal. But, you see, he was sly, he was clever— he made the raw deal work for him. It was part of the twinkle in his eye. He had what you'd call nowadays an old soul. Everyone loved Danny Weller. He was a short, homely guy. But, oh, the girls went for him, the nurses! People loved him. *Loved* him!

Freed from the domineering, overprotective Lena and Rosie, my father unfurled a compelling bachelor image. He knew how endearing his premature wistfulness was. So, too, was the mischief combined with the utter seriousness. There was also the extravagant self-possession that his medical school yearbook had noted—his selfishness and narcissism. Did the hint of a mean streak also surface—provocatively disarming in this round-faced, soft-fleshed, baby-blue-eyed man? Probably. It was always his secret weapon. Here in Hollywood, the newly arrived intern Danny Weller was perfecting his persona as surely as any newly arriving actor. The hospital on Sunset Boulevard was his version of his father's gates of Oklahoma.

There is a wonderful picture of my father, Dr. Newman, and Dr.

Newman's future wife Adele sitting in a study annex of their Cedars intern dorm. How luxe everything looks—the fancy brass lamp, the gold-embossed leather medical journals on the mahogany desk. Pretty Adele is perched on the desk, wearing a striped-sleeve silk top and wide-legged trousers. Her hair is held up on the sides with black bows, and her chin rests coquettishly on the back of her curled hand (red nail polish is very visible) as she looks over the handsome, dark-wavy-haired Dr. Newman's shoulder. He is sitting in a bentwood chair, stethoscope in hand, reading a medical journal so crisply reproduced I can almost smell its slick pages. Young Dr. Newman's chest hair peeks out of the scrubs he has on under his white jacket. Across from him, on a couch, sits my father with a pipe in his mouth, and the hair that had been abundant in his medical school photo is now receding. He is delicate and thoughtful—handsome (yes, *handsome*—not homely, Dr. Newman), the light to Irv Newman's dark. He is wearing a suit and tie; every crease and ripple in his pants casts a shadow. I can almost feel the fabric.

According to Dr. Newman's reminiscence, at night, in their dorm room after their rounds, the two interns would lie back and swap talks about honeys there and back East. They had a picture of Artie Shaw's singer Helen Forrest taped to the mirror. They believed America would be drawn into war and they were ready to go—Danny was enlisting as a seaman; the merchant marine was most likely to take him despite his "ticker problem." If worse came to worst, he planned to take Irv's EKG and fob it off as his own.

After the war was won, they would resume their career ascendancy. Their immigrant fathers' cramped career options—*shmata* maker, mender, or peddler—had given way to their own far wider choice: medicine or entertainment. All of Danny's brothers doctors, but Irv was born into more of a show business family. Irv's brother Alfred Newman, a former classical music child prodigy who, at twenty-nine, was Irving Berlin's film musical director, was the head of music for Zanuck's 20th Century–Fox.

Irv's kid brother Lionel had also been a prodigy. He had played piano for Mae West, Irving bragged to Danny, and he had contributed songs to Earl Carroll's *Vanities*. Now he was out here, too, tinkling the ivories for the movies. (Between them, Lionel and Alfred Newman eventually scored several hundred films and won dozens of Oscars and Grammys. The family's luster would extend into the next generation, to Irving and Adele's songwriter son Randy Newman.)

Lionel was selling songs to Carroll's Herman Hover for their new nightclub, Irv told Danny one night in the early spring of 1940.

"You think *that's* something?" Danny responded. "I've got a blind date with Hover's sister." (It is amazing to me that my father—ever disdainful, when I knew him, of his brother-in-law's frivolous work—had ever bragged about the connection.)

"Hover's sister? Jesus, don't tell her about the joy pills!" Irv said. "She's one of those gossip columnists."

"Keep your shirt on," my father reassured his roommate. "I never date Jewish girls." He planned to show up for the 7 P.M. date, then pretend to be called in for an emergency, leaving instead to meet the blond nurse he had been dating.

Dr. Newman knew my mother's name because she was making her mark in Hollywood, functioning as much as a critic and chronicler of the movie world as an interviewer. In the April 1940 *Screen Life*, her "Maureen O'Hara Follows Hepburn's Trail," occasioned by the remake of *A Bill of Divorcement*, focused on O'Hara's fraught ascension to a role that had brought two predecessors stardom. After a lead in which she described O'Hara starving herself to attain the properly gaunt look of "a modern English girl: nervous and full of complexes," Helen Hover wondered:

> . . . how Maureen managed the grueling role of Sydney Fairchild in *A Bill of Divorcement* on a rabbit's diet. Playing Sydney takes a lot of stamina. When Katharine Hepburn did it back in 1932 she was a limp rag at the end of each day's shooting. "She takes everything out of me, that girl," Katharine once said about the character. "Now she'd better give me something."
>
> She did—stardom. Stardom seems to come to every young actress who takes on the role of Sydney Fairchild. It's a role of such drama and poignancy, it gives an actress a swift spurt to success. The role changed Katharine Hepburn from a "queer duck from New York" into a serious dramatic actress. Katherine Cornell became the leading lady of Broadway as a result of playing Sydney on stage in 1921. Will it do the same for Maureen O'Hara?

The next month, in the same publication, she sounded a clarion call against drabness in "What's Wrong with Glamour?" (subhead: "When beautiful Lana Turner gives glamour the get-go, *Screen Life* decides it's time to investigate!") Her increasing fascination with Turner was the essay's focal point. "What's wrong with sex appeal? I ask you!" My mother challenged:

> According to the way Hollywood apparently figures it out, S.A. is okay for Annie Sheridan and Mae West and the stock girls who romp on the Santa Monica sands. But when a young girl hits the screen with a sock, then it seems to be the cue for her to do an about face and shun the nightclubs for her drahma lessons.

Take Lana Turner, recent bride of Artie Shaw . . . Lana's studio bosses (and some bright boys around Hollywood and Vine say the studio is behind Lana's battle against glamour) sit back and beam. Their Hot-Cha kid is becoming a Camp Fire Girl, and everything is ducky. But *is* it?

Helen went on to detail Lana's nightclub hopping, her stormy relationship with Greg Bautzer, her collapse from exhaustion on the set of *Dancing Co-Ed*, and her pious (studio-dictated) contention that "There is a certain responsibility in being in the limelight." She bemoaned Lana's new rectitude and said she hoped Lana would quickly get over it:

The new batch of starlets is pretty dull stuff. They knit, they follow orders. They represent the blues and the pinks in the Hollywood horizon. But Lana is red. As fiercely, spectacularly red as the car she drives. Come on, Lana—don't change!

The glamour she yearned for was back in the air when two new nightclubs roundly reversed what *Look* magazine had recently called the trend of movie stars staying home at night. On the southern side of the boulevard, Charlie Morrison, a lean, genteel former agent ("an elegant schmoozer," former Ciro's publicist Jim Byron called him) and his partner, Felix Young, had just opened the intimate, glamorous Mocambo, with its black-and-white-striped wallpaper and its aviary of parakeets, lovebirds, macaws, and cockatoos. The Mocambo—its italic, slanted logo bearing two big Os—was housed in the Montgomery family's building stock, with its village-like uniformity and uninterrupted line of black-shuttered windows on the second story. Like a New York club, the Mocambo's façade was preexisting, and its inside was mysterious and separate from its outside.

By contrast, Billy Wilkerson's stand-alone Ciro's was a creature of his own—and architect George Vernon Russell's—fantasy. The exterior was pure early forties Southern California sophistication: the second story, frosting white and shaped like a wedding cake with a slice removed, bearing dozens of appliquéd squares in bas-relief; the scripted logo (with its piquantly tilted, comically triple-oversized *C*) sitting on a swirling-edged white slab overhang, propped up by an elegant screen of white slats rising from planters bursting with tropical flora. Shirred glass doors opened into a dreamy interior. Designer Tom Douglas had covered the walls in ribbed thick silk of an applelike hue called Reseda Green and painted the ceiling American Beauty Red. Banquettes of that same rose red lined the walls. Bronze columns and urns were transformed into light fixtures.

Wilkerson's style of nightclub hosting relied on snob appeal; in ads he ran in his *Reporter* the week before the January 1940 opening ("Gala Premiere," one night; "General Opening," the next—with $7.50 for a "De Luxe Dinner"), a cool blonde sits at her dressing table, clutching a receiver to her ear, staring down at her Ciro's invitation through aviator glasses. Her dressing gown billows like the parted Red Sea, revealing extravagantly long gams crossed almost as high as her panty line. "Of course, darling, everybody that's *anybody* will be at Ciro's tonight!" she purrs.

The blonde in the ad was modeled after the first Ciro's cigarette girl, Mary Scott, whom I tracked down fifty-six years after the nightclubs's opening. There seem to have been certain archetypal forties-Sunset-Strip-cigarette-girl rites of passage, and Mary Scott went through all of them. In one, a girl acquires a job in wacky manner. (Mary, a teenaged movie theater usherette, was hiding in the bushes behind the club, looking for movie stars, when the parking concierge first shouted her away and then got a look at her legs and hired her.) In another, a nightclub owner's proprietary feeling for a cigarette girl's virtue imbues her with cheeky hard-to-getness. (Wilkerson, she said, "kept all the predators away so well that when Oleg Cassini kept asking me out I said, 'You want a beautiful girl? Here!' I pointed to Gene Tierney. 'Try her!' They ended up getting married.") In yet another, a cigarette girl's winsomeness leads to random acts of kindness from tough cookies. ("I said, 'Oh, Miss Stanwyck, you look lovely tonight.' The next day a package arrived at my house and the dress she'd had on was inside it.") Finally, a faux-Cinderella ending is followed by a vile comeuppance and eventually rewarded with a real Cinderella ending: Darryl Zanuck wooed Mary to his Fox office. (Not for nothing had Beadie Einstein gossiped about her boss's behavior.) He unzipped, and, says Mary, "terribly small accoutrement" in hand, he literally chased her around his desk. She escaped, her virtue intact—and her sense of her bargaining power enhanced enough for her to go after bigger game. She soon married Sir Cedric Hardwicke, becoming a British lady.

The melodrama that pulsed through the Troc was transported whole to Ciro's. Mary recalls, "George Raft and Betty Grable came in all the time together, but because he was Catholic he would never marry her." Also, in a shocking blow that rendered incredulous the many women who lusted after him, Ciro's handsome bandleader, Neil Bonceau, killed himself because his wife walked out on him.

My mother got her best items at Ciro's. "The blasé film colony, used to surprising twosomes, is raising its eyebrows at the friendship between Paulette Goddard and Anatole Litvak," she wrote. "Now Paulette and Charlie Chaplin, who were so busy denying rumors that they were married, in the first place, are now denying reports that they're about to separate."

After sitting through a show she would walk to Beadie's next door, kick off her shoes, and flop on the Murphy bed. Through Beadie's open window she could hear the fading bars of the set-closing music of Ciro's orchestra, as well as the laughter, the slamming Bentley doors, and the coyotes howling in the mountains. What a place was the Sunset Strip! What a dream Helen Laura Zlotchover from Brooklyn was living!

In the late spring of 1940, my parents finally agreed to the blind date that one or the other had kept postponing. He picked her up at Beadie's, and she saw his blue eyes glinting all the way from the back bedroom, where she was fastening her blouse's stock tie. Approaching, she saw his slow-spreading, almost sad half smile. He smiled with his mouth closed—a coolly withholding, grimly ironic, lazily confident gesture. She liked that.

In Irving's coupe, Danny drove her to nearby King's Restaurant, which nightclub employees, and the occasional cheeky, trysting movie star, claimed as their off-duty hangout. There they talked the night away. My mother would later say she didn't know a doctor could be so funny, and yet his humor wasn't shpritzy and hail-fellow, like those of the other men she dated. It was droll and life-worn. With his pink skin, round face, twinkly blue eyes, and ancient humor, he was captivating.

Despite her fascination with this blind date, she kept interrupting their talk to go to the coin telephone in the ladies' room and recite items to Fawcett's night editor, Sidney Safer. She also told Danny she had to get home early to hit the typewriter keys for a morning deadline—this date, it turned out, was a copy break. My father was struck that a Jewish woman could be so unpossessive and that a single woman could be so workbound. This was anything but the diamond-ring-obsessed brisket profferer he had expected. They got back in Irv's car and drove to a dumpy little jazz room called Jim Otto's Steak House and danced to a house band's rendition of "I Didn't Know What Time It Was." My father stood the blond nurse up.

In June 1940, on their third date, Helen and Danny took a trip to Yosemite. In a photograph of that day he's matinee-idol cool in tweed sports jacket with pocket hankie, sport shirt, and an ascot. She's wearing a head-draping snood, smiling girlishly, her high-peaked brows raised over wily sloe eyes turned triumphant. He had just asked her to marry him. His proposal was vintage Danny Weller: "You know, I have one foot on a banana peel, the other on the grave." She said she'd take her chances.

"Let's elope this weekend," he said.

She replied, "I can't! I have a deadline."

As it turns out, they waited five months. On Tuesday, November 5, the "Ramblin' Reporter," in Billy Wilkerson's *Hollywood Reporter*, ran this item. "Helen Hover, Fawcett's crack gossiper, and Dr. Daniel Weller, will be Yumated shortly. . . ."

"There was no Las Vegas then," my mother explained. "If you wanted to elope you drove to Yuma, Arizona—a tiny, dusty town with only two hotels. We woke up a justice of the peace who'd been sleeping in his clothes and had ketchup on his tie. He married us, and then we drove and drove, until we were in Texas.

"From Texas I called home. My mother said, '*Screen Life* just called—they want you to interview Bobby Stack; they're in a hurry for the story.' So I hopped on a two-engine plane in Dallas and three stops later I was back in L.A. I interviewed Stack, wrote the story while your father drove to New York to visit his brothers before they

enlisted in the army. Then, after I turned in my story I got a two-engine plane in L.A. and your father got a plane in New York, and three stops later I was back in Dallas, and so was he, and we finished our honeymoon."

Just after New Year's 1941 my parents took a real honeymoon—to Honolulu. They sailed over on the S.S. *Matsonia* and stayed at the Royal Hawaiian. Pictures show my father in an elegant suit, white sport shoes, and pipe, and my mother in a lei-ladened, padded-shouldered white silk pajama-slack ensemble. In one picture he is lying back in a rattan chair, in a tight white T-shirt. His upper body is taut. His hands are clasped behind his head, the soft undersides of his upper arms offered up to the tropical sunlight that splashes the photo. His eyes are tightly closed, his lips pursed; he looks half dreamy, half troubled. It is an achingly familiar look, even years later. "Daddy . . . ?" I want to take my index finger and stroke his underarm to wake him: to make sure he's just sleeping, that he hasn't had the Heart Attack. "Daddy? *Daddy!*" I'd ask. "Are you *okay?*" Our hearts were always hostage to that question.

It is the wistful, rueful second line my mother wrote, in white ink, on that crumbling black scrapbook page, under the picture of them in Yosemite, that seizes me:

Third date with Danny—June 1940. He looked happy then

She wrote "then." Past tense. Yet she wrote that line in the forties. Had his angry sadness really surfaced so early? He had a lot of life to cram into a reduced space of years, and his bitter understanding of that fact colored everything. Still, if she sensed it then, she did not care. She had waited a long time for love, and the waiting was worth it. She had found the man she was meant to marry, and, by God, she had married him.

Her life felt like a movie.

Chapter Six

HOLLYWOOD, NEW YORK, BOSTON, HOLLYWOOD: 1941–1943

Two conflicts were sparked in my father as soon as he married my mother. One was a conflict with the man who was his new wife's alter ego, on whom she had modeled herself; the second would be a war of values between his own serious, important work and the frivolous—but enormously seductive—nightclub world. Both conflicts burst out briefly and then went deeply underground while my father realized his life's dream and claimed his true vocation. But to bury a confict—or two—is not the same thing as to defuse it.

The first conflict, with the other man in his wife's life, Herman, was the more challenging. "Jewish families make princes, but they also make kings, and Herman was the king of that family," Irving Newman told me, suggesting that the Hovers' palpable dazzlement with Herman was off-putting to my father, so used to being a pampered family star in his own right. That family was a machine, a unit: too integrated, too closely knit, too bent to a single task—and to a single avatar. My father would walk into the house on DeLongpre, or accompany Helen to the Earl Carroll Theater, and the family's enchantment with Herman's world would viscerally offend this more serious, better-educated—and amply spoiled—young man. Irving Newman had put it simply, "Danny did not like his in-laws."

As for the second: Faced with the temptations of his new wife's world of nightclubs and movie studios, the young intern would have to clench his emotional fists in order to hold on to the somber, difficult life course he'd charted for himself.

My father's immediate solution for both conflicts was simple: to get out of Los Angeles and go back to the East Coast, where most of the programs that made up the rarefied orbit of neurosurgical residency were offered. Neurosurgical residency was part Socratic tutorial, part traveling supper: A small pool of acolytes spent three, six, or twelve months apprenticing with one or two august specialists before moving on to the next one, and then the next, and then the next. Over the course of seven years, a disciple would have worked closely with many of the giants in his field, who called those disciples their "boys."

While awaiting replies from several residency programs, my father approached a Los Angeles neurosurgeon, Mark Glaser, and offered himself as an unpaid helper in exchange for being able to watch him diagnose and operate. Glaser agreed to the arrangement. The then-late-middle-aged Glaser was what my mother called "an old-time neurosurgeon"—one of those pre-Cushing-era-trained men who had cobbled neurosurgery over a general surgery specialty. In his spare time, my father rooted around in Glaser's library, reading the bound presentations, clinic critiques, and scientific papers of the men who, unlike Glaser, he really wanted to be like: the members of the Harvey Cushing Society (Cushing's immediate followers) and the American Academy of Neurological Surgeons (the "generation" that followed the Cushing Society out of residency). Both groups' spiritual home was Cushing's Lahey Clinic, the young Boston institution whose neurosurgery department, though not even fully approved (and not as complete as, say, the Mayo Clinic's) was cutting edge. If you wanted to be a neurosurgeon, you *had* to do time at Lahey. When Harvey Cushing retired from Lahey's Peter Bent Brigham Hospital, Gilbert Horrax, who'd been Cushing's assistant for eighteen years, became head of Lahey's neurosurgery department. The tall, lean Horrax (he had been a track star at Williams College before going to medical school) was now neurosurgery's prince maker.

Still dining out, as it were, on Cushing's aura, neurosurgery in the late thirties and the cusp of the forties cloaked its considerable dangers beneath a veneer of glamour. Young neurosurgeons back then were "a breed apart from other doctors and surgeons," New York neurosurgeon Dr. Victor Ho said of his legendary forebears. "They were a step above everyone else. And they were a certain kind of guy: very egotistical, very opinionated, very independent, very hard living. You'd have to be, to go into a field in which even neurologists thought that assigning a patient for surgery was a death sentence. They called the unit's recovery room the Vegetable Patch because that's how so many of the postops turned out. It was surgery for cowboys."

It was, however, surgery for *smart* cowboys, since so much of the skill lay in the diagnostic work—the neuroanatomy, neuropathology, and neuroradiology that were the mountain supporting the peak that comprised the surgery. That's not the case today, when neurosurgeons are, as Victor Ho puts it, "end-point workers: technicians," going into the brain and doing the fixing after high technology has done much of the advance work—the sleuthing, deducing, and diagnosing. Back then, when CAT scans and MRIs were not even twinkles in practitioners' eyes, the primitive skull X ray was the only visual hint to the mysteries within the cranium. "There were no diagnostic tools," Ho says. "And magnification wasn't good. There weren't even diuretics to keep the brain from swelling. You *had* to know your stuff because there was nothing to help you. When you finished your training back then you were not just a neurosurgeon but a *neuroscientist.*"

Even as he longed to join those pioneers, my father was living in a way that almost mocked that life plan's seriousness. He and my mother had settled into a furnished suite in a hotel—the Hollywood Plaza, on Hollywood and Vine—that was straight out of Damon Runyon. For room and board, my father was house doctor to the chorus girls, actors, agents, stuntmen, gumshoes, and assorted hopefuls who lived in the building. "We ate three meals a day out, at the Earl Carroll or the Derby," my mother recalled. "Your father was always on call, forever rushing out with his black doctor's bag," as often as not reviving lachrymose private eyes after benders and fistfights, pumping stomachs full of overdosed phenobarbitol, and giving working girls injections of sulfa drugs to head off gonorrhea.

"Danny told me he worked at that hotel because he *liked* it!" my father's soon-to-be best friend during those years, radio star and hit ragtime songwriter Zeke Manners told me shortly before he died, in 1999. "He was never a typical doctor, he was too funny to be one. That's why he could be friends with a fellow like me!" Zeke—a San Francisco Jew and founding member of the wildly famous thirties western swing group the Beverly Hill Billies—had emphasized. "And that's why he liked being around those funny people in that sleazy, knockaround hotel." Yet, in sharp contrast with Zeke's recollection, my mother told me that my father would often rail contemptuously at the hotel job, "I didn't go to medical school for four years to give shots to hookers!" This conflict—between the serious and the nihilistic, the authoritarian and carefree sides of my father's soul—stands out clearly.

. . .

On April 2, 1941, with our country sending convoys to Britain, my father attempted, for the second time, to join the merchant marine. He had made his first application six months earlier but had flunked the physical. With the war drums growing louder and a second wave of the draft rumored imminent, it was thought that the physical-fitness bar might be lowered for those who were joining as support specialists rather than as combatants. So he drove down to the recruiting station at the Port of Los Angeles.

He applied for the post of ship's surgeon, armed with strong professional character references. "Dr. Daniel Weller is trustworthy, of good moral character, and an asset to the medical profession," obstetrician Samuel J. Klor wrote in one letter. He was "honest, of good moral character, and of excellent standing in the medical profession . . . a very capable physician," urologist Henry Bodner vouched in another. On April 10, my father received a telegram: Deputy Shipping Commissioner C. F. Walsh had approved his application.

Cautiously optimistic, he drove to the port to collect his processed papers. His brothers Milton and Alex had enlisted—he, too, would be anointed within a company of uniformed soldiers, just as their father had been in Oklahoma. Successfully proving one's machismo was not something Jewish men had great recent history—or ample confidence—in doing; serving in this war was an entrée to a long-denied and highly craved self-image. For a man who had been a sickly child, that validation was critical.

A week later another telegram from the bureau arrived: A second physical examination was required. That one my father failed. According to my mother, he perceived the turn of events as a bitter humiliation. The subject never came up again.

If my father's dream of becoming a seaman was a door slammed shut, another, more important door, sprang open. A hint of the good news lies in the look on my mother's face in a photograph taken of her with Shirley Temple four months later. Facing each other in adjacent director's chairs, the teenage actress (in an organdy party dress) and the journalist (in a swingy, shoulder-padded white frock) are smiling like best friends. My mother is positively glowing.

The good news her face projected was that at Massachusetts General Hospital a slot had opened up for a neurosurgical resident. My father was offered the position. He'd have to leave for Boston immediately.

"We jumped for joy!" my mother said. They placed a long-distance call to Mass General to accept and packed a trunk and valises. Days later, after kissing her husband good-bye on the Inglewood Airport tarmac, my mother dived back in: embarking on two weeks of back-to-back movie star interviews, cramming her steno books with material she'd turn into her first filed-from-the-East-Coast columns. The interview with Shirley Temple was the last one she did before getting on a plane to join Danny in Boston.

Boston meant the marriage had begun. My parents were away from both of their families—a couple on their own at last. They rented two rooms on the top of a rickety wooden triple-decker, and after Danny went off every morning, Helen sat rat-a-tat-tat typing her Hollywood copy while gazing at the billowing smokestacks of nearby Deaconness Hospital. As a break between Joan Fontaine and Mickey Rooney, she took strolls through Beacon Hill and amid the swan boats of the Boston Common, across from which pinch-faced doyennes issued forth from tea at the Ritz Carlton.

Boston's self-contained world furthered my mother's sense that she and her new husband were living in a bubble. Navigating through the cloakedly contentious city—its flinty Brahmins perched on the top rungs of a ladder being shaken by the colorful Irish Catholics—she felt like an invisible tourist, her own ethnic and social reference points so utterly beside the point. She and Danny were their own little country.

Once a week they'd go driving through New England, having boiled beef dinners in roadhouses while cheerfully listening to local bands clobber "Do, Do, Do," "Someone to Watch over Me," and my mother's favorite, "Embraceable You."

Embrace me my sweet embra-ceable you

"Your father hummed it while we danced," my mother told me. "Your unsentimental father, believe it or not."

During the week my father would get home at 10 P.M. after a day that had started at dawn, but he was so stimulated by all he had seen and was learning, he'd walk around the tiny flat for an hour puffing his pipe, verbally sorting out (his young mentor) Dr. William Sweet's introductory diagnostic demonstration. Though barely older than my father, Sweet was a bit of a Renaissance man—a classical pianist and an aviator, as well as a doctor and surgeon. Bringing his multifacetedness to bear on the art of diagnosis (and providing an enviable role model), Sweet taught his four acolytes how to calculate sensory loss in a face; assess a patient's cranial and auditory nerves; gauge four measurable sensations (light touch, pinprick, position, and vibration) in the trunk and appendages; measure bone and air conduction; examine the reflexes in the four quadrants of the abdomen; conduct a roentgenologic examination of the skull (a skull X ray); and perform a neuro-opthalmologic examination. That was just for starters.

Sometimes, after my mother put the final period on her Claudette Colbert or Humphrey Bogart item, she'd go meet my father in the Mass General cafeteria during his dinner break. With only a half hour to eat, the fellows—cloth napkins popping out over the neck prongs of their flashlighted retractors—would avidly spear their meat loaf and their Boston baked beans.

One night when Helen got there, Danny was over in a corner of the cafeteria, lost in talk, along with a few other residents, with a tall, almost gawky, intensely gesticulating, furrow-browed fellow, slightly older than he was. He had an impatient, inspired air of brilliance about him, and the residents fell silent when he talked. "He was so confident and idiosyncratic. He gave off excitement," my mother said.

His name was James Poppen, and he was the talk of Lahey Clinic. (Sweet had brought him over to help imbue the residents with passion for the field, and, since Lahey had no cafeteria, Poppen had stayed for supper.) He had a "touch," it was whispered. He was a surgical prodigy. He was already taking over operations—even some of Gilbert Horrax's—and with audacious style and confidence. He operated at twice, sometimes three times, normal speed, and he did not suppress that verboten component, emotion. "They say he swears—'Jesus Christ!'—when his rhythm is broken," my father told my mother that night, delightedly. "Poppen's like Gene Krupa!"

Gene Krupa, that is, by way of Tom Sawyer. Poppen was born a farm boy. He learned to shoot squirrels and deer nearly before he could walk, and was never seen in his hometown of Drenthe, Michigan, without his trusty dog and his even trustier rifle. A stint in prep school had knocked the country out of him, and natural talent led him to an inspired turn through his medical education, which he paid for by pitching minor league baseball. My father and his colleagues were taken by the man's originality, toughness, and aplomb. He would become the rebel star guiding the next neurosurgical generation.

Poppen treated the Mass General residents to thrilling, gossip-laden walks along the Charles River. He told the acolytes about the muffled battle raging at professional meetings between his own mentor, the virtuosic Cushing peer Walter Dandy, and the Chief, Cushing himself. Though former close colleagues, Cushing and Dandy weren't talking anymore. The cause of the rift was a controversial diagnostic tool called a pneumoenocephalogram, which Dandy had invented. The pneumo, as it was called, was a highly effective aid in roentgenography. An air bubble was shot, like a speedball, up a patient's spinal canal and into his brain; from the distortion of the structures on an X ray, one could infer hitherto-hidden tumors that might be present. It was a torturous procedure—

patients had to be strapped in their chairs just to bear it. Cushing had called it inhumane, even with the sodium pentothal injections given for sedation, but others (Poppen, among them) had taken Dandy's side against the Chief. Was it not a lesser evil to cause a patient excruciating pain in diagnosis rather than kill him by going in for a meningioma whose size and location was undetermined? Such Hobsonian choices were routine, yielding the common "neurosurgeon's personality": blunt, ironic curtness.

The Mass General posting was only a four-month-long apprenticeship. As a next step, my father secured, back-to-back, two second-stage residencies: the first, for November and December, as a postgraduate in neuroanatomy and neuropathology at New York City's Mt. Sinai Hospital, then a full year in neurology, neurosurgery, and psychiatry at Lenox Hill Hospital, twenty blocks downtown. To celebrate his acceptance, my parents bought a used convertible in which to journey to Manhattan. "It was a mongrel: a Ford in the front and a Chevy in the back," my mother recalled.

On October 15, my parents made the move. They rented a furnished apartment in the Westover Hotel on Seventy-second Street near Riverside Drive. Now my mother positioned her trusty Royal so she had a thimble-sized view of the Hudson. (In addition to writing her Fawcett columns from afar, she would start freelancing for Colliers as well as the new Liberty magazine.) My father reported to his new mentor, Dr. Joseph Globus, at Mt. Sinai Hospital, across from leafy Central Park, on Fifth Avenue.

Joseph Globus was urban, ironic, and theatrical—a Jewish émigré from Russia, different from the athletic, gentile American mainstream that had produced Cushing, Sweet, Horrax, and Poppen. After a raft of neurosurgeons who modeled a life he did not know, Danny Weller saw a man who could have been a member of his own family. Globus often carried himself as if the weight of the world was on his shoulders, and in a sense it was. He had made it his life-work to learn how intracranial meningiomas (the most common form of brain tumor—those located on the covering of the brain) form, change, and behave, and he was accumulating the case histories of every such tumor for which he could obtain a medical record. He aimed to produce a master classification for neurosurgeons, who were often surprisingly ill informed about these easy-to-remove tumors. Sweet had been an inspiring young teacher, but Globus was a careful master, and he was so committed to his chosen work that when, years earlier, Cushing had given him the flashier opportunity to become a neurosurgeon, he had refused. To Globus, the quiet work of neuroanatomy and neuropathology in his basement-level lab at Mt. Sinai was everything.

On the issue of whether or not to use the controversial pneumo-cephalogram, Globus (like most neuropaths) was a Dandy, not a Cushing, man. It fell to my father to strap Globus's patients into their chairs, give them their pentothal injections, talk them through their anguish, and help his mentor set the ventriculogram in motion. He also assisted with Globus's cerebral angiographies: shooting into patients' arteries the dye that behaved like a liquid Sam Spade, collaring hidden tumors and highlighting them so they'd pop out in the police line-up—the skull X ray.

By mid-November, the senior neuropathologist moved my father out of the examination rooms and into the histology lab. The morphology and microscopic anatomy of tumor cells—and the structure and movement of colonies of those cells—were now young Dr. Weller's concentration. Thus, my father would spend eight hours a day with coroner-fresh brain chunks. The ventricular slices were delicate, splayed, and nubby edged, like female genitalia; the midbrain views were hulking, angular, and masculine, like clenched fists or boulders.

Moving from macro- to microscopic views, the dense cells within the nodules were hypnotic. They could mass in rosette configurations around the blood vessels. They could be columnar or spindle-shaped—their nuclei, round or oval. Hordes of mitotic figures squirmed like tiny pollywogs. A crowd of blood vessels could rub up against the malignant *psammoma* bodies, resulting in a brilliant, swirling paisley of encapsulated globules. The most awesome tumors (of whose mysteries Globus was the absolute master) were the *spongioblastoma multiforme*, with their famously large quota of giant cells. These cells were the Enemy. Yet under the thick, imprisoning slab of microscope glass, they seemed gorgeously destructible.

My father's cerebral geography course (as a prelude to surgical search-and-destroy missions) allowed him to explore, in his own right, the brain's four fluid-filled chambers: the ventricles. There were two lateral ventricles, located in the cerebral hemispheres, which communicated with the third one, snuggled at the back of the brain between the thalmus and hypothalmus. The fourth, and lowest, ventricle extended to the central canal of the upper end of the spinal cord. It was a chamber of the third ventricle that interested Globus the most, the evocatively named aqueduct of Sylvius.

Obstructions of that part of the midbrain were common, the teacher taught the apprentices, but true malignant tumors growing from within the aqueduct's walls were exceptionally rare. Globus had found only four, out of 325 fully certified brain tumors in his database. He and a colleague, Hartwig Kuhlenbeck, of the anatomy department of the Woman's Medical College of Pennsylvania, had just received a foundation grant in child neurology research, to analyze those four aberrant cases. The resulting paper would be submitted to the *Journal of Neuropathology*. My mother remembered my father called her from the lab that day—he almost never did—and announced, "Globus asked me to be third author on the paper."

A dichotomy within those four rare cases struck a chord in my father that traveled way past the scientist in him, straight to the never-quite-placated angry child. Two of the four patients were men, adults aged twenty-nine and fifty-one, and the other two were teenagers, a girl, eighteen, and a boy, sixteen. All had died, but on maddeningly chimerical timetables, and here, to my father, lay the unfairness: The fifty-one-year-old man, a tough-hided syphilitic, had survived thirteen years of symptoms and had received fifty days of comforting hospital care before lapsing, pain-free, into a coma. Yet both teenagers had died, on the brink of their adult lives, in excruciating pain after risky surgery.

All his life, probably thinking back to his own infirm childhood, my father would get visibly angry when children suffered more than adults. So deeply did my sister and I absorb this specific melancholy, we soon devised a yearly custom of rewrapping our freshly received Christmas presents and leaving them on his study table each morning to take to his youngest patients. That sense of mission, and advocacy, for young tumor patients began with his late nights in Globus's office's anteroom, reading the reports of the struggles of the Sylvius teenagers. (The paper, with my father bylined as third author, was published in the April–May 1942 issue of the very periodical he had reverently perused in the Cedars of Lebanon library three years before: the *Journal of Neuropathology*.)

One day, in early December, in the middle of his work on the paper, an addled young resident entered Globus's office, the expression on his face was incredulous. The young man begged the doctor's pardon for the intrusion, and then he blurted out, "The Japanese have bombed Pearl Harbor!"

My father used Globus's office to telephone my mother. She'd been typing away on an article for *Colliers* on smart new ladies' trousers. She rushed to snap on her Philco, where America's entrance into the war was announced in stentorian tones over static.

My mother raced out of the apartment and through Central Park while my father rushed out to the hall, where the neurology staff were issuing forth from lab after lab, like evacuees from a fire, and huddling in front of the floor's several console radios, which were issuing news from Honolulu stereophonically.

My parents found each other on the northeast corner of Eighty-sixth and Fifth. "It was the first big event in our lives where we had only each other to turn to," my mother said. "We felt so close."

At the time of Pearl Harbor, Globus had been organizing an international conference of neuropathologists. (It eventually took place at Mt. Sinai Hospital in March, and papers on the subject were published in the periodical Globus founded and edited, the *Journal of Mt. Sinai Hospital*.) Over the months of autumn and early winter, corresponding with medical eminences all over Europe, often in their native languages, Globus had heard awful rumors of what was going on in Germany and Poland: Jews were denied access to stores, to pharmacists, to sides of streets, to streets, to neighborhoods. Next, Jews were denied wool, then butter, then hygeine aids. Homes were raided, families were beaten for hiding a half bar of soap in the bottom of a flour jar. Cabinets, tables, iceboxes, and jewel boxes were overturned and pillaged. People were committing suicide after the house raids, so certain of the futility of their lives. Jews were herded into trains for prisons.

"And they do not return from these places. The prisons are quiet. Too many go into these places, for the capacity," Globus would whisper, my father later told me. In his tutorials Globus often quoted the Jerusalem Talmud, "He who saves a single life has saved the world entire." Yet, privately, the man himself said grimly, "One life is not enough. There are too many lives that need saving."

What did my parents—thirty-one and thirty-two years old—
make of the dark bulletins that Globus's international colleagues
were sending him? From what I can deduce from my talks with my
mother, they received the news with a winded disbelief, and with a
frightened horror that they knew they had to quickly get hold of and
extinguish before it overtook them. The understanding that nothing
real or strong or earned—just the accident of their parents' emigra-
tion—had kept those European Jews' fate from befalling *them*: That
was too threatening. The energy they needed to climb ever higher
up the rungs of self-invention could not survive true comprehension of the tales they had heard. True comprehension would para-
lyze them with guilt over their breathtakingly arbitrary luck,
followed by a creeping fear that that luck was only temporary.

So they tried hard to push those stories—those never-doubted
rumors—to the periphery of their consciousness. There were
nights, however, when they couldn't. My mother told me she would
turn to my father and whisper, "We are too lucky. Why do *we* have
such luck? Why do we deserve to be spared like this?"

On January 2, 1942, in line with the fast-paced, musical-chairs
quality of neurosurgical residency, my father left his tutorial with
Globus at Mt. Sinai for a yearlong apprenticeship in Thomas
Davis's neuropsychiatric service at Lenox Hill Hospital. He was
going from research to practice, from academe to clinic.

Now, back at the Westover flat after his days at Lenox Hill, my
father would click open and shut his surgeon's bag—with its skull-
opening craniotomy burrs (a four-bladed perforating burr and a
seven-blade enlarging one); its Gigli saw and rongeurs—with the
nervous superstition of a brand-new parent making sure his infant
is still breathing. Before going to bed, he'd set the bag down on the
floor by the breakfront, a totemic placement that reminded my

mother of Herman's ritual with his lucky tap shoes on Arlington Avenue.

My father assisted two neurosurgeons, the senior Joseph King and the junior Frank Echlin. To be sure, some of the operations he attended them on were merely routine fare: the newly popular sympathectomies, whereby a whole nerve chain's sympathetic impulses (from chest to abdomen) were surgically interrupted, to relieve severe hypertension; the cordotomies, in which pain pathways were snipped, like phone cords by a thief; and, alas, the eventually disgraced lobotomies, to quell violent behavior. Any neurosurgeon who wanted to hang his shingle (and cut into a debt incurred from a decade and a half of schooling) needed to master these stock-in-trade bill payers.

Beyond these blue-plate specials were the procedures at the heart of the field—tumor excisions. As my father stood at the Lenox Hill operating table—working the electrocoagulating forceps to stanch cerebral bleeding, or affixing the metal suction catheter to the subdural burr hole that Eichlin or King had bored into the patient's skull with exacting twists of the wires of the Gigli saw—he saw, in situ, the tumors he had probed and measured in the laboratory. There, artfully plucked from the yellow-white cerebral cortex without disturbing the underlying grey tissue, was the real-life meningioma whose phylogenic and oncogenic history, whose earliest tissue forerunners, he had spent hundreds of hours studying. It was exhilarating, as heady as romance. "It's like standing on the edge of a cliff, in front of a steep drop, and the wind is at your back. One false move, a sixteenth of an inch, and it's over," Victor Ho said of the experience of doing neurosurgery. "It's very intense. It's not for everyone. But when it's for you, it's *really* for you."

Meningiomas, of course, were the easy ones. Most of them were benign, and they were cooperatively noninternal. It was the glioblastomas—troublesomely expansive and tenacious, infiltrative and often situated deep within the ventricles—that were challenging. Equally redoubtable were tumors on the spinal cord; their excision, via laminectomy, had to be fastidious. Then there were the difficult acoustic neuromas, tumors of the eighth cranial nerve that, though technically benign, encroached on the adjacent brain stem.

Nothing was more frustrating than the disorders one could not remedy—aneurysms. These were the pathological (overstretched and weakened) sacs (or "berries") in the wall of the internal carotid artery and other cerebral arteries branching into the brain's major blood superhighway. Often, if not diagnosed early, aneurysms could worsen and rupture, resulting in hemorrhage, from which the patient could die instantly. Neurosurgeons, those most aggressive of men, were left to nurse the furious guilt that they had known what was coming but could not prevent it. Back in the early 1940s, intervening to "trap" or "clip" an aneurysm (safely isolating the thin-walled sac from the functioning "parent" artery, by way of reinforcement or the affixing of the V-shaped, malleable McKenzie silver clip to grip the aneurysm's "neck") could save lives, but only in the hands of rare, talented practitioners. If intervention occurred after rupture, patients at times suffered a fate that Walter Dandy described by saying, "There could be no more rapid death or one so silent."

Dandy was American neurosurgery's principal early aneurysm pioneer. Five and six years after Scottish surgeon Norman Dott performed the first *planned* intracranial aneurysm operation, the Baltimore-based neurosurgeon performed his landmark trapping of a carotid cavernous aneurysm in 1936 and, more significantly, his McKenzie-clipping, in a 1937 operation on a forty-three-year-old alcoholic male. (Dandy, a bit of a daredevil, had located the aneurysm in that and his future surgeries without angiography to guide him—he thought the dyes involved would be harmful—leading some astonished peers to wonder if Cushing's continuing anger at him over the pneumoencephelogram might, at least partly, be displaced jealousy over Dandy's spotlight-stealing star turns.)

Dandy's relatively smooth maiden voyage had proved to be the exception, not the rule. The aneurysms he operated on were giant ones; surgery on smaller ones could be fatal. Postrupture interventions had such a high mortality rate that neurosurgeons practicing when my father was training often declined to publish their results, and "hopeless" was a word not infrequently heard.

"Is anyone doing promising work on aneurysms?" my father asked his Lenox Hill mentors, he later told me.

Only one person, King and Echlin told him: "Jim Poppen, at Lahey."

Hearing that, my father was more determined than ever to gain entry into that premier neurosurgical residence program, which involved being handpicked by Gilbert Horrax.

On February 9, a twenty-two-year-old nurse was admitted to my father's care at the Lenox Hill neuropsychiatric clinic. Her name was Alice, my mother recalled, "and she reminded Danny of nurses he'd dated at Cedars. Of all the patients he was getting, she was one he could relate to." Alice had mysteriously gone deaf four months earlier (the Lenox Hill staff had examined her but had discharged her without a diagnosis); now her deafness was joined by other, awful symptoms: "severe, throbbing frontal headaches" (as my father would later write in the paper that was eventually published in the 1944 *Journal of Neurosurgery*), as well as nausea, vomiting, and loss of strength in her right hand. During her week's hospitalization, the young neurosurgeon in training and the young nurse bonded. They probably flirted with each other. He had to write everything down since she couldn't hear. Sometimes he wrote jokes to make her crack a smile. He'd come home and tell my mother, "This is a hard one." That was surgeon's code for: If something bad happens to her, I'm going to take it personally.

The neurologic examination my father conducted on Alice yielded inconclusive results. The skull X ray and other diagnostic tests came back negative. All they could do was discharge her.

On April 22 Alice was back in the hospital, with clear neurological symptoms. Nerve sensations were weak up and down her right side. The deep reflexes in her eyes were hyperactive. Her abdominal reflexes were gone. Her condition plummeted. Her whole right side stiffened and lost sensation, and her "headaches," my father wrote, "became unbearable." She developed a dry, rasping cough, invisible in the chest X ray but occurring "at regular intervals during an hour." In a risqué-sounding move that was quite routine back then, my father swabbed her throat with cocaine to "to try to break the reflex arc." But the cough proved "resistant to all medication" and morphed into "a peculiar, rasping expulsive shriek." She "vomited and retched frequently."

My father bent over the deaf, semiparalyzed, frightened young woman. Pointing to her head with his left hand, he worked the index and middle fingers of his right hand like scissors busily snipping. Accompanying this pantomine, he broadly mugged with his facial expressions, like a clown making an exciting discovery. Alice smiled weakly. Then she nodded in capitulation. A little while later, the consent form for her exploratory brain surgery was presented to her, and she signed it.

My father had assisted in other suboccipital explorations, but this was the first one he'd initiated. My mother told me he came home that night sobered, even shaken. The first state was normal and appropriate; the second state was dangerous. Surgeons, especially neurosurgeons facing such bad patient survival odds, could not sink to emotion. Emotion hampered you. Bonding with Alice had been a mistake—and it had been unethical. Mugging at her bedside to get her to sign the release (even though the surgery was for her own good) meant that he had implicitly promised her relief. Could he deliver it?

The next day, as my father and Echlin stood over Alice, they discovered, he wrote, "a smooth, bluish, elongated mass . . . attached to the posterior aspect of the medulla" as well as "into and attached to the floor of the fourth ventricle, and attached downward to the level of the atlas." The atlas is the first cervical vertebra articulating immediately with the skull; it literally sustains the globe of the head. The tumor enmeshed in it was long, grasping, and unyielding. It was "attached firmly to the [spinal] cord and impossible to remove." They took the specimens of the tumor for biopsy, which yielded even worse news: The tumor was malignant.

Deep radiation therapy was initiated. "The patient ran a stormy course," my father wrote. She was in respiratory crisis for the forty-nine days she stayed in the hospital. Her "respirations were shallow, often simulating the panting of a dog [and] so labored that each inspiration and expiration was attended by a lateral propulsion of the head." Finally, she stopped returning for treatment.

"It broke your father's heart that he couldn't save Alice, and that he might have unintentionally misled her," my mother said. "What a difficult specialty he was in! There would always be more bad news than good news to deliver. You could comfort patients with your humor, but you had to be careful to not cross the line and get their hopes up with it." My father's trademark irony—his merry sardonic air, so much a part of his charisma—began growing expontentially in the vacuum created by his necessary suppression of other, less formed but nobler, aspects of his nature.

In the literature, symptoms like Alice's—bilateral deafness; persistent cough; sharp, spastic breathing—had never before indicated a tumor in the fourth ventricle. In fact, according to the received wisdom, such symptomology was, as my father later wrote, "misleading," even "bizarre." Alice's inoperable medulloblastoma was unusual enough to merit discussion by the Lenox Hill Hospital tumor board, and to win my father an interview with Gilbert Horrax.

"Dear Dr. Horrax: Thank you for the interest and courtesy you have shown me," Daniel Weller wrote in a letter on Lenox Hill Hospital stationery, dated June 1, 1942. Sounding simultaneously self-important and humbled, he continued:

> My tardiness in replying to your recent letter was due to the fact that we had a sudden rush of cases and with my intern out ill, I was kept busy all the time.
>
> I would consider it a privilege to work under you, and if a fellowship on your service is offered to me I would be only too happy to accept it.

His surgical mentors wrote recommendations. Tom Davis started his letter to his friend Horrax by remarking on my father's single-mindedness, "Dr. Daniel Weller . . . is interested hardly at all in psychiatry but . . . is keenly interested in neurosurgery." Frank Echlin also noted that same urgent focus, saying, "He is anxious to get as complete a training in neurosurgery and its branches as possible," something that would be "limited" at Lenox Hill. "Keenly," "anxious," "as complete as possible" all reflected my father's hunger and earnestness—and his understanding of the ticking clock. Joseph King weighed in, "He is intelligent, has imagination, is always willing to learn, doesn't think he knows it all, and he takes just as good care of a poor old ward patient as he does of a millionaire. I hope you take him on."

Horrax did. He told Echlin he was "very favorably impressed" with my father and admitted him to Lahey. The exact timing of the appointment was uncertain, but it could be as soon as January 1943.

My father had done it! He had won a Lahey fellowship. He had *willed himself* to become a neurosurgeon.

Armed with her husband's exciting and prestigious triumph, my mother took the train across country in August, while my father continued on at Lenox Hill. At Union Station she confronted a Hollywood radically changed from the one she'd left a year earlier. The hauntingly Spanish atrium that Herman had viewed as a looking glass into a halcyon land was now a packed-to-the-rafters waiting area in which hundreds of sailors were locked in embraces with their girlfriends and brides before taking the train up to San Francisco to ship out to the Pacific theater.

Everyone was a soldier now. Beadie Einstein had just had a whirlwind romance with Beverly Hill Billy Zeke Manners (who had dropped Eddie Cantor's daughter Margery for her)—and had married him after three dates, days before he shipped out with the air force. "Zeke's overseas! I'm a war bride!" she'd proudly told Helen, right after they hugged, boothside, at the Brown Derby, whose menu had been amended to obey the meat and sugar rationing laws. Later, stopping in to see her friends at all the wordsmiths' shops on the Strip—Fawcett, Dell, and the *Reporter*—my mother found her cronies tag teaming their regular fare with pro bono patriotic newsreel copy. She also saw the photos that studio publicists were proffering: female contract players showing off the jaunty black vertical stripes on the backs of their legs, faux-silk stockings to make up for the real ones they were happily forgoing.

The same fervor enveloped the nightclubs. With a massive influx of soldiers and defense workers flooding L.A., Herman (who had 1-A draft status and was waiting to be called himself) had put on a special War Workers' Late Show, with free rounds of drinks and a slashed-price cover charge; the chorus girls rose to the occasion with GI Joe costumes and plenty of marching and saluting in their choreography. The soldiers and shipworkers loved the Carroll—it became their Sunset Boulevard stop on a round that stretched from the jitterbug hot spot, the Zenda Ballroom, way downtown, to the betting palace, the Casino Gardens, in Ocean Park.

In between putting on these shows, Herman and his staff (everyone from the wine captain to the lighting chief to the busboys) were spending their spare time at the Old Barn, on Cahuenga Boulevard off Sunset, and so was just about every other entertainment craftsman and producer in Hollywood. John Garfield and Bette Davis had spearheaded a plan for studios, guilds, and unions to methodically turn the huge roadhouse-style club (and former livery stable) into a completely free, gratitude-filled pleasure palace called the Hollywood Canteen for Service Men. Billy Wilkerson and Columbia Studios had made generous behests to get the Old Barn leased. Studio set decorators were partitioning it and building the stage; studio soundmen were doing acoustics; studio animators were decorating the walls; and the staffs of the Mocambo, Ciro's, Earl Carroll, and the Cocoanut Grove were getting meal and drink service and show presentation up and running—tasks they would also continue after it opened.

The Hollywood Canteen was the best new idea Sunset Boulevard had. At least that's how Herman saw it. He was running the Carroll on automatic pilot by then (Carroll himself then held forth from a mansion in the hills, descending to view his work product only occasionally), and he was restless. The showgirl-based format and the overluxe room seemed of another era to him.

The other clubs on Sunset Boulevard were every bit as listless and suddenly off-message. Ciro's in particular had been suffering for months. After he had constructed the elegant club from scratch and made it the talk of the town, Wilkerson, characteristically, soon tired of it. He was, as usual, secretly mired in his gambling compulsion. By August 1942, Wilkerson let Ciro's slip into a doldrum, "temporarily" laying off the staff and draping the windows.

Ciro's siesta continued through late September's Indian summer—but every time Herman drove past the divalike boîte, it seemed a little bit less in repose and a little bit more abandoned. With the sun beating down on the parched trees atop the dirt-dry King's Road cliff behind Ciro's parking lot, it seemed to Herman that one carelessly tossed match by a passing vagrant could destroy all of that thoughtful elegance—instantly and completely. He felt dismayed and protective.

He was pouring his heart into the Hollywood Canteen, which had its grand opening on October 3. The Hovers—Celia, Lenny, Herman, and Helen (Isidore, who'd had a stroke, was housebound)—attended, passing through a door emblazoned with the legend: Through These Portals Pass the Most Beautiful Uniforms in the World. "Jesus, Herman!" publicist Irving Fein marveled. "Your saying's got more legs than the showgirls you wrote it for!"

The evening was unforgettable. Bette Davis and John Garfield gave welcoming speeches. Abbott and Costello did pratfalls. Duke Ellington led the orchestra, playing "Stompin' at the Savoy" and "In the Mood" for the dancers—and what dancers! Loretta Young, Joan Crawford, Marlene Dietrich, and Rita Hayworth jitterbugged and cheek-to-cheeked with the soldiers, sailors, marines, and airmen. Betty Grable was the queen of the floor; she swing-danced with (somebody counted) forty-two GIs in eight minutes. Bob Hope stood up to wash dishes, and other celebrities, even celebrities' mothers, followed.

Herman saw that it was the chemistry between the glitterati and the proletariat that made a good club work. It was emotional and sensual camaraderie linking disparate types who secretly needed each other for validation. That's what made a club sexy. It was the social registrees' urge to prove themselves "Jazz Age" enough to be accepted by the gangsters at the Slipper, and the white Broadway stars' awed fealty, on Sunday night, to the race-room virtuosi at the Cotton Club. Longing, envy, lust, and glamour were the staples of a club you never wanted to leave, but those were just the basics. There was also an overlay that was required, at least there, at least then, and Herman realized it was bonhomie, wholesomeness, a pinch of schmaltz, and a dose of heart-lifting barracks democracy. That's what that moment in Hollywood demanded.

Meanwhile, on the opposite coast, the Lahey Clinic was altering its agenda in order to help the war effort, training doctors for battlefield work. In late October, my father received a letter from Gilbert Horrax explaining that fellowships were now temporarily on hold: Would he kindly agree to change his start date from January to April 1943? On October 30, my father replied that while he was "anxious and prepared to start on January 1," he fully understood "the recent problem that has arisen due to the present national emergency" and would wait until April 1. He closed with, "Respectfully yours."

"Anxious," "prepared," "respectfully," the words poignantly describe a man so near and yet so far—praying that nothing else would further delay this hard-won flight of his, which had just been delayed, minutes from takeoff.

Then, surprisingly, in February, my father did a turnabout. He suddenly requested an extra month's delay in commencing his fellowship. The cause was personal dislocation after his temporary move, with his wife, to Los Angeles—and the letter in which he made his request was late in being written and had an addled, pleading quality. My father wrote:

Dear Dr. Horrax,

The task of moving to California and adjusting myself prevented me from writing to you sooner. However, may I say that my plans are the same and I am very anxious to start my appointment with you. However, I wonder if it would be acceptable to you if I came East the latter part of April or May 1st?

What occasioned this move across the country, which would end up throwing off the start date of his coveted Lahey fellowship? The answer, at least in part, is this: a radical move by Herman, prince of the Hovers.

By November, Billy Wilkerson's siesta-ing club was showing desperation in spite of itself. To my uncle, as he put it in his memoir, Ciro's appeared "like a once-rich dowager in frayed furs, who has run through her inheritance but is still trying to keep up appearances." He went to Wilkerson and asked for the grand lady's hand. He wished to save her.

My uncle gave Wilkerson a twenty-five-thousand-dollar deposit for a three-month, nine-hundred-dollar-a-month lease with an option to renew for three years. Ciro's was his! He planned on a day-after-Christmas opening. He had six weeks to revive the abandoned queen of the Strip and infuse it with a new identity. He had already reinvented himself; now he would reinvent the idea of the Hollywood nightclub.

When he told this to his sister, she said, "I'll help you!"

My father came out for the opening, and, by doing so, bumped himself farther down the list for Lahey—there wouldn't be a spot for him until the summer of 1943, if he was lucky. He would have to bide his time by working with Mark Glaser.

Whose idea was it to come out for the opening? I wonder. Was the decision his? Was his serious side temporarily overcome by his trumpet-playing, hooker-inoculating alter ego? Or had the Hovers inveigled him to join them? Eventually, they would be financially supporting his residency. Was the Ciro's opening when that arrangement started?

However it happened, my father interrupted his own dream for Herman's dream. In that first, key round at least, glamour had trumped seriousness. Show business won out over neurosurgery.

Chapter Seven

HOLLYWOOD, BOSTON, NEW YORK, HOLLYWOOD: 1942–1945

The first year of operating Ciro's proved to be an ecstatic trial by fire for my uncle and a turning point for his character. It was through negotiating with an assortment of wily colleagues—and a fair dose of fate—that Herman finally shed the last vestiges of his surprisingly resilient naïveté.

Nightclubs customarily reaped their profits in the last wee hours of the morning, midnight to last call: 2 A.M. That's when people drank most seriously, and drinks sales were where the clubs raked in their proceeds. A week after he'd plunked down his twenty-five-thousand-dollar deposit, however, the California State Board of Equalization cut back the liquor-sale curfew to *midnight*, and Herman felt like he'd just bought an expensive racehorse, only to find it had a broken leg.

My uncle paid a second visit to Billy Wilkerson. "I want out," he said. "A club can't show a profit up to midnight. *You* know that! It's impossible."

"The law will never be enforced!" Wilkerson countered. "It's unconstitutional! Anyway, I won't *let* you out." Wilkerson, my uncle recalled, was "a nonstop talker whose words had the impact of a jackhammer. He had been tapping on the desk with a pencil as he spoke, and the cadence of his tapping seemed to emphasize every

word. 'You know why I won't let you out? Because you're just plain
yellow! *I won't do anything for someone who's yellow!'* "

More to the point, it was later made evident that Wilkerson had
already forked over the supposedly escrowed $25,000 to his gam-
bling creditors. The pages of Ciro's inventory Herman received
were dizzying:

> *224 Louis XIV demitasse spoons*
> *196 Regency demitasse spoons*
> *189 Marie Antoinette demitasse spoons*
> *99 International Silver Company demitasse spoons*

This list convinced him he needed someone to take over the restaurant end while he concentrated on the showmanship component. Marcel Lamaze, the Earl Carroll's pixieish headwaiter, approached
Herman, offering to put up 50 percent of the operating costs. "Here
was the perfect partner," Herman marveled. "Marcel was a connoisseur
of vintage wines. He could pass a blindfold test sniffing *bernaise, espag-
nole, duxelle,* and a dozen other sauces. And he had a suavity, an impec-
cability, a savoire faire that customers loved." But "one week before
opening night, Marcel still hadn't paid for his share of the partnership,"
Herman wrote, although Herman had "defrayed Marcel's rent, bought
him a new tuxedo, and furnished him with spending money." Instead,
he announced to my uncle, "I've been thinking it over. Ciro's hasn't a
ghost of a chance. I won't squander my time on a failure."

Seven days before opening night, Herman was thus stuck with no
one to run the kitchen, the wine list, the bar, or the service. He was
about to succumb to hysteria when, forty-eight hours later, Lamaze
sashayed back in with a new declaration: He had no money to
invest, but he'd still like to work at Ciro's. "His nerve won me over,"
Herman wrote. He hired Marcel and paid him handsomely.

With Lamaze taking care of cuisine and libations, Herman finalized his plans to turn Ciro's into a combination of the Silver Slipper, the Cotton Club, the Hollywood Canteen, the B. F. Keith vaudeville palaces of his childhood, and the Latin nightclubs in then wildly popular Havana. Ditching Wilkerson's no-entertainment policy, he hired dance team Sue Barat and Don Loper (Loper later became a *le tout* L.A. women's fashion designer) to augment the Al Donahue Orchestra. He booked Eddie LeBaron's Latin band for good measure.

Picturing happily inebriated couples rhumbaing away, he had a few square feet of wooden slats of the dance floor removed—he *shrank* it. Bumped derrieres made dancing sexy. This counterintuitive idea became his number one axiom: Small dance floor, to produce intimacy. Several other axioms followed:

- Remove mirrors from main room—don't let women and men notice the physical ravages of overcarousing.
- Put lighting fixtures on special theatrical dimmers, so light slowly fades with the passing hours.
- No tall headwaiters. It's ego crippling for a small man to follow a towering headwaiter to a table.

On the club's exterior, up went a marquee (Wilkerson considered neon advertisements tacky): *H. D. Hover Presents.* Down came the ballustrade and entranceway slats; Herman wanted fans to be able to watch the celebrities alight from their vehicles. Then my mother came up with an idea that would add immeasurably to Ciro's nightclub-confidential sizzle. She had a small toilet–cum–empty storeroom that was attached to the tiny cigarette-concession office enlarged and refitted as a hidden proper ladies' lounge. Celia made chintz slipcovers for a chaise longue found in the basement, and Beadie Einstein Manners got her boss Zanuck to part with a bare-bulb-studded makeup mirror from one of the studio's dressing rooms. Lenny got involved, too, working with the contractors there and on other phases of the restoration.

Finally, Herman tweaked Wilkerson's original opening night display ads. (Wilkerson was giving him a free ad in the *Reporter*.) He retained the sketch of the silk-pegnoired woman seated at her dressing table, talking on the telephone, but, instead of the "Everybody that's anybody will be at Ciro's" tag line, the legend was the more inclusive "An Evening of Revelry."

The ad ran on Christmas Eve. The only phone call Herman got was, he said, "from the *Daily Variety* [Wilkerson's *Reporter*'s competitor], telling me I should advertise with them. The forty-eight hours to opening night passed like an eternity. Ringing in my head, those two sleepless nights, were the words of singer Margaret Whiting at a dull Broadway premiere, 'I've seen more people at the opening of an umbrella.' " Would that be Herman's fate? Happily, no. Recent events on the war front—U.S. troops had just invaded North Africa; Guadalcanal had reached its climactic moment; and the Germans were poised to lose the Battle of Stalingrad—left Americans chewing on the good feeling fed to them by Winston Churchill a month earlier: that if this was not the end of the war, it was at least the beginning of the end. They *yearned* to go out and cut the rug the night after Christmas.

Consequently, "they came in in twos and fours and sixes," Herman recalled. "They thronged the place." Joan Crawford was there. So was Cary Grant. Lana Turner came with her new husband, restaurant owner Steve Crane, and my mother—supervising the cigarette and coat-check girls with one eye, sleuthing for column items with the other—got the actress she most avidly chronicled to sit down with her in the cigarette girls' lounge.

The movie stars of the forties had a combination of qualities that are the mirror opposite of their counterparts today. On the one hand, they gave off a glamour unheard of in our era, when ten-million-dollar-a-picture actresses wear jeans on David Letterman. But the jeans-wearing actresses are sophisticated; those glamour girls were not. They were often socially naive contract-worker bees completely beholden to studio bosses. They were raised in a culture that still inculcated obedience and in an America deeply gridded by the class system. A lot of them were insecure about their rough edges (high school dropout Betty Hutton told my mother she kept a dictionary on her bedstand to look up words whose meanings she didn't know) and their recent poverty (ex-elevator operator Dorothy Lamour remembered when she and her mother had to stretch $1.75 to last five days). However, they were still able to be human beings. They didn't have minders or bodyguards; they opened their own front doors; they worried about getting pregnant; and when they got drunk, they would pour out their hearts in a powder room.

Fawcett was by then billing their columnist "Helen Hover Weller, *Ace* Hollywood Reporter," and my mother's ace-iness had much to do with her willingness to sit on stories if her sources asked her to. So when my mother asked Turner what was wrong, the star went off the record—and broke into tears. She regretted the recent demise of her marriage to Artie Shaw, she blubbered. They had eloped, on a lark, the night of their first date because both wanted babies. (Their press agents pretended they'd had a few dates, so it would look better.) Then she'd gotten pregnant, but instead of telling Shaw, she first broke the news to her boss Louis B. Mayer. Mayer made Turner have an abortion. Shaw found out about the pregnancy only after it was terminated, and that betrayal spelled the end of their marriage.

As opening night wore on, Herman's waiters running behind, and the celebrities-as-waitstaff spirit that had defined the Hollywood Canteen took root at Ciro's. "Mickey Rooney pinch-hit as a headwaiter and was taking orders," Herman remembered. "Jimmy Durante stepped in to help out." In addition, the then barely known "Desi Arnaz was there in his army uniform"—with his soon-to-be-wife, former Earl Carroll showgirl Lucille Ball. As the *Herald Express* reporter noted, Arnaz stepped up to the band-stand and played conga drums with Eddie LeBaron, and then led a samba line that included Ball, Grant, and even a few GIs who'd been up in the back, chowing down their Serviceman's Specials. (Two years later, when Arnaz was discharged from the army, Her-man immediately snapped him up and headlined him at Ciro's. Ball, newly married to him, was ringside almost every night, making it hard for Arnaz to drink, which he liked to do with abandon and of which she disapproved. "So he would sneak champagne—hide a few glasses around the club, excuse himself and quaff them down—when she wasn't looking," Herman recalled.)

In a 1998 TV documentary about the Sunset Strip, Billy Wilker-son's son, businessman Willie Wilkerson, said that, under his father, Ciro's had been elite and exclusive—not a populist place, by any means. "Hover had a more egalitarian vision: 'Come one, come all.' And I think the Sunset Strip was ready for that."

The bonhomie that ignited opening night allowed Herman to rake in profits of twenty-five hundred dollars to four thousand dollars a week in the early months of 1943. He was featuring a new headliner every two weeks, and he had a way to measure audience response to the entertainment, "During the show, I didn't even glance at the performers. Rather, I trained my eyes on the darkened audience. If I observed more than two cigarettes being lit, the song was not scor-ing. My theory was that those captivated by a show do not light up fresh cigarettes."

Herman didn't wangle his first name attraction until spring, when

William Morris agent Ben Holzman called and asked, "Interested in playing Joe E. Lewis?" The comic was on his way to entertain the troops in the South Pacific and had two weeks to kill. Holzman gave Herman a bargain rate, but when Herman bragged about it to his colleagues, they told him that Lewis had last closed a Sunset Strip room before an audience of twelve people.

Somehow, though, in the new Ciro's Lewis was different—he clicked. The engagement was a huge success. On a roll, Herman booked "a young Danish piano player named Victor Borge, whose sense of comedy at the keyboard was fresh and unrivalled," he wrote. "I paid this ingeniously clever performer five hundred dollars weekly for a two week stand in June. He packed them in the first week."

Herman had just locked up after that first week's engagement and was asleep in his Hollywood Boulevard apartment when the phone rang. It was 4 A.M. The new orchestra leader, Emil Coleman, was agitatedly saying, "Better come over to Ciro's, Herman. The place is burning."

By then Herman's attachment to the nightclub was intense. As he threw on his clothes and got in his car, he realized, he said, that "Ciro's was my woman, my undying love." Driving down Sunset, "I saw a glow in the sky, and two blocks from my establishment police and fire trucks blocked the road. I parked and sprinted. Ciro's looked like a stage set in hell. Huge clawing flames were spurting from all three stories."

In an interview Billy Wilkerson gave the *Herald Express* in 1957, he blamed the lack of control of the fire on confusion between the L.A. City and County Fire Departments over who was supposed to put out the blaze. "Part of the building is on city property and part on county," Wilkerson told the paper. "While the two outfits were trying to decide who had jurisdiction, Ciro's practically burned down." Perhaps a likelier reason is that "restaurant kitchen fires" (as this was officially judged to be) were always looked at gimlet-eyed by the local fire departments, back in that randy time and place. Whatever the reason, the fire was not subdued until 7 A.M.

The damage broke my uncle's heart. His version of what came next was this: "For the first few days after the appalling disaster, I had no time for anything but the removal of the charred wooden rafters, the loose bricks, and the ubiquitous plaster." Wilkerson was carting off the rubble and saving what was salvageable, but Herman was charged with hiring and paying for site watchmen. "Then I sat back and waited for Wilkerson to phone. He said he would call as soon as he got the insurance money."

The wait lasted four months, but Wilkerson proved true to his word. "No sooner had Wilkerson collected for the loss then he phoned. He wanted to see me right away."

Herman drove to the *Reporter* with visions of Ciro's redesign and hopes that Wilkerson would approve them. "After clapping me on the back and bidding me to take a seat, he dropped a blockbuster of a sentence: 'I've sold the property.' The good man paused to blow his nose. 'You may remove your watchmen.'"

Herman shot back, "Why didn't you give *me* a chance to buy it?!"

"Oh, come off it!" Wilkerson responded. "You would have been nuts. Griffith bought the property and he'll rebuild at his expense." Albert Griffith owned movie theaters, oil wells, and the Last Frontier Hotel in the then obscure Nevada town, Las Vegas.

Wilkerson's eagerness to unload Ciro's had much to do with his own imminent pursuit of Las Vegas, in concert with a man he had become inextricably bound up with: Bugsy Siegel. The alliance, based on Wilkerson's gambling addiction, was several years old. (In 1942, just before Herman leased Ciro's from him, Wilkerson had been sending meals from Ciro's kitchen to Siegel's L.A. County Jail cell, where he was awaiting trial for the 1939 murder of fellow mobster Harry Greenberg.) Soon, with Siegel backing him, Wilkerson would open the Flamingo Hotel and eventually be forced to turn it over entirely to the mobster.

A week after Wilkerson agreed to sell Ciro's to Albert Griffith, as fate would have it, Griffith dropped dead of a heart attack. Hearing the news, Herman again went straight to Wilkerson's office. "He greeted me effusively; he obviously had a guilty conscience. The executor of the Griffith estate wanted out of the contract. Wilkerson was capable of changing his mind in the middle of a sentence if it was better for him. We made a deal."

Herman took Isidore Hover's entire estate—the reinvested assets from the real estate holdings he'd sold before he left Brooklyn—and poured them into Ciro's, making it truly a Hover family business. Wilkerson lowered the purchase price because Herman took on the $210,000 postfire refurbishment that wasn't covered by insurance. The deed to the nightclub became Herman's immediately; the deed to the land reverted to him after a land mortgage was paid off in full two years later.

Herman knew his postrenovation opening night act had to be sensational. He gambled on an emerging Spanish-Cuban violinist and tango bandleader (and accomplished caricaturist) named Xavier Cugat. Volatile and charismatic, Cugie had the squinty eyes and the huge, downward-tilting nose of a wickedly playful anteater.

"On opening night, Carmen Miranda did an impromptu number," Herman recalled. "Tony Martin got up on the floor, and Judy Garland and Van Johnson joined in the incipient pandemonium." Of course, "Desi Arnaz—still in the uniform of Uncle Sam—got into the act. He had been one of Cugat's boys not too long ago."

Opening nights were *the* big occasion in Hollywood; the studios liked to send all their stars and arrivistes out in gowns, tuxes, and furs.

They were there to be photographed for the magazines, newsreels, and newspapers (and, not incidentally, to plug their about-to-be-released films). So, as Herman put it, "Cafe society was out in full strength: Esther Willians and Ben Gage, Lana Turner and Steve Crane, and Ava Gardner with Howard Duff. Rudy Vallee, Gene Kelly, and Cary Grant were in parties. Mary Livingston and Jack Benny hosted George Burns and Gracie Allen, and were seated next to the table occupied by Roz Russell and Loretta Young with their respective spouses."

Cugat called Jimmy Durante up on the stage and the two engaged in verbal dueling ("which requires," as Herman put it, "both deftness and esprit"), ending with "Schnozzola throwing Cugat's sheet music in the air and putting on an impromptu show," Herman recalled. With Durante hoarsely belting out nonsensical lyrics to "Pasodoble," which Cugat played with his feet planted in a wide straddle (his body bobbing and the bow of his fiddle looping and spinning and diving like a twirled baton), the kitchen staff edged toward the opened door and peered into the main room. "Seeing them, Durante shouted, 'Stop da music! All youse cooks and waiters, come on over here!' They crowded into the room—'See, everybody *wants* ta get *inta da* act!' Durante crowed—and he got them up on the stage and Cugie gave them percussion instruments."

Cugat was also, as Herman put it, "the wiliest man my staff and I ever worked with." He liked to dance so much (with a vampy little girlfriend named Angel, whom he plunked down at ringside), he would often abandon his band to get on the floor. Soon, he started taking his set breaks across the street at the Mocambo, sambaing with Angel to the rival club's orchestra.

Toward the end of Cugat's second booking, Herman was on a talent-scouting trip to New York when he got "a premonition," as he put it, "that all was not kosher." He immediately called his club and asked for Cugat. The headwaiter admitted that Cugie had changed the schedule so his last set was over by 11:45 instead of 2:00. Then Cugat was off to the Mocambo with Angel. Herman next called Cugat's agent at home. " 'By the time I get to Ciro's, I want to see Cugat on the bandstand!' I roared. He put in a call to Cugat at the Mo. Cugie was sore as a pup, but he returned."

Not one to suffer humiliation lightly, Cugat immediately plotted revenge. At his next afternoon's rehearsal, he ordered his band to play the introductory verse of "Begin the Beguine"—a single note repeated for thirty-two bars—and *nothing else* through all the evening's sets. When Herman asked what the hell was going on, Cugat whipped out his contract to prove that nothing in it stipulated he had to play more than one song. It just said he had to *play*.

It was four hours to showtime. Herman took a breather to figure his options. He remembered a just-up-from-Tijuana pauper musician he'd seen on Olvera Street. In those days of uncopyrighted stage names, the fellow had a gimmick. Herman drove down to the pungent alleyway, plucked up the unwashed fellow, his serape, sombrero, and one-man-band accoutrements, and drove the clangy assemblage back to Ciro's. "This performer's name is *also* Xavier Cugat," Herman announced, ushering the fellow to the center of the wooden dance floor. "Here's his birth certificate." The man obligingly displayed the crumpled, and possibly fraudulent, document. Then Herman ceremoniously unfurled the man's serape, and the star and the club owner watched this other Xavier Cugat sit down cross-legged on it to play a monkey grinder's organ with his hands, toot a harmonica stuck between his teeth, clang the cymbals attached to his knees, and honk the car horns wedged under his armpits. "I'm playing him," Herman said. "The contract just says 'Xavier Cugat'; it doesn't say *which* Xavier Cugat."

Cugat caved. "It was the only time I ever got the better of Cugat," wrote Herman, who, during Cugat's subsequent (and

increasingly valued) engagements, was hoodwinked into gifting
Angel with a mink coat, while the Mocambo's Charlie Morrison was
hoodwinked into buying her a sable one. Still, the triumph, singular
though it was, launched a new stage of self-creation for my uncle.
He'd gone from lean and earnest dancer/choreographer to still vulnerable nightclub second in command. Now he was morphing into a
more powerful if less sympathetic character: H. D. Hover, the
shrewd, puffed-up, consummate Hollywood honcho.

One day at the end of that summer of 1943, my mother ran into
flamboyant studio publicist Russell Birdwell, who had done the
Gone with the Wind campaign for the Selznicks, as she was dropping
off copy at Fawcett. "I'm going to Boston tomorrow!" she told him,
excitedly. Danny was *finally* starting at Lahey! The rash of post-
ponements of this jewel-in-the-crown assignment had been painful
for both of them, even though the thrill of helping Herman launch
Ciro's had somewhat taken my mother's mind off it. (My father had
bided the time impatiently working with Mark Glaser.)

"Well, dear," Birdwell replied, "you must call my friend at the
Boston American. He'll set you right up with a job!"

As soon as they landed and rented another tiny apartment, my
mother approached Birdwell's friend and got a job as a "senior
rewrite" at the *American,* which pumped out five editions a day. She
loved the camaraderie with the mostly male and Irish writers ("I'd
walk them up and down the city room when they were drunk; I was
very protective of them," she told me), the macho rhythm (" 'Weller!
Pick it up!' the city editor would shout when a story was breaking"),
the hourly adding of emerging details to early-edition stories about
fires and murders and mayhem. It was my mother at her best: hanging out with guys, laughing and taking their ribbing ("F'Pete's sake,
you don't start a St. Patty's Day's piece with '*Begora!*' Not even *here*

you don't!'"), and punching out copy on deadline. Never mind that her New York friends were by then settling into wife roles and having the requisite two babies in the suburbs. Reporting is what she loved, and her disdain for the doctor's wife convention was palpable. Sometimes it was a little too much so. "Your mother was a very rude and preoccupied guest," Esther Kaufman recalls of the time she and my father visited Esther and Danny Kaufman at Ft. Devins, where Kaufman was stationed. My father had urged the visit, not just because he and Danny were close but because Esther's brother, Mel Allen, was lead announcer of the Yankees, making inside stories on Joltin' Joe DiMaggio abundant in that household. My mother, however, disdained Jewish Southern Belle Esther as a smug phony. (The animosity between the two would have occasion to intensify years later.) "I spent the whole day making chopped liver appetizers and a pot roast," Esther says, "but when your mother came, it was like she wanted to fly right out again. She spent the evening in our bedroom to make phone calls for those stories of hers."

It was her work that kept my mother busy and happy during my father's grueling morning-noon-and-night stints at Lahey. "They didn't have interns or medical students to do the histories and the physicals. It was a tremendous amount of work; you never saw your husband if he was a Lahey fellow—but, oh, were the fellows glorified!" recalls Dr. Jean Hawkes, whose husband, Doug, was in my father's group there.

The dozen handpicked Lahey fellows absorbed and exuded the prevalent line about their chosen field. "Neurosurgery was the ultimate medical specialty but it was so young, so technically difficult, with so little leeway for mistakes, you had to be crazy to go into it," Hawkes recalls. "Gilbert Horrax was horrified at how they'd all earn a living!"

Despite (or because) of that combination of machismo and self-deprecation, the Lahey neurosurgeons were storied and pampered. "We had our very own scrub nurses at Deaconness and New England Baptist," recalls Lahey's neurosurgery department's chairman emeritus Dr. Charles Fager, who arrived just after my father left. "Most of the nurses were spinsters. They were devoted to their jobs, as if they were nuns. They'd go around to the hospitals with us and carry our instruments, which would then be delivered to us in the operating rooms. And they'd come to the clinic and see our patients with us. Neurosurgeons at Lahey were *gods*." Fager laughs. "Oh, it was very elite! It was marvelous!"

Ceremonial perks were the least of it. Lahey was a scholar's program, and the breakthroughs published by the faculty when my father arrived were estimable: clinic founder and surgery chief Frank Lahey on stomach cancer and thyroid surgery; neurologist John Dynes on Parkinson's disease; and radiologist Hugh Hare on pulmonary metastatic testicular cancer. Then, of course, there was the neurosurgical wonder boy James Poppen, by then a living legend. "He was developing a whole new school of surgery," Fager says. "He had a natural aptitude—a gift. It had nothing to do with training. He was like Jascha Heifetz to the violin, Tiger Woods to golf: It was a level of skill that was just incredible. We'd often have three or four residents and three or four fellows who were ready to leave Lahey, but they stayed an extra year, without pay, just to watch Poppen. Then they took his incredible techniques all over the country."

The revolution Poppen fostered had to do with speed and simplicity. "Most neurosurgeons—Horrax, for example—were slow, tedious, fussy, plodding, necessarily as a result of their classical training by Harvey Cushing," Fager continues. "Oh, it was dreadful! Poppen gave us the attitude, 'Don't fool around——get it *done!*' But he was also delicate and neat. He didn't bruise the brain. He was expeditious, aggressive, *and* careful."

Poppen and Horrax were opposites. Horrax was "courtly and soft-spoken," Fager says, "with a very, very bland, humorless aspect." "He was refined and kind," says Hawkes. "In a field full of prima donnas, where others threw things and swore, the most Horrax ever said was, 'Goodness gracious.' " And he was so sensible, "he ate lunch every day at the corner drugstore because he could get a meal for 35 cents," says Hawkes.

Next to this flinty, straitlaced gentleman, "Poppen," Fager says, "was ebullient, engaging, emotional—cursing and making remarks"—a regular Gene Krupa, as my father had put it, "even though there might be six or seven people watching him." The odd-couple neurosurgeons created a kind of dog and pony show. Fager recalls, "If there were two operating rooms going and Dr. Horrax had started a case, Poppen would have finished his first case and he would go in and say, 'Dr. Horrax, can I give you a hand?' (He treated Horrax as the boss.) And Horrax would say, 'Oh, sure, Jim, come on in.' In the next half hour, Poppen would take Horrax's patient's tumor out and go back to his next case."

At the time, Poppen was tackling the specialty's most stubborn challenge: how to make aneurysm surgery safer. Aneurysm surgery "is what gave us the reputation of being cowboys back then," Dr. Fager says. Even today, sixty years later, when greatly improved clips and soaring technical advances have completely transformed the enterprise, it is still fraught with risk. "You're working with a very thin membrane," explains neurosurgeon Victor Ho. "With any misstep, any slip of the instrument, the thing ruptures and you've got blood jetting straight up from the heart, right in your face. A quart of blood [can be lost] in a few seconds."

Poppen's early contribution to aneurysm work had been to surround aneurysms with strips of muscle. At Lahey he was working on a theory: A patient's chance for long-term survival would increase substantially if the artery was ligated—tied off—before-hand. With Hugh Hare, the eminence in Lahey's radiology depart-ment, he embarked upon a special project to test that hypothesis by way of radical ligation techniques. My father was the Lahey fellow chosen to assist them.

The first stage of the job was evaluating patients who presented obvious aneurysm symptoms: severe headaches, pain around the eye, impaired vision, nausea, fainting, bleeding, or convulsions. If his testing proved the presence of an aneurysm, my father would assist Poppen with the procedure that was the heart of his experiment—and it was almost harrowingly primitive. Using a strange trussing contraption called the Light collar, Poppen would essentially "train" the patient's carotid artery to tolerate surgical occlusion, much as a novice swimmer trains his lungs to hold his breath underwater.

Poppen would fit the patient into the Light collar, which put tremendous pressure on the clavicle above the carotid artery. Then, positioning his hands carefully on the collar, Poppen would com-press the carotid artery, cutting off blood flow while the seconds ticked by on the counter. At thirty seconds, Poppen would spring open his hands and quickly unstrap the patient. A half hour later he would repeat the process with the count running to sixty seconds. Immediately afterward, my father would assess the patient for cir-culation damage.

Over the next few days Poppen would apply the Light collar to the patient several times a day, each time for thirty seconds longer than the last time. Finally, the patient was able to tolerate occlusion of his carotid artery for an uninterrupted ten minutes.

Once the patient was able to survive "preoperative fractional compression of the artery" without brain damage, it was time to find out exactly where the incipient saccular rupture was hiding. In a black-walled chamber, Hugh Hare slowly injected four to eight cc of the dye thorotrast (later discovered to cause cancer) into the patient's artery and tracked the liquid's progress through the artery by staring at the depleting color in the drip vial. At precisely the instant the last two cc of fluid was entering the artery, Hare clicked the switch. The aneurysm's location—somewhere along the artery's juncture with the circle of Willis (the confluence of the vascular structures at the base of the brain, giving off the vessels that feed blood to the brain)—lit up on the arteriograph. When Hare squeezed the bulb, the site was captured on stereoscopic film. Poppen slapped the developed X ray up on the view box and studied it carefully. Then the patient was given local anesthesia. Poppen dissected the muscle until the artery was exposed, sterile and naked. Then came a snap decision: Could the patient tolerate a complete blocking of the artery or just a partial one? The surgeon made the assessment and performed the appropriate ligation of the artery.

After the wound was closed, the patient was turned upside down and fastened in acrobat's rigging to keep him that way for an uninterrupted *seventy-two hours*. Round the clock, nurses helped the patient endure the hysteria-producing disorientation and kept him from turning himself right-side-up, even for a few seconds. As Poppen, Hare, and Weller warned in their subsequent paper ("Diagnosis and Treatment of Aneurysm of the Internal Carotid Artery"), published in the 1944 journal *Surgical Clinics of North America*, "Maintenance of normal blood pressure is important to prevent circulatory changes that may be disastrous."

Sometimes Poppen went further. If inaction meant the patient would die, and if the arteriogram showed the aneurysm to be in a position favorable either to "trapping" or to reinforcing the whole wall, then he performed a craniotomy to get to the site of the threatened rupture and employed the McKenzie clip to stanch the dilatation. That was the cowboy work Fager was referring to. As Poppen,

Hare, and Weller bluntly put it in their paper (which was written by my father since he was the junior researcher), it was "hazardous."

"There's an artery leading to the brain that we hold our breath for when we operate," my father once told Lizzie and me. "We call it 'the artery of cerebral hemorrhage'; that's how prone it is to rupture." (Tragically, decades later, that very artery would rupture in Liz's husband's head; he would die instantly of an undiagnosed aneurysm.) "I used to hold my breath for it when Poppen clipped," my father said. "Now my residents hold their breaths for it, when I do."

Decades later, when she knew she was dying, my mother typed a message on a Post-it note and stuck it on her *Boston American* staff portrait, which had long hung in her home office. She was flagging that picture for my sister and me, to show us that it was important. The sloppy Selectric-typed note (she could barely move by then) read, "This photo, one of my favorites, taken when I was a writer (rewrite desk) on *Boston American,* Hearst's top-flight paper in Boston. Your dad had a fellowship in neurosurgery at Lahey Clinic—and it was one of the best years of our lives." Those last eleven words—a note in a bottle, tossed from the drowning ship of her soul—still have the power to stir me.

Even then, as Esther Kaufman tells it, my father was restless. Esther remembers going with her husband, Danny, to visit the Boston apartment. "We were invited to go out to dinner with him and Helen, but when we got there, there was no Helen. Danny Weller and Marty Lasoff [the womanizer of the old Brooklyn trio] were there, with two ladies, nice-looking young ladies. Danny Weller served drinks and said we were going out to dinner.

"And then the phone rang.

"Danny took the call and then he said, 'You all have to leave now! Everybody! Hurry!' "

Lasoff, the Kaufmans, and the two young ladies hustled. "We all got in the elevator," Esther Kaufman recalls, "and Danny was rushing us out of there and we got downstairs and we were walking to the exit of the building, and your mother arrives. And Marty says, 'Oh, we were all just upstairs! We were going out! We stopped to see Danny, and we were just going out!' And she did *not* take this very graciously. She was very curt to us. She was very upset. Marty considered this a close call for your father." (Decades later, Esther Kaufman still seems perturbed by my mother's lack of etiquette.)

At the end of 1944 the Lahey fellowship ended, and my parents moved back to New York so my father could complete the next stage of his residency. My mother had turned down the job of women's page editor of the *American*, but no matter: Danny's career was the one that counted. They rented an apartment in a doorman building on Remsen Street in Brooklyn Heights. Being back in Brooklyn struck a sentimental nerve, yet every time my mother set off across the borough to Arlington Avenue she found a reason to stop and turn around. Life, for her, was only forward motion.

My father returned to Mt. Sinai as a "voluntary assistant in neuropathology." Globus had asked him to participate in the preparation of his life's work—his collected case histories and master classification of meningiomas—for publication. A South American neuropathologist—Jorge Gomez Jaramillo, up from Medellín, Colombia, on a fellowship—shared the chore with my father. Both were picking up from the extensive start-up that had been done by Avraam Kazan, my father's coresident with Globus from the year before, who was then an army lieutenant.

Under Globus's tutelage, my father spent four months studying the embryonic development of the three membranes (subarachnoid, *dura mater*, and *pia mater*) that envelop the brain and spinal cord, and organized Globus's twenty years of research, which had led him to contend (back in the days when others were misguided) that those common, noninvasive meningeal masses actually had their origins in *skeletal* tissue. There were "bits of bone in the tumors," as Globus used to put it, a fact essential to understanding them.

Then, with Globus guiding them, Weller and Jaramillo examined the multitude of unevenly documented meningioma case histories that Kazan had been pulling together and reclassified them according to a single consistent measure. The result was an enormous article—twenty-five published pages—titled "Intracranial Meningiomas," in the *Journal of Mt. Sinai Hospital*.

With Kazan off in battle and Jaramillo not a fluent writer of English, it fell to my father to sum up his mentor's thesis in the opening two paragraphs. These clear but impassioned words are his:

> Until recently there was great diversity of opinion as to the origin and classification of meningiomas. The . . . observations . . . resulted in many different names applied by different investigators to tumors of similar structure. This led to an accumulation of unreliable morphologic data, and the classification of meningiomas was in a chaotic state. . . . [I]n 1935 Globus presented his theory as to the formation of these neoplasms and offered his histologic classification. This theory, we believe, made possible a clearer insight into the true nature of this type of tumor and the varying pattern often assumed by it.

He told me that he waited nervously while Globus read them. Then Globus had smiled, approvingly. The paper remained definitive in the field until about 1950.

My mother was so proud of my father's work that she tried her hand at putting her enthrallment with her husband into the form of a novel. Her characters "met cute," fell quickly in love, and, of course, the man proposed by warning, "I have one foot on a banana peel . . ."

My mother revealed the existence of the (by-then-long-abandoned) novel to me when I was ten. It had a nautical setting, she said: The man and woman go off on a trip around the world; he is signed on as the ship's doctor. "Why didn't you finish it?" I asked. "Oh!" she'd slapped the air dismissively. "I'm not a good enough writer." Then she added, "But I should have finished it, anyway. I *did* want to write that book." Her surprising earnestness, and her regret, touched me deeply.

The man and woman go off on a trip around the world; he's signed on as the ship's doctor. "I have one foot on a banana peel, *the other on the grave.*" Why, I wonder now, did she put those two thoughts together? During those intense residency years, would my father lie in bed at night, frightened, angry, feeling his heart beating weakly? Did he express that alter-ego wish: to chuck it all and go off to sea for adventure? Years later my father would do just that—and wind up finishing her novel for her.

"Danny is doing such wonderful, important work!" my mother would rave during the several trips she made to L.A. in that period. It was as if she were using the seriousness of the East—and the integrity her marriage assumed there—to shield her from Celia's overstrong embrace, and from the rush she got whenever she entered Ciro's. It was a high-pitched time in Hollywood. The town was both draped in patriotic bunting and laced with heavy-breathing intrigue. Handsome stars were in the service—Lieutenant Tyrone Power, Colonel Jimmy Stewart, Captain Clark Gable, Lieutenant Robert Taylor, Colonel George Montgomery, even Russian count–turned–U.S. Lieutenant Oleg Cassini (on base at Ft. Riley, Kansas, no less)—and their female counterparts were dutifully role-modeling frugality. ("Thrifty by nature, Lucille Ball saves all bottles and jugs and hand paints decorative designs on them," read *Motion Picture*'s caption of the actress wielding paintbrush and pottery.) At the same time, the films rolling out of production were dark melo-dramas (Charles Boyer, Ingrid Bergman, and Joseph Cotten in *Gaslight*) and tales of sexual betrayal and murder: Fred MacMurray, Barbara Stanwyck, and Edward G. Robinson in *Double Indemnity*, as well as the emerging film noir genre.

My mother justified her trips west by working, visiting the com-missaries and homes of the stars daily, notepad in hand, and typing up her findings on thin paper to be sent by airmail back to New York. Some of the best skinny came from Ciro's—often items that had eluded the grasp of Hedda, Louella, and Winchell (and most of which my mother could not bring herself to write, but could only enjoy as part of the backstairs-Ciro's grapevine):

- Howard Hughes packed the room with tablefuls of guests. Then he'd go out to the parking lot and huddle with women in an old Chevrolet, having his tournedos ferried through the car window in a center-thumb-holed covered silver serving dish.
- Joan Bennett was always on the phone in the ladies' lounge, hav-ing loud, romantic conversations with agent Jennings Lang, even though she was married to producer Walter Wanger. (Years later, Wanger would retaliate by shooting Lang in the groin.)
- Jimmy Roosevelt, Franklin D. Roosevelt's son (and, by coinci-dence, Harvey Cushing's son-in-law), then an L.A. business-man, often stopped in, sometimes with his mother, Eleanor, whose young female friend (and controversial Office of Civil Defense appointee) dancer Mayris Chaney just happened to have taken a little apartment right up King's Road. The pied-à-terre's purpose was never mentioned.
- Just before she married businessman Bill Howard, Dorothy

Lamour ran into the ladies' room and cried her eyes out because tall, handsome lawyer Greg Bautzer, who was quickly becoming the town's biggest lady's man, had just told her he didn't love her. (Bautzer—who represented Howard Hughes and Bugsy Siegel—romanced Lamour, Lana Turner, Peggy Lee, and, as veteran Hollywood journalist and Ciro's ringsider Jim Bacon told me, "was such a good lover that, after one performance in bed with him, Joan Crawford bought him a Cadillac.")

• The pièce de résistance: One night Paulette Goddard and director Anatole Litvak (who had "raised eyebrows" before, my mother had noted in a column) were practically fornicating on the dance floor. After Herman escorted them off, they repaired to their table, under which Litvak crouched, and—unmistakably to the diners nearby—performed cunnilingus on her.

My mother double-dutied, under two different bylines, a pair of lengthy monthly features for *Motion Picture*: "Popping Questions At . . ." and "Let's Pretend You're . . ."

In "Popping Questions At . . ."—"by Helen Hover"—my mother popped fifty questions at a star. These Q-and-As are a time capsule of a bygone culture. In contrast to celebrity interviews of our feelings-worshipping present, where everyone knows how to answer a question like a conflict mediator, the stars of that era could be cracklingly blunt. Here's Joan Crawford:

Q: Why have you been off the screen for more than a year?
A: I wouldn't do any more war stories. That was the reason for my argument with MGM.
Q: Is it true you have a wristwatch with the hands stopped at the exact moment you met your husband [Phillip Terry]?

A: No. How silly! A columnist invented that story and it's made me feel like a fool.

Q: What do you want that you have so far failed to achieve?

A: I wanted to be a singer. MGM discouraged me.

Q: What is your most temperamental demand?

A: I *scream* for quiet in the house on Sunday morning.

Although Crawford's last statement hints at violence, the full extent of the abuses that this woman later known as "Mommie Dearest" visited on her children was still hidden. (My mother left that interview in tears after hearing her scream at and spank them.) Other deceptions that would, decades later, be blasted open in stars' kids' memoirs were also being fomented for my mother's delectation in the living rooms of these graceful Spanish and neo-New England houses. For example, her article about adopted children in Hollywood leads with:

Loretta Young was telling a friend about a conversation she overheard the other day between her adopted daughter, Judy, and Irene Dunne's twelve-year-old adopted youngster, Missy. The children were discussing plans for a circus party Loretta was giving them.

"Who shall we invite to the party?" Missy asked.

"Oh," answered Judy loftily. "Let's have kids that aren't adopted, too."

More than anything else, that explains the magnificent job both Irene and Loretta have done in telling their little daughters not only that they are adopted, but that to be adopted is something to be proud of, not a fact to be hidden.

Loretta Young's daughter Judy was not adopted; she was Young's child with Clark Gable. Young foisted the adopted-daughter fiction on everyone, especially her daughter, for years. A devout Catholic, she cared desperately about her career, her image, and her studio's approval. The truth had to be pried out of her.

My mother "popped questions" to "the Swoon King," Frank Sinatra. The skinny, big-eared singer had just moved to L.A. with Nancy and Nancy Jr.; his swing-flick *Higher and Higher* (in which he sang "I Couldn't Sleep a Wink Last Night" and "A Lovely Way to Spend an Evening") had just hit the screens. The interview leaves no doubt as to who was the precursor to Elvis and the Beatles:

Q: What is your honest opinion of your more hysterical fans?
A: I'm grateful to them, but I wouldn't mind if some of the noisier ones controlled themselves. I'm afraid some of the more exuberant kids may get hurt.

It also suggests why Sinatra always stayed close to Nancy Sr.:

Q: What quality attracted you to your wife?
A: She built up my ego. When I told her I wanted to quit my job as a sportswriter [at a local Jersey paper] to become a singer like Bing Crosby, she thought it was the right thing to do even though everyone else said I was nuts . . . I don't have to explain things to her.

Previews of the nascent, crass "Chairman of the Board" flicker:

Why do so many girls overdo the sloppy [clothing]? Some of those rolled-up sweater sleeves and run-down saddle shoes make a girl look like a washwoman ready to do a job on the floors.

Much more apparent, however, is the scrappy, loyal Hobokenite whose best friend is one Hank Sanicola ("I met him about ten years ago when he was a song plugger and no music publisher would let me near the place") and whose "proudest possession" is his prize-fighter pal Tami Mauriello's ID bracelet, which he's wearing on his wrist until Mauriello comes home from the war.

My mother asked, "What is your ambition for the future?" Earnestly, he replied, "I'd like to have a large office with a mahogany desk and rows of push buttons, like in the movies."

My mother's other feature, "Let's Pretend You're . . . by Helen Weller," set Hollywood marriages in picture frames the female reader could vicariously step right into. "Here's a game you can play each month in MOTION PICTURE magazine," the blurb each month explained. "The author writes intimately about one of the famous Hollywood wives, as she knows her, and, neatest trick of the month, she puts you right in the shoes of the person she's writing about. Read it and have some fun."

Writing the series, my mother ascended from "ace reporter" to featured and photographed one. Fawcett photographer Len Weissman accompanied her to each interview, and she's pictured in the pages—thin and pretty, in a snappy ensemble. Her hair is expertly rolled up and spilling in curls over her forehead, and she is smiling and taking notes with the movie star's wife.

Written in the intimate, portentous second person, the eighteen stories in the series exude wartime romanticism and the coy pragmatism of the days when even tough, admired women played marriage like a chess game. If you're Mrs. Harry James (Betty Grable), for example, you may be a diva ("Among the fur coats in your closet are a mink, a beaver, a lynx, white fox, and silver fox"), but:

Whatever your husband does is okay with you. You fall right in with his plans. Playing baseball with the men in his band is his idea of a perfect Sunday afternoon. Instead of staying home, you dash off with him, sit in an empty grandstand and yell your heart out gleefully for your husband to make a home run.

You also love to talk about how:

Before you were married, Harry gave you an identification bracelet marked "Betty Grable." After your marriage he said he didn't like it and took it off your arm. Then he replaced it with an identical bracelet marked "Betty James."

Only half tongue-in-cheek (her ridicule about this ethos would surface later), my mother assayed the cheeky shrewdness of these strong dames who rose early to cook breakfasts for their hubbies (Dinah Shore's meal for George Montgomery could have demolished the arteries of a truck driver) and fawned over any domestic assistance. Mrs. Sonny Tufts—"a tall, exotic" chorus dancer— thinks "he's an angel for helping out: He dries the dishes, waxes the floor, scrubs the kitchen linoleum."

Weak though he might be, the husband was indisputably in charge—or else you let him think so. Even if you're spitfire Jane Wyman, a.k.a. Mrs. Ronald Reagan (she possesses "the temper in the family—Ronnie lets you blow off until you get it out of your system"), you say, "Although you've a mind of your own, your husband makes the decisions in the family. That's the way you like it." (Wyman, of course, eventually dumped Reagan because she found him insufferably boring.)

In her own marriage, my mother was woefully undomestic (there were no Dinah Shore breakfasts from her), but *her* husband, unlike

Jane Wyman's unflappably genial Ronnie, had the temper and the complexity in the family. She had also quietly begun to take its measure. She knew to leave Danny alone when a difficult—or unsuccessful—surgery had left him tense and melancholy. (He had segued from Mt. Sinai to his most demanding and experience-intensive neurosurgical residency yet: a year's appointment at bustling, public Kings County Hospital.) She tried to hold her tongue when anxiety made her repeat a remark—he was unforgiving of neurotic tics and lack of verbal discipline.

Yet, for all his diffidence and hauteur, there were times when she was unquestionably (and unquestionedly) winning, and the issue of where they would settle down after he finished his training constituted her main victory. L.A. was home to her, but it didn't feel that way to Danny. He disdained Hollywood (even as he enjoyed it), but she longed to help Herman and Lenny run Ciro's, making the club a re-creation of the Hover siblings' childhood afternoons at the Orpheum. Besides, moving east to west seemed to her the only natural progression. You followed the sun—it was that simple. You could get your medical education among the great minds back East, and you could work in the city rooms of crumbling Eastern cities, but you couldn't move back East. That was going backward.

My father did not subscribe to his wife's sense of geographic progression. To him the East was the base, the cultural and intellectual center of things. Still—uncharacteristically for this strong-willed, narcissistic man—he let himself be pulled along by the depth of her feeling on the issue. Maybe there was something he wanted in balmy Hollywood—some license, some opportunity for the unleashing of his alter ego—that he couldn't bring himself to acknowledge openly. It was better to pretend to be dragged there half against his wishes.

By then another issue had also reared its head: My mother desperately wanted to have a baby. She had endured one miscarriage, so when she became pregnant early in 1945 she was ecstatic.

Yet while my mother was as blissful as the wives of "Let's Pretend You're . . ." series, for my father having a pregnant wife may have represented other realities, such as: a fat wife, a suddenly conventional wife, a motherlike wife—a wife like the mother he'd been escaping. He was a man with a shortened time frame, with the right to use his time as he chose, the right to invent himself. If he didn't like something, he would avoid or reject it and make no apologies. My mother went into labor on September 16. "Your father took me to the maternity ward and just *left* me there," she later said incredulously. He went back to his own patients. He *was* dedicated, yes, but he also had this *streak* in him. This coldness, this *cruelty*. There was no anesthesia, I was in the most *god*-awful labor—and he just *left* me there!"

She was quick to add that it was the lack of anesthesia that "made you such a beautiful baby. Such blue eyes! So alert! You were so beautiful, you inspired Danny's brother Alex to get married and have a baby, too." (Alex did Danny one better: His daughter, Mary Louise Weller—born ten months after me—grew up to become a Ford model and an actress, best known for her role as John Belushi's sorority girlfriend in *Animal House*.)

My mother's overchampioning of me, a tic she had all her life, started with my birth. "Such a *beautiful* baby, you inspired Alex . . . !" She felt her restless husband moving away from her, and here was a baby—a girl, to boot—to have and hold instead. She was, however, anxious in her love of me, and anxious *for* me. She loved me in a desperate, too-eager, openmouthed way—as if she perpetually had, on the tip of her tongue, one more way to sing my praises to get the man whose back was turned to face her.

I became her too-eager, openmouthed, turned-male-back-facing daughter. The phatic communication I had with my mother until the day she died—the lack of a border between us, the never-articulated but powerful sense of mutual failure with the man we both loved—is why I was so relieved, when I was pregnant twenty years ago, to learn that my baby was a boy. I couldn't bear to repeat that poignant, loser's cycle.

Baby or no baby, my father seemed to be pressing ahead with his own agenda. On December 14, he wrote to Dr. Paul C. Bucy, a founding Cushing Society member who was in charge of qualifying exams for the American Society of Neurological Surgeons:

> My dear Dr. Bucy,
>   I am desirous of knowing whether my training in neurological surgery to date in addition to an anticipated two years of practice in the specialty is sufficient to make me eligible for the board examinations.

He enumerated every one of his ten years of postcollege training in medicine and surgery, and listed his publications. Counting the year with Mark Glaser, and counting to the projected end of his Kings County appointment, his neurosurgical residencies added up to six, not seven, years. But his published papers added weight to his resume. He ended the letter, "Anxiously awaiting an early reply . . ." "Anxiously," "early": These words show that his quest to become a neurosurgeon was always so consciously time sensitive. Six days later Bucy wrote back:

> I think it is not unlikely that the Board will find your training sufficient. However, this is a question which only the Board as a whole can answer. I would, therefore, urge that you fill out an application blank and return it.

Although my father promptly filled out the application in detail, he never did get around to taking the board examination that year. Perhaps he was thwarted by a crisis in his wife's family, pulling him west into their seductive web. Perhaps he was afraid he would fail. Whatever the reason, that letter marked the beginning of a cycle that would persist until the end of his life. "He had this *cruelty* . . ." my mother said. Draconian as he could be to others, he could be equally cruel to his own earnest self.

Just about the time my father received the letter from Bucy, my mother was on a train to L.A. With her was her three-month-old baby, Sheila Joan, and her devoted housekeeper, Mary "Molly" Doherty, whom she'd turned into my even-more-devoted nanny. My mother was euphoric during the train ride, eager to show off the new baby she loved. Arriving at Union Station, Molly held me up like a trophy while she and my mother peered through the crowds, searching for Herman's countenance. My mother expected him to greet her with a triumphant smile, but he was somber—very somber. My mother felt a key, rusty from twenty-seven years' disuse, turning a catch in a lock in her chest and opening a chamber of dread inside her.

Herman approached, his deliberate steps themselves a warning. He looked at his sister a long time. I can just hear her screaming, her words like fists: "Tell me, tell me, *tell* me! *TELL me!*"

Lenny was very sick, he said. Tubercular meningitis. It had just come on—like *that!* He was quarantined in a wing of the new house with a private nurse and doctor.

Herman and my mother fell into each other's arms, as they had the night that Sadie died. With the sun beating down as inappropriately and sadistically as the stubborn lamplight had beamed under her childhood door, my heartbroken mother cried for her younger brother.

Part III

Chapter Eight

HOLLYWOOD AND BEVERLY HILLS: 1946–1951

Can anyone remember a moment from infancy? Or do we reconstruct such memories in early childhood—from the evidence we felt and knew—until they are as real as life?

I remember being lifted high in the solarium-turned-nursery of Uncle Herman's Bedford Drive home, in a torrent of light glinting off the dark-watered swimming pool. My whole childhood was bathed in that crystaline, dry, unblinking L.A. basin sunlight, and it seems the outpouring started there: light jumping through the window, bouncing off the white nursery furniture and Molly's starched white uniform, and beaming off her soupy bifocal globes. Molly was my guardian—my everything—for the three months that my mother tended infectious Lenny elsewhere in the house.

Those first three months in L.A. had been a nightmare for my mother. Right after she had run in and kissed Lenny, his doctor had forbade her to touch her baby, so infectious was Lenny's disease deemed to be. So she could do no more than wave at me through a window Herman had constructed between one wing of the house and the nursery, while she spent most of her time watching her younger brother writhe in the throes of an unspeakably painful illness that left him weaker in body and mind every day.

The family did everything they could to try to save him: My father connected Lenny's doctors with the Lahey chieftains and sent them sheaves of Globus's meninges research, talking them through the mysteries of spinal-cord membrane arcana on the phone. Herman dispatched couriers to San Francisco and Tijuana for wonder drugs. My mother got the names of touted doctors from Harry Cohn and her now-friend Lana Turner, but nothing worked. One day in April 1946, Lenny slipped into a coma and died—at thirty-two.

After he was buried and my mother was out of quarantine, she started singing me lullabies—"Lavender Blue" and "Over the Rainbow"—her voice breaking all over the place. Her vulnerability was as tactile as my teething ring, setting up a bond that eventually made me as much her caretaker as she was mine.

My father came out to L.A. in June 1946, as soon as his Kings County residency was up, and while he was setting up his practice we lived as a family in Herman's house. He couldn't afford to buy us a house right away, and, besides, Helen felt comfortable at Herman's—pampered and assisted by the servants, as a new mother and a grieving sister, having her family around her again, just like on Arlington Avenue. Herman was a prince of L.A., and every day he surveyed his domestic domain, with its grand piano at the street end and its black-and-white harlequin tiles toward the back, in a maroon bathrobe with a monogram on its breast. Telephones were always being handed to him as he sat at a massive oak table facing the olive-treed brick patio, beyond which was the swimming pool, its water bottle green. When Uncle was busy, everyone had to be quiet. ("Sshh!" Molly would say.) The deference accorded him quietly piqued my father's anger. Herman was, to Daniel Weller's thinking, a mere herder-together and promoter of publicity seekers and ex-vaudevillians. He contributed nothing of seriousness to society.

Starting six months after Lenny's death, Herman often entertained. In fact, now that I think of it, the blinding light of my first conscious image may have come from my sheer dazzlement—as an eight- and ten- and fifteen-month-old—at the goings-on in that, my first real home. Everywhere I crawled and stumbled, everywhere Molly carried me, every time I awoke or drifted off to sleep, there seemed to be, just past the nursery door, a gust of luminosity—a party going on. As a 1948 *Modern Screen* article put it, "Everyone is welcome at Ciro's, H. D. Hover's glittering night club, but to attend one of those celebrated revels at his bachelor home, you've got to be somebody special!" The article waxed on that Herman's "bachelor home [was] ideally arranged for festive gatherings, with the cocktail room, dining room, sun room, patio and rumpus room all flowing into one another" and that he had "one of the most extensive knowledges extant of who's who in Hollywood and an unrivalled party-giving know-how."

On Sunday, Uncle Herman hosted brunches outside by the pool, which became a tradition extending through all the years of Ciro's. Musicians from the club would be there, always with someone fabulous at the piano. There'd be tables set up around his olive trees— the expansive leaves serving as the umbrella. It was always hot. A bald black butler in a tuxedo passed around hors d'oeuvres on silver trays—the cream cheese in the celery hollows was my favorite. Molly would sit me on her lap amid the gorgeous, flirty people: the dreamboat men, the women in Mexican peasant tops or sarongs over bathing suits, their pool-wet hair stuffed under sombreros or turbans. (Later, while rocking me to sleep, she'd call her friends at the New York convent to which she'd eventually retire and incredulously whisper, "I sat across from Ava Gardner! On the Blessed Virgin, she was here! With Howard Duff!")

Looking at the pictures in that *Modern Screen* layout tumbles me back to those long-ago days, with their exotic textures and smells. I glance at the bench Carmen Miranda is sitting on . . . and the distinct aroma of wet, chlorine-doused canvas overlaid by gin and hibiscus fills my nostrils, like it did when I was two. Mention of Howard Hughes brings back images of the tall, dark man who used to stand in uncle's low-ceilinged den talking Molly out of her fear of airplanes while his aide-de-camp, a man named Johnny Meyer (whose function at Ciro's was to dance with Hughes's girlfriend, Terry Moore), fascinated me by cracking pistachio nuts with his teeth. (Soon after, Hughes accidentally crashed his airplane in the middle of Beverly Hills—my parents heard the crash from Herman's patio—and, as Ciro's maitre d' Johnny Oldrate told me, "After that, Hughes couldn't even read a menu.")

There, in the *Modern Screen* story, is a handsome Roy Rogers oaring a raft in Herman's pool, smiling under his cowboy hat, and Egyptian royalty—"Prince Mohammed Aly Ibrahim and Princess Hanrade Ibrahim." There's a pageboyed blonde in a cotton eyelet ("Way up on Hover's preferred list is Diana Lynn") and a group around the piano. "The inside of Hover's house is open to those who tired of the sun. Abe Burroughs (at piano) sang some of his clever parodies for John Payne, Glo De Haven, Hover and Hover's date Lyn Thomas"—the latter, a comely blonde. Yet another— decolletaged—blonde is playing with a toy monkey beside a turbaned, hirsute man in military getup. The caption reads, "All the way from India came the Rajah Paul Satypal (above with Ann Sterling). A young fellow came up to him, and asked, 'Is that Ciro's combat uniform?' 'No,' said the Rajah. 'It's Mocambo's.' "

In the layout's now campy pièce de résistance, Herman's guests pose for an overview shot (the photographer must have mounted the swimming pool's high diving board)—lolling, theatrically, upside down in the swivel chaise longues.

At more than a few of those parties someone would be pushed, fully clothed, in the pool, and the cameramen would come running to record the event. Nick Sevano, who was then Frank Sinatra's on-and-off-again manager ("I had the pleasure of being fired and rehired by Frank four times," he says), told me about one of those theatrical splashings. The young lady "was in her bathing suit," Sevano recalled, "but she was all coiffed. Herman said, 'Grab her and pull her into the pool.' The photographer got a shot of me pulling. Oh, she got dunked! She looked great, wet, by the way." She should have; she was Marilyn Monroe.

Monroe was good natured about the dousing because it was at Ciro's that she'd recently been treated to the impromptu makeover that so radically changed her image. My mother recalled the evening, "She was just starting out, painfully shy, dressed drably. She came into Ciro's with her mentor, Johnny Hyde. Xavier Cugat's girlfriend Angel took pity on her and decided to dress her up." Angel grabbed socialite Dorothy Jameson, a fixture on the best-dressed lists, and the two women took Marilyn into the cigarette girls' lounge, whipped off her glasses, redid her hair and makeup, and dressed her in one of Angel's gowns. "Marilyn emerged and everyone gasped," my mother said. "It was the first clue to her sensuality, hitherto hidden."

Another Sunday afternoon party—which Herman hosted to celebrate one of his favorite bits of matchmaking: the marriage of A&P heir Huntington Hartford and Ciro's cigarette girl Marjorie Steele—is described in a "Cholly Angelo" society page column in the *Los Angeles Times*:

Two dance bands provided music. A staff of sixteen servants and cooks handled the food and drinks. There were 300 invitees. Clark Gable was there and he is a hell of a man! Carmen Miranda was sitting with Douglas Fairbanks Jr. Ava Gardner kept on her striped brown and white stole over her brocade dress as she glanced at the ice sculpture of the bridal couple. She had come with Peter Lawford but was in pleasant conversation with Australian sportsman Freddie McAvoy. In a small group with Esther Williams and Ben Gage and Tony Martin and Cyd Charisse was Sheilah Graham. In animated conversation with Arlene Dahl and Joe Perrin was Liz Whitney, horsewoman to the manner born.

The glamour of Herman's house parties was spillover of the glamour of the evenings at the club. By 1948, in an article headlined "Herman's Place" (in its cinema section), *Time* magazine was touting Ciro's as *the* place to be for Hollywood evenings, and a few years ago Andy Williams recalled to me how dazzled he, a teenage hopeful from Iowa, was to have been rushed by the patrons when he opened there, backing singer Kay Thompson, in 1947.

Herman may have been the consummate host both at home and at the club, and he may have decorated his arm with many a (publicity- and access-seeking) pretty young thing—the aforementioned Lyn Thomas was one; model and starlet Greg Sherwood (who had small roles in late forties–early fifties movies) was another. As Reggie Drew, a Ciro's cigarette girl, later told me, "Your uncle liked young, pretty women. They'd come in for an interview and off he'd go with them." Still, a lady's man is the last thing my uncle seemed to be. More than that, he seemed devoid of sexual chemistry. His body had become heavy—his dancer's leanness long gone—and he had no personal charisma. There was a diffident loneliness at his core. As two separate people—his then publicist Jim Byron and Ciro's radio-show host Johnny Grant—told me, "He was absolutely married to Ciro's."

My father was his opposite. He was as naturally charming as my

uncle was flat-footed, and, for as long as I can remember, the contrast between the two men was striking. Herman pontificated, but
to no particular effect. My father insinuated and spoke softly and
sparely. His was the understated chuckle, the long pause during the
contemplative puff on the pipe. The Hovers—my uncle, mother,
and grandmother—were overeager, too available. They leaned forward. You always got a little too much of them. My father leaned
back. He left you wanting more. "That twinkle in his eye was something you saw from a great distance," is how Zeke Manners put it.
"It stayed with you and got right in your heart."

My father had plunged into his friendship with Zeke during
those months living at Herman's. Helen's friend Beadie's Beverly
Hill Billy husband had tickled Danny's own self-image with the

quip with which he was regularly opening his new weekly ABC
Radio show. "People ask, 'Zeke, how'd you become a hillbilly?' I say,
'I got tired of my old job: being a brain surgeon.'" (I never knew
how important Zeke was to the development of syndicated radio
until his death in 1999, when the *New York Times* gave him an
almost-half-page obituary.) The idea of palling around with the
accordian-playing songwriter of the hits "The Pennsylvania Polka"
and "Sioux City Sue" was as appealing to the brain surgeon as having a brain surgeon friend was to Zeke. The two men bonded.

This was useful, because my father needed a person with whom
to escape that house, that temple of his brother-in-law's ego.
"Danny would call me in the middle of the night—he was always
restless—and ask me to drive with him to Bakersfield or get on the
ferry boat to Catalina," Zeke said. "For some crazy reason I'd go.
You couldn't say no to this guy! He'd have amphetamines with him,
and we'd take them. 'I'm gonna have fun because today may be my
last day.' That was Danny Weller. We were like brothers. I loved
him as much as one man can love another man."

We were still living at Herman's house when my little sister Elizabeth Lee (the preponderance of L sounds in her name was to honor
Lenny) was born on March 15, 1947. She was my father's daughter.
It was as if, living among the Hovers, he needed an ally, and so he
claimed her as his own, just as I was fixed in his mind as my
mother's child. Shortly after my birth, we'd departed for Los Angeles, leaving him essentially a bachelor for the first six months of
1946. Thus, there was a break in his process of bonding with his
firstborn infant. Now, this second baby—this fat, blond-ringleted
newborn—would be *his*. As if to clinch the deal, she happened to
have inherited those slant-lidded, troubled Weller eyes. "Little
Danny," she was nicknamed.

As we both grew from babies to toddlers, and from toddlers to little girls, our developing personalities cemented my father's tie to Lizzie. I was a Hover: jumpy, talkative, insecure, and overbearing. Lizzie was gentle, cool, and solemn—Weller calm. She would be the scientist, the scholar, the imp—his heir and confidante. He would make sure of it.

A few months after Lizzie's birth, my parents purchased their own house, eight blocks east, at 520 North Elm. My father's old mentor, Dr. Mark Glaser, had just died of leukemia, and my father was in the process of buying his practice from his widow, with money borrowed from Herman.

As fate would have it, our move out of Herman's house, in late summer 1947, came not a moment too soon—and involved a close call with someone who wanted to kill us.

My father had recently assessed a brain injury case for the state insurance commission. A miner and laborer named Bill Ward attributed his brain injury to an accident he had while working for the state. After examining Ward, my father concluded that his injury predated the accident. The claim was denied. The examination was forgettable to my father, but apparently not to Ward. As former Beverly Hills police chief Clinton H. Anderson put it in his 1960 book, *Beverly Hills Is My Beat*, Ward "was what psychologists call the nonverbal type. He preferred action to words in settling arguments. He obtained the names and addresses of all the individuals involved in the [insurance claim] hearing and began plotting their immediate extinction." Specifically:

He purchased a large supply of dynamite and fuses and fashioned a bomb for each of his intended victims, packing two-gallon Coca-Cola cans with dynamite sticks. His plan was to cut the fuses in varying lengths, making the first ones long enough so that he would have sufficient time to plant bombs at all the houses and be safely out of the area before the first one exploded. If his scheme succeeded he would wipe out seven homes and thirty-five people, including some small children, and be on a freight train headed north before any suspicion could touch him.

Those "small children" included, foremost, my baby sister and me. Ward made sure that the first bomb he set was the one at Dr. Weller's house. He got our address from court records: 606 North Bedford, Herman's home. Eleven days earlier we had moved to 520 N. Elm—thankfully, Ward was unaware of that.

Ward set the fuse at Herman's house at 3 A.M. He was apprehended in the act of laying his second bomb, blocks away, and brought to the precinct. "As he was being interrogated," Anderson wrote, "a terrific explosion shook a wide area of Beverly Hills. A bomb which he had planted a short time earlier had gone off as planned. The explosion, at the home of Herman Hover, famous in Hollywood as the owner of Ciro's, lifted the house two inches off its foundation and blew a two-by-four through the ceiling of the bedroom, narrowly missing the occupant."

Ward was charged with attempted murder, found not guilty by reason of insanity, and shipped off to the state mental hospital at Camarillo. When he was about to be released, Chief Anderson offered us special police protection. My parents declined the police guard and said they didn't want Ward to even be in the state. Ward was paid a large sum never to set foot in California again. He took the money, went to Montana, and died shortly thereafter.

The incident sent shock waves through Los Angeles's small neurosurgical community. (When, in 1999, I interviewed Dr. Aidan Raney, one of the few living neurosurgeons who'd practiced there then, he remembered the fifty-two-year-old incident in detail.) The front page of the *Herald Express* showed an unscathed Herman surveying the rubble in his bathrobe. What *was* demolished was the nursery wing that my baby sister and I had so recently vacated. "Your father and I were beside ourselves with gratitude that we'd already moved," my mother said. "We kept saying, 'The children could have been killed, they could have been *killed!*'" The next day the *Beverly Hills Citizen* ran a picture of the four Wellers, captioned, "The family that was saved."

The family that was saved. So that is how we began our life as a family of four: with a sense of having been plucked out of the jaws of catastrophe. Indeed, there was a sweetness to those first four and six and eight years on Elm Drive—a sense of love and closeness and peace that is best personified in a photo of us sitting on a swing for four in the backyard: I, pigtailed as always, on our mother's lap; curly-haired Lizzie on our father's.

In the late forties and the earliest fifties, it still was an adventure to live in Los Angeles. Air-conditioning hadn't arrived and swimming pools weren't heated. During the 105-plus degree days we'd barricade ourselves in the dark-walled living room. (My father sometimes rented an oxygen tank for himself, so labored was his breathing.) Mountain lions and coyotes roamed the canyons. So did "nature boys": hippie precursors who lived on roots and berries and migrated down from their huts to pick up day work within the booming swimming-pool-building sector. (When my father glimpsed the hairy specimen my mother had hired giving Lizzie and me a ride in his wheelbarrow, he reeled around and punched him. The dazed and bloodied fellow—Figaro Gypsy Boots was his nom de plume—left that racket fast and soon surfaced as a regular on *The Steve Allen Show.*)

It was an era when America had a gruff naïveté—a time of fatty prime rib and overcooked, olive-drab vegetables; of ASBESTOS stamped proudly on school auditorium curtains; of children's shoe stores that gave you balloons when they X-rayed your feet—in which well-being was something presumably attained by pledging allegiance. Still, as Americans, we Angelenos knew we were marginal, a piece of the country that did not count. Our black-and-white TV screen, our first-grade workbooks, our Nancy Drew—all of those fed us images of the "real" America: the gold-standard East Coast, an exotic place of close-together buildings, unimaginably steep skyscrapers or dumpy wooden houses, crisscrossed by laundry-flapping clotheslines. Our land and history seemed more primordial, yet that other America was deemed the origin point, and who were we to dispute it? It was the motherland; we were just the colonies.

The colony of Jewish Angelenos was even farther removed from the mainstream. In California, two generations before multiculturalism, there was only one official religion—Christianity. The Jewish families that comprised 50 percent of Beverly Hills may have had their temples (ours was the beautiful Temple Israel, where somber Rabbi Max Nussbaum, whose eventual claim to fame was converting Elizabeth Taylor, was the more traditional Reform antidote to Wilshire Temple's controversially assimilationist rabbi, Edgar Magnin), but, come December, every Beverly Hills Jewish kid stood on the auditorium risers and piously sang out "Adestes Fideles" and other religious hymns—and no parent dared complain.

For the most part, our lives had a genteel rhythm back in those late forties days, when men wore hats to work, women would raise their voices an octave to speak in bell-like tones with slightly Anglicized accents, and maids and nursemaids wore uniforms. Lizzie and I were girly girls. In our princess costumes, we would go out on the balcony of our shared bedroom and wave our scepters over our front-lawn kingdom of unknowing subjects: the paperboy, the

Arden and Adohr deliverymen, and the gardeners. We wore matching dresses at our birthday parties (there was always a clown, and
Nancy, the Ciro's photographer, took pictures). We also attended
Miko's, the tiny, exclusive nursery school where elegant Hungarian
Miko gave tea parties, cutting the crusts off our sandwiches. After
graduating from Miko's it was off to Hawthorne, where the offspring of big-screen femme fatales, my classmates, endured identi-
ties 180 degrees from their mothers'. Rita Hayworth's daughter was
the sad, fat, plain Rebecca Welles; sarong-clad Dorothy Lamour
had a son as prim—and primly named (Ridgely Howard)—as a
miniature English barrister. My first-grade tormentor was Michael
DeToth, a boy so wild, his voice, at six, was already gone from years
of screaming. He was the son of the icily cool Veronica Lake. (Sitting behind me, he'd yank my ponytails into his gluepot.) On the
first day of spring, the Hawthorne kindergarten girls—in our pastel
organdy dresses, our soft hair gleaming in the sunlight—performed
the Maypole Dance, braiding the long ribbons around the pole
while our dressed-up parents ooh'd and aah'd and the *Beverly Hills
Citizen* photographer jumped around, click-clicking.

By five years old, I came to a terrible realization: My father had
moved toward my little sister because she was the quieter, sweeter,
and calmer—the more *good*—of the two of us. The only way I
knew of getting his attention was to make those very cutesy-pie
imprecations (which my mother encouraged)—"Daddy, watch me
tap dance! I'm like Darla Hood on *The Little Rascals*! Daddy,
Daddy! You aren't *watching!*"—that I knew had alienated him in
the first place. It would have been better if I'd been obtuse—
unaware of the fact that I was turning my father off—but I was a
consciousness-cursed child. (I remember walking around the
Hawthorne School playground on the first day of first grade, whis-

pering to myself, with alarm, "Why can't I stop thinking? I'm the only person here who can't turn her mind off!") I knew what I wanted—a look from my father that told me he adored me—but between cup and lip was a torturous slip. Toward my goal I would entreat, "Daddy, Daddy, I heard a funny joke!" "Daddy, I'm going to do *pliés* for you—watch!" "Daddy! I'm entering the Cheerios limerick contest. Listen!" I helplessly watched my own backfiring behavior the way a transcendental meditator watches her thoughts flicker across her mind.

One sign of favor my father had bestowed upon Lizzie was a nickname: Twerpy. "Hi, Twerpy," he would say. "Twerpy, come here"—and she would climb quietly onto his lap, her head nuzzling under his pipe. He called her Twerpy, he said, because she was like a little bird. Little birds are delicate, with fluttery wings; they glide over places others plod through; they have high, enchanting voices.

"You call Lizzie Twerpy," I whined one day, as we were all driving to Lake Arrowhead. "What can *I* be?"

"Danny . . . ?" my mother turned toward him, verbally poking him in the ribs. "Give her a nickname."

He was puffing on his pipe, driving us through the sentrylike evergreens. I hung over the front seat, my knees banging his seat back, my cheek grazing his, waiting for his selection.

He smiled rabbinically. With exaggerated pomp, he serenely announced: "You shall be 'Brooksie . . .' "

Brooksie—the name seemed to radiate his affection, but his sentence did not have a period on it. After he'd taken the full measure of my satisfaction, he continued, ". . . because, like a brook—you *babble*."

I knew that my father had insulted me and had even timed the insult for maximum impact. I knew I had provoked him. I also saw I had no choice but to pretend that none of this had happened.

Whether my father meant to project annoyance at me, or he was being benignly sarcastic, or my insecurity about our relationship led me to be hypersensitive, I do not know. Either way, our relationship was already problematic.

In contrast to Lizzie, I became increasingly hyperactive. I developed the tic of flapping my hands: literally holding my arms out and shaking both my wrists, simultaneously, as fast as I could. The urge to do this would come over me when I got excited. (I was probably a good candidate for one of those drugs, nonexistent then, but now routinely given to hyperactive children.) Usually I tried to hide this from my parents, but sometimes my father would see me.

"I am very disturbed by Sheila's behavior," my father told Beatrice Cole, one of my mother's former New York editors, when she visited California during that time. "And Helen spoils them both badly. Sheila, especially." He had purposely pulled Beatrice aside to make this worried complaint, feeling that she was a sensible presence he could get on his side. "I saw his point," the almost imperiously refined Bea told me, decades later. "You did seem very spoiled, and you were hyperactive. I might have suggested to Helen that she not encourage your antics so much. It *was* quite an honor to have been taken into Danny's confidence, but . . ." Bea went on to say that my mother seemed puzzled and crestfallen by her negative picture of me. Not wanting to hurt or offend her former student, Bea promptly dropped the subject. Hearing that account, I felt as red-faced and humiliated as if that long-ago day in 1952 were yesterday.

As much as one would expect me to have viewed my little sister as a kind of rival, she was too sweet and vulnerable for that. If our father was my dismissor, our mother was hers, so in some Solomonic way, Lizzie and I were even. She remembers our mother driving us home from Hawthorne one day, harrumphing (about the unquestioned leader of the "popular girls" in my second-grade class), "That was *some* dress Kathi Weisz had on—*much* too ornate for a school day! And she has a narrow face. You're much prettier than she is, if you ask *me*." I was the horse she had her money on, in a race that conspicuously didn't include Lizzie. Humiliated as I felt about alienating our father, to Lizzie's benefit, I felt as guilty about overcharming our mother at her expense, about welcoming her desperate overestimation of me, because I was the daughter who emotionally resembled her.

Thus positioned to never compete, Lizzie and I were free to be true best friends. We had picnics in the backyard weathered wooden "monkey house." We were inveterate door-to-door salesmen. No Christmas card line advertised on the inside back cover of an Archie and Veronica comic book failed to entice us as Willy Lomans. (Before the unspeakably sad day she left us for the cloistered life, Molly, along with the maids, Virgie and Alberta, were our best customers, favoring the pinecone motifs and the bas-relief white crosses.) We branched into notions, fashioning carnations out of Kleenex and bobby pins, hawking them door-to-door for a nickel. Finally, we tried agribusiness (our Waterloo): plucking the honeysuckle off the backyard vines, spending hours squeezing the liquid from the buds into a jelly jar, minuscule drib by minuscule drab. When we had a quarter inch of honey on the jar bottom, we hurried off to make our fortune. "Honeysuckle for sale!" we sang out at the first doorstep. When Mrs. Moran, the kindly bohemian widow opened the door (gray braid down to her rump, a dozen cats, dates and cocoanut forever whirring around in her Osterizer), my sister got so excited she let the jar drop. It crashed on the stoop, bouncing gooey, jagged shards everywhere. I scolded her all the way home; she cried her eyes out.

Of course, that was exactly the kind of episode that, in our father's view, bifurcated us—me, the bad sister; she, the good one. One Kodachrome of us—I was eight, she was six—says it all. I'd been playing Ping-Pong with Lizzie, and I had either disputed a point or complained that she wasn't a good enough player. Whatever my beef, I was making it ungracefully. Our father heard the dust-up and rushed to Lizzie's side. The photo shows me sulking while they walk off with chins high—her face is serene and wounded; his is judgmental. His arm is around her shoulder. The message in his face is clear: He disapproves of me.

At that point, part of the reason was my sister's bad luck with health. At five, she fell out of her bed and broke her arm. Another time, she had to have a piece of her skin cut out of her back because the pediatrician feared it would turn malignant. One night she whimpered to me from the bathroom. Blood was streaming down both nostrils. Daddy came and comforted her (I was jealous). Later, blood tests revealed her to be anemic. Finally, after one joint

appointment we had with the pediatrician, our doctor heard a murmur in her heart. She had an ailing heart—a further tie to Daddy.
Lizzie bore these infirmities with such aplomb, our mother dubbed
her "the Iron Butterfly." Oh, why was it always *she* who elegantly
weathered such dramatic bad luck, while I—with my obnoxious
flapping hands—was so tediously bereft of poignance and heroics?

Despite the schism in our family, we had our happy rituals: bagels
and lox on Saturday morning, then a trip to the pony rides on Beverly Boulevard and La Cienega, where Lizzie and I, in our matching overalls, would ride around the ring on our bouncy steeds while
Mommy (who rode English saddle quite decently) cheered us on as
Daddy smiled behind his hand-cranked home movie camera. In
these movies I am a pint-sized coquette between my full-cowboy-
costumed boyfriends, little Randy Newman and little Charlie
Manners (the latter of whom, fourteen years later, leaped to his
death off a roof during an acid trip). Then, for lunch, we'd hit the
then landmarked-statused hot-dog-shaped hot dog stand before
heading home.

On Sunday morning, my sister and I would jump on our father in
bed, pummel him, and ride him like a pony. Then he'd grab us and
tickle us under our neck and armpits until we begged for mercy. (I
squealed the quicker and louder; unlike my little sister, I had no
threshold for physical discomfort.) However, he hadn't won—we
did, with the next round: verbal taunting. "Fet-*or*-e! Fet-*or*-e!" we
would giddily sing, elaborately holding our noses. (He had recently
bought a pocket-sized Italian-English dictionary to communicate
with a tumor patient who spoke no English. Entertaining us with a
translation lesson one night, he'd stopped and smirked at the
humorously succinct *feh-TO-re: to stink*—and that of course had
instantly become our nickname for him.)

Next in the Sunday morning ritual came his removal of his trumpet from its resting niche in the back of his closet. Pushing aside the neat row of wooden-hangered flannel, linen, seersucker, and denim, he would reveal a hidden wall indentation, built for a family's safe but now protecting the treasured props of his persona. "You see?" he would say, waving an old ribbon-bound portfolio. "Your grandpappy's cavalry papers. From when he—" "I know, I *know*," I would wiggle my head as I cut him off (there were some acts of daughterly brattiness he did enjoy indulging) and droningly finish his sentence, ". . . when he opened the gates to Oklahoma." He seemed to like that I didn't believe the tale; perhaps that way, Louis's years on the plains stayed all the more his safely secret lodestar.

The trumpet was gleaming brass. (He polished it regularly; my nostrils would remember that thick liquid's metallicky smell anywhere.) Stiff, tall, with those funny protruding plugs, it seemed to stand for his manhood. Rabbis removing the Torah from the Ark were not as reverential as my father at this moment. He fitted the mouthpiece on, popped his 78 of Louis Armstrong's "When the Saints Go Marching In" on the Victrola, strode out on the landing, lifted the horn to his mouth, and belted and belted. Off-key, on-key, off-key, on-key, his eyes closed, his cheeks fattened, his face reddened. He looked so defiantly happy, and he looked as if he would explode at the very same instant.

Like any self-respecting West L.A. Jewish family, it was then off to breakfast at either Canter's or Cohen's on Fairfax (the legendary former exists to this day; the latter inexplicably failed), where we'd run into everyone we knew, either at the booths or the crowded glass take-out counter, vying for whitefish and sturgeon from the charmingly gruff deli men.

Sometimes, on one of those two days, while our mother was at Ciro's (or home typing a story about Robert Mitchum or Farley

Granger), our father would take Lizzie and me to the hospital with him. We would sit in the staff cafeteria, eating cubes of green Jell-O the consistency of Goodyear tires. Then he would take us to the famous Skeleton Room, a rank little chamber in the bowels of the anatomy wing, where Mr. Bones jangled about from the wall hook by his skull, like some skinned, elongated Howdy Doody. After the hospital rounds, he led my sister and me from the parking lot to a shabby hot pastrami sandwich stand on Vermont Avenue.

"It's the doctor!" the old pastrami man would bellow from behind his smudged sliding-glass window.

"You've heard of Captain Pinafore?" my father would ask grandly, taking off his yachting cap and placing it on the little man's head. "*This* is Admiral Pastrami!"

"Ach . . ." The little man blushed and flapped his hand. "The kibitzer."

"And"—my father placed a hand on our shoulders—"the kibitzettes."

"So what will it be?" The little man smiled conspiratorially. "Three dips?" (Gravy-loaded "pastrami dips" were his speciality.)

"Three *dippy* dip dips." My father paused, then sang operatically, "Three dippy . . . dippy . . . diiiiippy dips."

"Only for the doctor and his girls, all that extra sauce." The pastrami man, mock aggrieved, ladeled. "Here, take your hat back. It shouldn't get soiled."

During the week, our father worked almost around the clock. He had taken over Glaser's office, downtown on Wilshire, near MacArthur Park. The building was so old-fashioned, when you got off on the floor, you expected to see Philip Marlowe in his trench coat: tiny diamond-shaped white hall tiles (such as are found now only in ancient grammar school bathrooms); heavy, smelly, sand-filled canisters in which to stub out your cigarette while you waited for the lever-operated elevator; and DR. DANIEL WELLER, NEURO-SURGERY stenciled on the beveled door glass between the dark wood framing.

Inside, Della the nurse-secretary ruled. She was brunette and spunky—deep voiced, with a wry, hoarse laugh—the equal to my father's wit and temper. She did everything from strap and soothe patients during pneumocepholograms (while puffing on her ever-present Pall Mall), to take my father's dictation, to do the billing. Once, after he bawled her out for something, she handed in her resignation in a rage of tears. "*Della* quit!" my mother whispered, in panic, to her friends on the phone for several days, so essential was she to Danny's practice. After struggling on a few days with airhead temps, my father called Della at the tract house she shared with her mother in the then rural San Fernando Valley, pretending to be an old Yiddish crooner in the middle of a Romeo audition to a hard-of-hearing Juliet on a balcony. Della was won back in a heartbeat.

I recently learned, with no small shock, something that my mother never knew: My father carried on an affair with Della over a good many of their years working together. I was told that by a witness, my father's niece-in-law Fran Douglas, who, with her then husband (my father's sister Rosie's son, Lewis), had what can only be called several double dates with the two, who were openly affectionate. Even all these years later, both my father's brazenness and the casual participation in his infidelity by others in his family quietly stuns me. Yet both things were a warm-up for what would come later.

There were so few real (i.e., Cushing-heir) neurosurgeons in L.A. back then—only six to eight, says Aidan Raney, who was one of them, as was his brother, Rupert. It was Aidan who influentially proved, by way of his paper in the *American Journal of Neurology and Psychiatry*, that a high percentage of headaches originate not in the head (as previously thought) but in the neck region. Raney told me, "Dan Weller was a very fine man, considered to have done very good work. Everyone thought very highly of him."

These surgeons serviced not just sprawling Los Angeles County but also the surrounding ones, often coming to the rescue of patients on whom flawed surgeries had been inflicted by their poorly trained, pre-Cushing elders who'd cobbled the specialty onto a general-surgery background. So my father operated not only at Cedars of Lebanon, Queen of Angels, and County General, but also at San Bernardino County Hospital, Kern County Hospital, Harbor General Hospital in Torrance, and the City of Hope in Duarte. Half of the time he got home at 10 P.M. Often he spent the night at the hospital; the speeded-up neurosurgeries of James Poppen had given way to slower methods, and my father could be on his feet for ten hours straight excising an acoustic neuroma.

Fellowship in the American and International Colleges of Surgeons was my father's chief ambition, and he was working hard to amass the one hundred cases each required for admission. He spent most of his evening hours at home holed up in his grasscloth-lined study, hoarsedly recording his cases on his Dictaphone. The study was a serious, masculine room, with low shelves of shiny-papered medical journals, yielding horrors: photographs of open abdomens, deformed faces, and amputated limb stumps. (Lizzie and I would dare each other to peruse them.) Book-ended by heavy gold anchors, on the pride-of-place shelf behind his swivel chair, were his bibles: *The Life of Harvey Cushing* and James Poppen's *Atlas of Neurosurgery*.

The rest of the house, even with the clunky Early American furniture so in vogue in the early fifties (and which my parents would replace, room by room, with pointy-legged modern), had a lightness to it—people laughed and chattered there. That room alone, despite its sliding glass door that gave off to the olive tree and the monkey house, was solemn, as if the emotional waste matter of my father's daily work had filtered down and coagulated inside it like a sediment. I rarely went in there. It was scary and depressing.

Besides, it was unofficially off-limits. It was his private lair. One night I had tiptoed down for a midnight snack, and he had left the door partly open. There he was, bent over the Dictaphone, his shoulders hunched, his bald spot moist, his pipe set down in the leather-trimmed copper ashtray. I paused at the door. He paused in his dictation. My heart skipped—but he hadn't seen me eavesdropping on him; he had just paused, for no particular reason I could figure. He stared straight ahead and sighed deeply. What was he thinking at that moment? He had become the man he had fought to become, and yet there was an unmistakable tension and melancholy about him. What in this good life we had—what in the noble, complex work he did—*gnawed* at him so? I wondered as I stood there.

I hurried up the stairs so he wouldn't see that I noticed.

My father plunged into medical association membership. He had been on the rosters of the California, American, and L.A. County Medical Associations since his intern days, but in the early fifties, he also joined the Southern California Society of Neurological Surgeons. ("At meetings Danny didn't gab at all, didn't waste a lot of words. His comments were right to the point," Aiden Raney recalls. "And he was always nicely dressed, always nice looking.") Yet he continued to dance around the only society that really counted—the American Board of Neurological Surgery, to which he had first written in 1945. In January 1950, he wrote the board's Dr. W. J. German, in Connecticut:

My dear Dr. German:

I should like to take the examinations for the American Board of Neurological Surgery and would appreciate your sending me application blanks for same.

Thank you.

Yours very truly,
Daniel Weller, M.D.

Dr. German immediately wrote back:

Dear Dr. Weller:

Enclosed is the application form which is to be submitted in applying for the examinations of the American Board of Neurological Surgery. In order that this may be reviewed by the Credentials Committee before the Board meeting in March, I would suggest you fill out and return the form as soon as possible.

Also enclosed is a pamphlet giving the requirements for certification by the Board. If there are any further points with which I may help you, please do not hesitate to let me know.

Sincerely,
William J. German, M.D.

Despite Dr. German's great solicitousness, my father never got around to taking the exam in March 1950. At the time, he was also flexing that alternative side of his personality. As if the running around to all the far-flung hospitals was not enough, he briefly signed on as house doctor at the Statler Hilton Hotel. "I don't know why Danny did that; it was beneath him," Irving Newman told me, with a disapproving look on his face, in the early 1970s. Now I see it, of course, as part of a pattern. The Statler Hilton was an update of the Hollywood Plaza, and his work there was a means of burnishing the eccentricities in his invented self. Working, even one night a week, in that trysting place of executives and their secretaries was my father's way of keeping the contrarian niche in his personality filled with a relatively benign act of rebellion. The real rebellion, with attendant self-destructiveness, would come later.

At just about the time that he was writing to Dr. German, my father and I achieved our most intimate moment. One rainy winter Sunday, in the middle of a child's birthday party, I was suddenly struck with a high fever, violent stomach pain, and nausea. An ambulance rushed me to the hospital. As I lay strapped on the hard table in a frighteningly overlit room, there was Daddy: his eyes twinkling above the sterile mouth-mask, his cheeks even pinker than usual from holding his head horizontal. I pointed to my sterile hair cap, then to his.

"We're twins," he said.

I smiled, relishing the notion.

He continued. "Dannele," he said, using Lena's Yiddicized endearment for him, "and Brooksie."

Now that nickname didn't seem like an insult at all! It was perfused with all the tenderness the world could hold.

"Are they going to . . . ?" Too afraid to even say the words, I made a slash across my stomach.

"You won't feel it. They have to take it out."

"Why?! *Why* do they have to?"

"There's a little man at the beach who wants to sell it."

"Dah-*deee* . . . !"

" '*Frank*furters . . . *Eski*mo Pies . . . ap*pen*dixes . . . ' "

"No, really, *why?*"

"It is infected," he said, as firmly as if I were any old patient. "It must be removed, or the entire cavity will become infected."

"But I'm scared!" I whimpered, fidgeting and kicking, despite myself. (Lizzie, the Iron Butterfly, wouldn't have done that.) I needed the twinkle in his eye back; I needed soft reassurance, not censure. If he disapproved of me *now*, just before I went under, I would *die*—I just *knew* it!

Waiting a seeming eternity for his reaction, I peered into his eyes, which popped out at me with almost spooky candor—so bas-reliefed were they against the obscurement of his head, nose, and mouth by the sterile swathing. His eyes seemed to reveal too much for a little girl to know about her father. They pulled me right into his heart—the same heavy heart I had glimpsed that night when I had come across him in his study. Life is uncertain and sometimes unfair, his eyes reluctantly admitted.

Finally, he spoke. "I will be here the whole time," he said. "I will take care of you."

He gave instructions to the anesthesiologist. His rubber-gloved fingers inched around the taut sheet for the bump that was my hand. As the needle pierced my vein, and as the room's scary harsh lights went all liquid and blurry, he squeezed it, and squeezed it, and squeezed it.

Chapter Nine

HOLLYWOOD AND BEVERLY HILLS: 1948–1952

During the same years that we were living out our ordinary lives on Elm Drive, Ciro's—*our* Ciro's—was in the midst of its spectacular heyday, and Herman had become not just a noted host but a famous talent-launcher. "Oh, it was *the* place to go," Army Archerd told me. He is now a *Variety* eminence, but then he was a legman for columnist Harrison Carroll, of the *L.A. Herald Express.* "The stars came out, they dressed beautifully, they enjoyed the show, they had dinner—there was no hiding away. Stars went there to show off their romances, and Carroll and I were there, every Tuesday and Friday night, at the number one table, on the rise, as you came down the steps on the left—to get them."

"The late forties and early fifties at Ciro's: there was not another time, or place, in Hollywood—or anywhere—like it," mused Nick Sevano. "The club was a world unto itself, and in that world your every emotion got exaggerated—by inebriation, by music, by the beauty of all the people around you," said Jim Byron. Byron was the club's publicist, but he was in his early twenties—so young, curious, and handsome, he was seized as a confidant by the female staff and patrons. "If that was the world you lived in every day, you had to be extra careful to keep your bearings."

During those bearings-keeping hours of the afternoon, I'd accompany my mother to Ciro's. While preschool-aged Lizzie was home with the housekeeper, mom would pick me up from Hawthorne and take me along on her daily visit. We would come in the kitchen entrance, by the busboys' time clock. She would be holding a bag of lipsticks, green plastic matchbook covers, and compacts, all with *Ciro's* emblazoned on them. Maybe we'd run into Tom Pryor, the ever-aggrieved accountant, kvetching as he walked downstairs from his office next to Herman's, "That Maurice Chevalier, was there *ever* a cheaper talent? We give him a valet, and he doesn't tip him! Now he's billing us for the cologne he puts on before he goes onstage!"

In the cavernous steel-and-iron kitchen, the *sous*-chef had half the burners going with a dozen sauces percolating toward their final gustatory destination. Round knobs of tournedos, fat filet mignons, and mounds of steak tartare sat in their own blood on the white marble meat counter. The fish, for which someone had to go down to the airport to meet three separate small planes daily, occupied its own briny-smelling pantry, sink, and refrigerator. There were bins of crushed ice everywhere. Slatted crates of Cornish hens, escargots, and fluffy frizzy vegetables were stacked along the sideboards of the long wide main work island and then knifed at, torn at, prettied, and washed by a half dozen kitchen men while, away in his Santa Monica home, the master chef (who had arisen at dawn to go to market), was just getting up from his nap, taking a shot of Pernod for good measure.

Down the cellar-dank hall, Bobby the bartender was whistling in his pungent hutch as he briskly plucked out bottles and shifted his stock around—the Haig & Haig here, the Smirnoff there (he had his reasons)—and he stabbed the cork ends of the silver spouts into the line of favored A-shots on his low shelf. Bobby looked like a jockey;

he had the same beat-up, middle-aged face disconcertedly attached to a tiny, youthful body. I loved to watch him double-dunk the glasses, lickety-split, in the side-by-side sinks mandated by the health department. "Hey, Squirt!" he'd say, snatching my nose off with his two fingers; then he'd put his hand to his mouth and pretend to turn me in ("Psst! CBE! Over here!") as I brazenly twirled around, touching things. The California Board of Equalization—the liquor authority—could close the place down if a minor was caught handling liquor: That fact was my family's eleventh commandment. Bobby added the touch that I'd be arrested as well, making my daily stop at the lair an irresistible flirtation with mayhem.

Herman's show producer and protégé George Schlatter might come down from the office then, bearing importantly a small, heavy, knotted white sack. Everyone would clear the way for George—and my mother would nervously rub her fingers together and half open her mouth, a tic of hers (which projected the sentiment "Get it *over* with!") when Herman was ordering something untoward but not unnecessary. Schlatter took the bag to the kitchen door, where a messenger from the expensive haberdashery shop several doors down Sunset Boulevard stood. Schlatter gave the man the bag and the man gave Schlatter a stack of haberdasherers' boxes, which, from the way Schlatter was carrying them, seemed a little too light to be holding heavy garments. "As far as I was concerned, *I* was legitimately buying *boxes!*" George Schlatter told me recently. The boxes were empty. Bugsy Siegel heir Mickey Cohen (who came in whenever he wanted, got his ringside meal for free—and always used a mountain of napkins) owned the haberdashery shop, and he was extorting some kind of protection money from my uncle. (The protection money, however, didn't keep Cohen from getting shot in the shoulder right outside Ciro's in 1949 by a rival gangster, who killed one of Cohen's lieutenants and wounded the U.S. attorney general's agent, who was guarding Cohen after he'd "flipped" to the feds' side in a mob prosecution.)

I would hang out with Bobby a little longer—help him empty the vat of pimento-stuffed green olives and the jar of baby onions into small inlaid silver tubs, try to figure for the life of me how he skinned those lemons, so fast, with one stroke, with one hand—to yield such thin, unbroken curlicues. Then he would let me sack his cache of plumed toothpicks and green maraschino cherries. I would join my mother in the main room, so dark that the bandstand's white leatherette gleamed like teeth in a coal mine. As the piano tuner was coaxing out atonal thuds and plinks, electricians teetered high on ladders, doing a million things with both hands while managing to keep their lit cigarettes pinched in their fingers. Kindly head busboy Manuel Reyes would roll in the rack of steam-cleaned, white-paper-packaged waitstaff uniforms, waving to me as he passed.

We would seat ourselves in one of the corner booths, 6 and 9, which were "holds." Proxy patrons (sometimes presentable members of our family, like my father's nephew Lewis Douglas and his pretty wife Fran, or my mother's cousin George Frankel and his tall, blond, bosomy wife Ruth) would be up and out in a flash, so that, as Schlatter told me, "No matter how booked we were, if Clark Gable or Gary Cooper walked in we'd have a table for them." Herman's own bare half table—tucked in the troubleshooter's wedge between the main room, the kitchen hall, and the dressing room—was where you'd put unfussy friends of the house who stopped by, like Bullets Durgan, who was Jackie Gleason's manager and everyone's buddy, or Bob Hope's agent Louis Schurr, who always brought a full-length coat in case a lady who had only a stole or a wrap had an accident.

Herman, huddled at the maitre d's stand, sipping his "morning" coffee from a brown-striped china cup, and his maître d'/bouncer

Johnny Oldrate would have their daily powwow. Their urgent strategy talks would be muffled by the drone of the huge canister vacuum cleaners that uncoincidentally snarled around the carpet at exactly that moment, blocking eavesdroping capability. Together, like generals, they plotted the evening's rules of engagement.

Herman had a three-strike rule—the third time a patron threw a punch, he was banned for life—but the rule was problematic. It didn't matter if a two-bit toughie like agent Sid Luft (then married to actress Lynn Bari, soon after to Judy Garland) pushed the envelope. But no one wanted to three-strike-rule Frank Sinatra. There was a time, in 1953, after his breakup with Ava Gardner, when "he'd come in drunk a lot," Johnny Oldrate told me. "The rumor around Ciro's was that he wasn't a good enough lover for her. One night a newspaperman from New York"—*Daily News* entertainment writer Lee Mortimer—"made a remark to Frank, and Frank went for him and started beating him up. I had to pull them apart and cool Frank down a little." Before that, Sinatra had thrown a punch at Peter Lawford (again, over Gardner), and his final strike was a whack at Ciro's publicist Jim Byron for a minor slight. To wiggle out of the dilemma, Herman found a loophole to his three-strike rule, reasoning that the punch didn't count if it landed on the jaw of an employee. (George Schlatter told me that he and Sinatra's widow Barbara had a recent laugh over that one.)

Herman's edicts to Oldrate usually started with a yes or no. *No*—don't seat Errol Flynn at table 4; that's the vantage point from which he had recently smiled across the dance-floor corner at Rita Hayworth, triggering her complaint to her fiancé Aly Khan that Flynn was leering. *No*—don't let Howard Hughes book another whole row of banquettes for himself and Elizabeth Taylor—find some excuse to dissuade him. Vic Damone was playing at Charlie Morrison's club across the street—Taylor had a crush on Damone; she'd be ringside at the Mocambo, and Hughes would be stood up again. More complex were the ladies' wars over Greg Bautzer. As Peggy Lee put it in her autobiography *Miss Peggy Lee*, "Herman Hover's Ciro's was *the* most elegant place you could go and it was inhabited by the most eligible bachelors. Easily one of the most handsome was Greg Bautzer," over whom Lee admitted competing with Lana Turner, Ava Gardner, and Joan Crawford. One recent night, Crawford called Ciro's and learned that Bautzer was there with Lana Turner (their on-again, off-again romance had spanned the forties, notwithstanding Turner's several marriages) and so had stormed in with *four* handsome escorts to show Bautzer up. Everyone in the room *except* Bautzer seemed to take notice.

While Herman and Oldrate strategized, tall Reggie Drew (the cigarette girl) and tiny Nancy Caporel (the photographer) would whisk in in their street clothes—the two were best friends—and sometimes stop to pass along gossip that could have curled the edges of the linen napkins stacked up on the banquette arms. With her shutterbug's gut, Nancy always knew which particular smooching celebs framed in her lens were really female beard and raving fairy (Phyllis Gates and Rock Hudson, for example). She knew it could work the other way, too: Flaming queen (and Herman discovery) Liberace had actually, unaccountably, groped a chorus girl in the broom closet. Everyone recognized actor Dan Dailey—under the makeup, wig, flowered dress, and high heels—the night he sneaked into the room as a transvestite and tried to get AP reporter Jim Bacon on the dance floor with him.

Reggie was the wolf magnet—Duke Ellington barnyard-talked her; Johnny Stompanato hinted at the bulging manhood beneath his full-length vicuña coat; Rory Calhoun would turn around and hit on her whenever his wife, Lita, stepped into the ladies' room. Herman had hired her after inspecting her gams, in the presence of his legs-vetting secretary Miss Miller, and predicted "big things" for her. While nothing huge had materialized, she at least had some interesting opportunities. One night at closing time, Reggie and the hatcheck girl were invited for a nightcap at the hotel of the ringsiding Shah Reza Pahlavi of Persia and his brother. When they arrived, President Truman's Secret Service agents interrogated them, and then advised them that it would be profitable for the women to spend the night with the Pahlavis. (The U.S. Secret Service, pimping for the shah? No wonder there was an Iranian revolution!) "The other girl went along with it, but I said, 'I'm sorry, but I'm not a call girl,'" Reggie told me. "The shah's brother drove me home. We stopped at a drive-in and he gave me a kiss good night. The next night, as we set up our cigarette tray, the other girl showed me the jewels and money the shah had given her."

My mother and I would spend another two or three hours in the club—she was upstairs doing business with Herman, while I flattened out my *Weekly Reader* and my arithmetic workbook in a downstairs banquette. Manuel would sharpen my pencil and bring me a Shirley Temple from Bobby and a small reading lamp. One after another, the spanking white tablecloths were waved over and patted onto all the adjoining tables, turning the room formal and celestial. Then the staff emerged, suited up—Reggie, in her satin bustier, thigh-length skirt, and fishnet stockings; Nancy, in her low-cut floor-length taffeta gown, the hem hiding the built-up shoes she wore to give her the height to bend down on her beaming photo subjects; the busboys in their burgundy monkey jackets (brass buttons glinting off the chrome of the drum stand); the waiters in their tuxedos—all costumed like actors in a theater drama. Here were the backstairs sages, poised to catch their betters at their most craven and most vulnerable. Secret power rippled through the room like a presence.

Next, in would come the Talent, for the light and sound check. Now things got exciting! The Ciro's staff's favorite performer and nominee for Nicest Star in the World was Nat King Cole, often accompanied by his lovely wife, Maria. His smile so sweet, his hair like ripply licorice, he'd stand at the keyboard and play call-and-response chords to Dick Stabile, who would echo him on clarinet. If the Condoli Brothers were also playing that night (they backed up Peggy Lee but sometimes freelanced), the sound check could turn into a minijam, good enough to be recorded. Then Cole would sit down and do some gentle jazz, too subtle to waste on the worked-up audience that would later fill the noisy room. The clank of silverware in the rubber tubs would taper off as the busboys allowed themselves a respite, and other staff inched forward from the rear Ciroette Room and trickled in from the kitchen, to gather close and savor the private concert.

As I sat there, I got to see all of this, I got to watch the magical transformation of this room and these people; and I would feel so high—it was like a spoonful of hot chocolate pudding had just slid into my mouth on a perfectly empty stomach.

Too soon, my mother would come for me, holding a brown paper bag of lyonnaise potatoes and lamb chops with shirred-cellophane slippers: Lizzie's and my dinner. Even with our live-in maid to do the cooking, she was too intimidated by grocery shopping not to fetch us Ciro's takeout almost every night for dinner. As we left, she'd call out to the staff, "I'll be back in with Doctor for the show!" Sure enough, later on, she and my father, all dressed up, would kiss us good night, then reenter. This place, by now fully grown-up, with flashbulbs popping, perfume in the air, and no longer rehearsing, was a fountain of glamour and longing.

My father was ambivalent, at best, about his wife's partnership with her brother. "Helen is always with that brother of hers," he

would often complain to Zeke. Even though there was no question
of her pride in being a neurosurgeon's wife, she seemed too
entranced with the cheap accomplishment that was Ciro's. However, and this was the kicker, so were his colleagues. My parents
socialized abundantly with my father's doctor and surgeon friends
(although my mother thought the men were intimidating and felt
she had little in common with their boring wives), and these couples
always leapt at the chance of going to Ciro's. ("No matter how
'high-minded' people are," my mother often said, from a lifetime of
experience, "they're always agog over movie stars.") For my proud
father, the implicit ability of Herman to reach into *his* sacrosanct
world and lure his brethren was a bitter pill. So, his rivalry with and
resentment of Herman percolating inside him as he entered Ciro's

with my mother at night, my father would always stop at Johnny Oldrate's stand and unnecessarily remind the deferential maitre d', with a voice like a finger in the face, that if his exchange should call with a patient emergency, Oldrate *must* go get him *immediately*, no matter *what* point it was in the damn show. No matter *who* was singing.

That was his way of telling Oldrate—telling *all* of them—that he had far more serious things to do than be there. And that a suddenly declining postoperative tumor took precedence over the hush in the room required by the last bars of an encore performance by Peggy Lee.

In 1948, Herman had brought the team of Dean Martin and Jerry Lewis to Ciro's after watching them open for Cugat at the Capitol Theater. Jerry was funny and wacky, but smooth crooner Dean was the glue of the act. "He was a terrific *feeder*," Herman wrote in his memoir. "When he tosses his partner a line to respond to, he makes the audience perk up and pay attention to what's coming." Their wildly successful Ciro's engagement helped catapult the unlikely duo—suave crooner and antic comic—to fame. During the course of the engagement, Hover and Martin became friends. Despite his reputation, "Dean never drank that much," my uncle told Martin biographer Nick Tosches, for his book *Dino*, but the easygoing part was right—"he was a good guy, very easy to get along with." Despite the patina of polish he would later attain with the Rat Pack, "he was rough, uncouth, not educated—I don't think he ever read a book." By contrast, Jeanne Bieggar, the beautiful twenty-two-year-old blond model that thirty-two-year-old, just-divorced Martin seemed smitten by, as they sat and talked between his shows, was cultivated and educated.

Bieggar would stop by Ciro's and sometimes sit with another

new-to-town model, an equally fetching young woman from Illinois who was looking for a job as a chorus girl, model, or actress. Although she was of Norwegian ancestry, this young woman's hair was almost black, which strikingly accentuated her milk-white skin. Like Jeanne Bieggar, she had quietly mastered the manner of the upper classes, and when she held her head high she radiated a natural hauteur. Her sheeny, abundant hair was held back in combs at the sides and wrapped into a figure-eight chignon in the back of her head. "She was lovely and ladylike," Reggie Drew remembers. "She was *very* pretty," says Jim Byron, whose aesthetic standards were high. Her name was Yvonne Ealy.

Although Martin only had eyes for Bieggar, plenty of actresses had eyes for *him*. Ann Sheridan sat ringside four nights in a row, and when Martin ignored her "she fled into the ladies' room in tears," my mother recalled. According to what Herman told Tosches, Lana Turner (apparently ever on the prowl) was so "stuck on" Martin that at one post-closing party at Turner's canyon home, "I saw her pull some raw stuff on Dean, with her own husband, Bob Topping, right there. She went pretty far."

In September 1949, Dean Martin and Jeanne Bieggar were married at Herman's house. It was Molly's final week of work with us before flying back East to board in a convent, and she couldn't bear to miss this last thrilling party at Mr. Hover's, so she packed me up, and there we stood, in the postbombing-refashioned room where my nursery had been: she in her thick-soled nursing shoes, me in my Mary Janes, amid the $8,000 worth of white gardenias Herman had brought in, watching Jerry Lewis, solemn as best man, and Herman's friend Judge Griffin perform the ceremony.

Martin and Lewis performed again at Ciro's in 1950 and brought the house down. A year later, when they were making $100,000 a week and enormously famous, they insisted on holding their Ciro's fee at its original pittance. Lewis told my uncle, "Tell our agent you want to play us and you'll pay $7,000, and if he raises any squawk, he can fuck hisself." That agent, Larry Barnett, head of MCA's Act and Band division, was hardly a sucker; still, Hover and Martin and Lewis decided to pull his leg a bit. When Barnett called Herman, Herman said, "Seven thousand for two weeks, take it or leave it." Minutes later Barnett called Herman back, and said, in bewilderment, "They agreed! How long will you be home? They want me to draw the contract right now and have you sign it before you change your mind."

"This Martin and Lewis engagement was going to be the biggest event in the history of the club," George Schlatter told me. "They rehearsed. Everything was great. Six hundred guests are there at the opening (and Ciro's openings were tuxes and long gowns and jewels and champagne: a major social event), sitting down to their dinners . . . and all of a sudden Jerry calls at about seven o'clock: He has a fever of 104!" In Herman's memory, it was Dean who called, on sick Jerry's behalf, and it was 8 P.M. At any rate, some of the patrons "were already halfway through an expensive dinner, quaffing jeroboams of champagne—with a potential gross of $40,000 for the night."

Herman's version of the frantic remedy starts with a series of phone calls. "George Schlatter and I got busy. We called Bob Hope to help out. 'Sorry, Mr. Hope is not home.' Judy Garland. 'Not home.' Liberace. 'Not home.' (All three would wind up in the room as patrons.) Danny Thomas. 'He's at the TV studio.' I bounded out of the office with George close behind. We were Basil Rathbone and Nigel Bruce in the Sherlock Holmes series, pounding down the stairway of Baker Street."

They jumped in the car and tore down Sunset Boulevard, trying to find Thomas before he left the studio, but were too late. A few more phone calls were fruitless. There seemed only one thing to do. "Herman and I drive up to Chasen's to find substitutes," Schlatter told me, picking up the narrative. Herman's old *Vanities* stooge friend Dave Chasen understood their dilemma and waved the men in. "We find Tony Martin having dinner at one table and Alan King having dinner at another. We figure, Tony Martin, Alan King— that's close enough! I say, 'You gotta help us!' They say, 'We're eating!' I say, 'I'll feed ya between shows!' " Both men were steam-rolled into it.

The two men "put on a great show," Schlatter recalls. "Then Dean showed up and joined them." "As Dean stepped up on the stage"—now the story's back in my uncle's words—"the audience applauded as if for a leading pitcher coming in from the bull pen to win a tight one for his faltering teammates. Dean peeled off his bow tie and unbuttoned his shirt to where the undershirt showed." By then no longer a teetotaler, Dean "was a little fried, but he called up every star in the room—and every one of them performed." Finally, Dean called Herman onstage, whereupon my uncle attempted his old twelve-step-double-pull-back. His date for the evening (and most evenings now), Jeanne Martin's friend Yvonne Ealy, assured him they were applauding because his performance was over. Nevertheless "Desi Arnaz, swilling a glass of champagne, said, 'Hey, you sonuvabitch, trying to put us all out of business?' "

Herman wrote, "As I look back at that unforgetable evening, I feel like the Irish peasant who said to John Keats, 'Sure, I believe in faeries. Never seen any, but it stands to reason.' " He was a happy man.

Big, theatrical, gimmicky evenings like that one were what distinguished Ciro's from its across-the-street competitors, the Mocambo and, by then as well, Crescendo. The three clubs formed a circuit.

(Andy Williams told me, "What was special about that time was, when you went out, you had all of them to hit in an evening.") Those were intimate supper clubs with a starkly lit singer clutching a microphone—Vic Damone, Julie London, Eartha Kitt. Herman retained the B. F. Keith gene—the vaudeville hankering. It was novelty he was looking for. Ciro's went through a circus craze—Sonja Henie entered the club riding an elephant; Alan Young brought in a lion on a leash; clothier Sy Devore, a cheetah; and, during the opening night party for the acrobatic Corsoni Brothers, in a famous pose, Darryl Zanuck hung upside down over the dance floor from a trapeze bar. Then, reverting to his Earl Carroll days, Herman decided to bring in a stripper. "While she didn't have to be pure," Herman wrote in his memoir, "I did not want anyone looking like a doorway hooker."

He heard of an aloof Canadian blonde with Slavic eyes and an extraordinary figure. Her name was Marie van Schaark, but she'd become a legend in Montreal calling herself Lili St. Cyr. She had just moved to New York, where she was posing for art magazines and stripping at one of the jazz clubs on Fifty-second Street, at which (since this was 1951) bebop was premiering while people at the small tables were sucking pads cut out of benzedrine inhalers.

Herman booked a flight east.

Herman was involved with Yvonne Ealy, but on trips to New York he also dated a blond ex–Debutante of the Year named Margot Morris, whom he'd met through his friend Oleg Cassini. (Oleg's brother, Igor, wrote the New York society column, "Cholly Knickerbocker.") Herman took Margot to see Lili St. Cyr. He was struck by her "cold dignity, an elegant beauty daring anyone to lay a hand on her." It was a persona he liked; Margot Morris had it, and so did Yvonne Ealy. He wanted St. Cyr for Ciro's.

Carving a loophole into the law criminalizing striptease in New

York, Lili did *backward* striptease: She emerged onstage wearing pasties and a G-string and proceeded to clothe herself, caressing every part of her body in the process. The wit of her managing to stoke the audience's excitment with every *added*, not subtracted, garment made her act more Dada than burlesque. Borrowing H. L. Mencken's term, Herman would bill her as an *"ecdysiast."*

Just as he had for Joyce Hawley's appearance at Earl Carroll's fateful party twenty-five years earlier—but more elaborately—Herman had a marble bathtub rigged up on a specially built supersized stage. Jamie Ballard (L.A. society's premier interior decorator, whom Herman entrusted with completely redecorating Ciro's every two years) designed the set, a diaphonous curtain sliding over all. On opening night, Lili emerged in a mink stole over a mink coat. First one wrap then the other one slithered off her body. She would methodically throw off her jewelery, piece by piece, then slowly unencumber her torso of every scrap of clothing until . . . "she was *nude!*" Army Archerd recalled, with a bit of a start all these years later. "It was the most daring thing on the Strip. It was startling for those days."

The audience beheld her; then into the tub she went.

Just as St. Cyr was artfully jackknifing her leg up through the bubbles and pulling her knee to her chin, L.A. sheriff's officers stormed the main room, flashing their badges. They arrested St. Cyr for public indecency, hustling her out in her robe. The arrest made front-page headlines in the next afternoon's *Examiner* and *Herald Express*. But Herman—and an L.A. undersheriff—had fooled the newspaper editors (not to mention the readers): Jim Byron had made the tip-off call. "Everybody on the Strip knew everybody in the sheriff's department," Byron recently told me, laughing. (How else could Mickey Cohen use a haberdashery store as a front for his illegal enterprises?) "They knew what was going on. They weren't seriously interested in giving Herman a hard time."

Yet Herman was arrested—and the district attorney was less inclined to dismiss the case than the undersheriff had actually assumed when he ordered the arrest. The lewd-and-indecent charges against St. Cyr and Hover stuck. In court, represented by powerful defense attorney Gerry Geisler, Herman got up before the jury and demonstrated the difference between a lawful "bump" (a pelvic protrustion) and an illegal "grind" (a circular hip move- ment)—Lili had only done the former. Still, it certainly wasn't H. D. Hover that the all-male jury wanted to see as a witness. The defense obliged them by busing them to Ciro's, where Lili did her show. The twelve lucky jurors perused the prosecution evidence thor- oughly. Then (since she did her trademark reclothing) they voted to acquit her, as well as my uncle.

If vice squad raids (albeit manipulated ones) and indecency arrests were Exhibit One of the scandal-mongering spirit that, in the early fifties, was draining the postwar elegance out of L.A., there were also other signs. Johnny Oldrate barred *Confidential* maga- zine's "reporters" from the premises, but sometimes these old gumshoes idled their cars across the street until closing time. Ciro's was the rare club in still-segregated nightlife L.A. whose after-hours parties crossed the color line. (Lena Horne wasn't allowed to sit in the Cocoanut Grove between the sets of her own engagement, and Billy Eckstine could only purchase the Crescendo, the club adjacent to the Mocambo, by enlisting a white man in Philadelphia to sign the papers.) So waiting to tail Ciro's headliner, ringsiders, and staff to some canyon lair at 2:30 A.M. was worth the paper's time.

Spies from the House Un-American Activities Committee (HUAC) and the McCarthy committee were also sniffing around Ciro's, on the hunt for Commie screenwriters who might, they imagined, be sneaking Marxist messages into, say, the songs of Patti Page, the adagio lifts of Veloz and Yolanda, or the fiddle antics of

Cugie and his new girl, Abbe Lane. One of J. Edgar Hoover's agents even slipped a tape recorder into a heat duct in the men's room, and then got too drunk to go back to retrieve it.

Newspaper columnists could be as feared as Hoover's men. These were the days when Walter Winchell would come in with Marilyn Monroe, on actual dates, and no one dare let the news out of the room. Syndicated columnist Florabel Muir, who had taken a bullet in her derriere during a hit on Mickey Cohen and had reported the story of Bugsy Siegel's Coldwater Canyon murder a few years earlier, was another Ciro's regular whose eagle eye made patrons extremely wary. "She was a nasty lady," Jim Byron says. Florabel would not sit on a story.

Shortly after the Lili St. Cyr bust, actor Franchot Tone, a Cornell Phi Beta Kappa from a scholarly eastern family, started coming in a lot with notoriously promiscuous ex-chorine Barbara Payton. As my uncle put it, "Tone fell hard for the ravishing sexpot and told friends he wanted to marry her. The tables at Ciro's were humming with them trying to talk him out of it."

Payton had started a simultaneous fling with weightlifter and B-movie actor Tom Neal, a beefy opportunist who was everything that gentleman egghead Tone was not. Tone challenged Neal to a fight, and they went at it on the lawn in front of Payton's home. Neal was unscathed but Tone was pummeled. In an uncharacteristic act of nuance, Payton decided to marry not the winner but the loser.

Florabel Muir wrote a column item that opened, "What an eye opening Tone will get if he goes through with having Neal arrested and tried for assault and the juicy news of the rather sordid Neal/Payton romance goes over the wires for the world to read."

A few nights later, Franchot Tone (still bandaged from his honor duel) and his new wife Barbara Payton spotted Florabel Muir at her table 2. "Tone walked over and bent down in a gesture, which

looked at first as if he were going to kiss Florabel," Herman remembered. "Then he grabbed her hands and kicked her shins under the
table and spat in her face." The room went silent with awe. Muir,
more ruthless than Louella and Hedda (who often sat on stories),
was second only to Winchell in the power to destroy a career. Muir
jumped on the phone, and once again sheriffs swooped into Ciro's
with handcuffs—this time not for the naked stripper but for the
bandaged actor. Tone was charged with spitting in a public place.
Muir stood up on the banquette and demanded, "Since when in hell
has my *face* become a *public place*?!" (Tone and Payton divorced
forty-five days later.)

With all that happened at Ciro's in 1951, no event was more
exciting than my uncle's launching of one particular career.

A Harlem tap-dancing threesome had been playing in a Las Vegas
hotel lounge in 1950, wowing the patrons but collecting the crushing
indignities that befell any African-American act in that Jim-Crow-
in-the-desert (where a hotel swimming pool had recently been
drained and scrubbed after Dorothy Dandridge had inserted her
toe). "They were paying more attention and giving us more respect
than ever before," said the youngest and most talented member of
the troupe, in the book he would later write, "and after every performance I was so exhilarated by our acceptance onstage that I really
expected one of the owners to . . . sa[y], 'You were great. To hell
with the [segregation] rules. Come on in and have a drink with us.'
But it never happened. The [white] acts could move around the
hotel, go out and gamble or sit in the lounge and have a drink, but we
had to leave though the kitchen, with the garbage."

My uncle had heard of the group's leader, Will Mastin, and had
remembered the second lead from his own dancing days. An agent
Herman trusted, Art Silber, was trying to talk him into booking

them for their Vegas fee of $550 a week. None of the Sunset Strip clubs could compete with the high-volume Vegas fee scale. Herman told Silber he could only pay his opening acts $500, but that he'd use the trio to open for Janis Paige on Academy Awards night, when every star in Hollywood came to the club after the ceremonies.

The older members of the trio were offended by the lop-off of $50 from their standard fee. "I'll quit show business before I go in there for $500!" Sammy Davis Sr. said. "Herman Hover was a dancer for Earl Carroll when I was [dancing in vaudeville], and he knows we can outdance him every minute of the day."

Mastin agreed, noting, "We're not starving. No point taking a cut just to work a place."

"A *place!?*" said the youngest member, Sammy Davis Jr. "This is *Ciro's*, for God's sake! [It's] the best club out here, and we need to play it."

But Mastin and Davis Sr. refused to budge. Finally, Art Silber told Herman he'd make up the $50 a week if Herman would book them. The highly unusual move of an agent willing to go out of pocket to land a booking did the trick. "All right, you win," Herman told Silber. "If you believe in them that much, I'll go for the $550."

The deal was made; an engagement was booked.

Late afternoon on opening night—during that span of hours I often sat in the banquette doing my homework—Davis Sr., Davis Jr., and Mastin arrived at Ciro's. As Davis recalled the conversation in his 1965 memoir (with Jane and Burt Boyar) *Yes I Can*, the three first exchanged incredulous looks at the crummy, atticlike second-act dressing room they were led to and, Davis said, "burst out laughing" at this "part of the glamour of Ciro's the public didn't see."

The club itself was something else. Just before going on, Davis recalled:

Will came upstairs [to the dressing room] in a run. "Well, I've seen it all now." He was out of breath from excitement. "I walked around backstage and took a peep out front and you oughta see what's going on. The place is loaded with the biggest names in the business from Martin and Lewis right on down the line. . . . We never played anything like this before. . . . It's got the French menus and the captains in tails and the customers are dressed to the teeth. This place is about as high class as you can get."

Standing in the wings and hearing the nightclub sounds ("hundreds of forks and knives scraping dinner plates, a thousand swirling ice cubes, the like-no-other-sound of champagne corks popping," Davis said), he and his father and uncle lapsed into their "deepest Amos 'n' Andy talk, something Negroes do among themselves when they're nervous but happy."

Dick Stabile introduced them, after cautioning, "Nobody pays any attention to opening acts here, but I'll gag it up a little and get their attention for you." Out they came in their trademark "dancing shoes." "And we might have been barefoot on hot sand," Davis remembered. "Our feet weren't onstage as much as they were in the air. We'd started probably faster than any act this crowd had ever seen and we kept increasing the pace, trying as we never had before. We finished the opening number and, characteristic of colored acts, we didn't wait to enjoy the applause before we were off dancing again. We were fighting for our lives, and our frenzy of movement got to the audience . . . until soon it was like they were out of breath trying to keep up with us."

After a few more numbers, Davis Sr. and Mastin stepped back, and Sammy Davis Jr. started doing impressions. "I did Sinatra and they screamed. I went through the rest of the singers, and by the time I finished Satchmo they were pounding the tables so hard I could see the silverware jumping up and down. I switched into the movie stars, first Bogart, then Garfield—suddenly I felt the whole room shifting toward me. They were no longer just sitting back watching, amused. They were reacting to everything, catching every inflection, every little move and gesture, concentrating, leaning in as though they wanted to push, to help. I was touching them." Next, more dancing with his elders. Then:

> When we finished, after being on for forty minutes, they wouldn't let us stay off. It was as if they knew something big was happening to us and they wanted to be a part of it. They kept . . . screaming for us to come back. . . . We'd already taken two bows but a man with a gun couldn't have held me back. I looked at my father. "To hell with [Janis Paige's] contract. I ain't gonna miss this for *nobody!!!*" We went out twice more. They kept shouting for an encore. I'd already done every impression I'd ever tried. But we had to do something so I did Jerry Lewis. . . . The sight of a colored Jerry Lewis was the absolute topper. It was *over.* When I heard that scream, I knew we'd had it. There was nothing we could do that would top that!

"Sammy got carried away, and the whole room went crazy!" George Schlatter remembered. "Janis never got on. [Davis said she did, but late, angry, and so disconcerted she was hitting wrong notes.] She waited out her whole show in the hallway."

My parents came home from the club that night and my mother announced, as if winded, to no one in particular, "That was the biggest night. Something just *happened.*"

The morning papers concurred. The *Los Angeles Mirror* said,

"The surprise sensation of the show, the Will Mastin Trio . . . left the audiences begging for more." The *Daily Variety* opined, "a walloping success." The *Los Angeles Times* chipped in, "Show-stoppers." Most important, the review in the *Hollywood Reporter*, by Herb Stein, said, "Once in a long time an artist hits town and sends the place on its ear. Such a one is young Sammy Davis Jr. of the Will Mastin Trio at Ciro's."

Herman had the marquee changed; he put THE WILL MASTIN TRIO FEATURING SAMMY DAVIS JR in block letters the same size as JANIS PAIGE, and he changed the order of the show: Janis opened for *them*; they became the main act. Then he did more. "Herman found and leased a home for Sammy," George Schlatter says. "It was Judy Garland's old home, on Sunset Plaza Drive"— just above the Strip. To get around the "no Negroes" real estate policy, "The leasing had to be made in my name," Schlatter said, "because the Realtors would recognize Herman's name as connected to Sammy and they wouldn't go through with the deal. So it was rented with Herman's help, by me, and then transferred to Sammy." Davis hosted postshow parties at the house, with its sweeping views of L.A. and its white furniture and carpets; the parties overflowed with black celebrities, including Louis Armstrong. George, Herman, Reggie Drew, and other Ciro's folk were also in attendance.

"Women found Sammy fantastically sexy," my uncle wrote in his memoir. "I never saw a man attract women the way he did." Even within the entertainment world at the time, interracial romances were rare and avant garde, so all of backstairs Ciro's was party to the high-running emotions—and risks of physical harm, incurred by Sammy—that these liaisons, including one with Ava Gardner, occasioned.

Davis grew to like and trust Herman. Over the years of their friendship, my uncle thought Sammy complex. He could be bitter and retaliatory for all he had endured—once rejecting a Monaco charity engagement because Princess Grace would only send a limo, not a helicopter, to get him at the airport—but he was democratic in seeking career advice (listening, for example, when the Ciro's busboys thought he had bought the wrong material from a gag-and-patter writer and should return to his original). Despite his success, he was often broke. After the lease on the Sunset Plaza house lapsed, he would hole up for months at a time in the dumpy Sunset Colonial Hotel, as if he were a local gumshoe, not a headliner.

It was during one such desperate moment that Davis planned his uneasy return to the stage after the 1953 car accident in which he lost his eye. From his room in the Colonial he read the point-blank question in the *L.A. Times*: "Can Sammy run again?" Down the street at Ciro's, Herman, Johnny Oldrate, Manuel Reyes, and the crew were reading the article, too. "Sammy Davis Jr. is scheduled to begin a four-week engagement at Ciro's in mid-March [1954]," the story opened. "The announcement by Herman Hover causes one to speculate as to whether the Sammy Davis Jr. who'll open at Ciro's can possibly bear any resemblance to the dazzling figure of perpetual motion whose career only two months ago loomed as one of the brightest in show business."

All of Hollywood turned up to cheer Davis on. Frank Sinatra strode out to introduce his friend to the audience. Davis sneaked a peek through the curtain, and, as he recalled, "From one end of Ciro's to the other were the giants of the motion picture industry— the Cary Grants, the Bogarts, the Edward G. Robinsons, the Spencer Tracys, Gary Coopers, Jimmy Cagneys, Dick Powells. . . . People were shouting 'Bravo' and whistling."

The show lasted two hours. During the final standing ovation, Davis recalled, "Herman Hover was walking onstage followed by every waiter, busboy, every cook and kitchen helper in the club.

They formed a semicircle around me, the band began playing 'Auld Lang Syne,' and they were singing to me. The audience fell apart. I just stood there, crying like a baby, deep racking sobs."

It was my infatuation with evenings like that—with how Ciro's dazzled my little-girl eyes—that led to a terrible miscalculation I made with my father when I was about nine.

I was sitting on the side of my parents' bed. My father was reclining on his pillow, half under the sheet, in his seersucker pajamas. Wint-O-Green LifeSavers, pipe tobacco, and sample packets from Lilly and Pfizer were scattered on his bedstand. A tube of sunlight streamed in the window. It felt like we were floating in the caramel center of a chocolate bar—until I asked, in the Daddy's Girl voice I adopted, hoping I'd become one: "Dah-dee, why can't you own a nightclub, like Uncle Herman?"

His reaction shocked me.

Drawing himself straight up, his face flashing red, he whispered, like a threat, "One day you will be proud that your father is a neurosurgeon." I flushed with panicked sorrow. I was used to pushing the wrong buttons with him—looking for affection and getting annoyance or disdain—but now I'd really done it, gone and pushed some much deeper button. I hadn't realized how eclipsed he felt by Herman, how bitter he was at the contrast between my uncle's high-profile fame and his quiet, serious accomplishment. I felt as if I'd set out to utter one word . . . but a different word had slid out of my mouth instead, and when the shock of it settled I was left with deep humiliation. *How could I have gotten things so wrong? How could I have no touch for this?*

The sunlight through the window was a mocking irony—flaunting, as it so often did, the contrast between the discomfort of my inner state and the comfort of my body. "Oh, I am proud. I *am* proud! I was just kidding, Daddy!" I said, once I recovered from the mortification. But it was too late. He was out of the room by then.

On Christmas Eve 1951, my uncle married Yvonne Ealy in Las Vegas. The wedding picture of them in the *L.A. Examiner* shows a heavyset man, looking older than his forty-five years, protectively sliding a mink coat onto the bare shoulders of a strikingly beautiful, fresh-faced, and elegant young woman who is wearing a strapless, peplum sheath suit, with lots of tiny covered buttons on it. She is smiling at him adoringly. A week later I went to their house to meet Aunt Yvonne—as I would call her, from that day forward.

She was the most beautiful woman I had ever seen up close. Her coloring—black hair, white skin—was startling. In a cocktail dress you'd see in a fashion magazine, she strode across the harlequin-tiled floors of Uncle's house—my old house, my Mollyland, now *her* house—with an imperious serenity.

My mother and grandmother were a little stiff around her, as if the occasion itself was awkward. For so long they had been a closed unit with Herman—especially my mother. She was his one remaining sibling, his twin in dreams and life trajectory, and by then his business partner. She had gotten—perhaps unwisely—used to having her bachelor brother all to herself. Now there was a stranger, come to claim half of what they'd made together.

Then there was her hard-to-swallow, untrustworthy physical presence. Absorbing new women into the family usually didn't have that component. As with many westward-migrated New York Jews who'd struck it big, Herman had made a momentous break with the centuries-old tradition of the men in the family marrying only Jewish women. Yvonne was a different kind of sister for the Hover women—calm, cold, and, most of all, beautiful—and that newness made my mother feel provincial, disarmed, slightly wary, and even a little hurt. Jewish women were sensitive to the phenomenon of their successful men choosing wives from the supposedly fairer-faced group. Why should a *shiksa* nab a "catch" like her brother? Was she just after his power and money, or the world of connections he offered? (Some of the Ciro's staff, like Latin band leader Gerry Galian, thought Yvonne an "operator.") Would she return his love and trust? As my mother's cousin Hilda Stone recalled, "Your mother and grandmother didn't really like or trust Yvonne—none of us Hover women did—but for Herman's sake they were nice to her."

As for me, I was simply fascinated. An hour later, when I saw a light coming from their bedroom suite, being the nosy kid that I was, I entered.

I heard her high-octaved, not entirely friendly "Hello . . . ?" from an inside chamber. Following the sound, I walked into the part of Uncle's bathroom that was my new aunt's boudoir. She was sitting there in a satin pegnoir, her face still queenly even with splotches of cold cream dabbed on it. Spread out before her were perfumes and ointments, in porcelain, silver, and cut-glass containers. The wall of mirrors in front of us reflected the mirrors on the folding mirrored doors behind us. There was a throne room of vanity. It smelled of meadows and islands.

"I just came to say hi," I said. What was I sniffing around for? Immersion into the exotic? Tutelage? Validation? I was coming at her with my most ham-handed self, and I almost knew it.

"Hello, dear," she said briskly, turning back to her mirror.

I saw my eyes in the mirror looking at her, but she did not meet them. She didn't want me there.

I turned and left, of course.

Chapter Ten

BEVERLY HILLS AND HOLLYWOOD: 1952–1955

A conference on aneurysms was being held in Boston. James Poppen was speaking; my father *had* to be there. Part of his urgency in going was the subject matter—I always knew when my father had just performed an unsuccessful ruptured-aneurysm intervention; he was furious (sometimes taking out his rage on an overdone steak or my parakeet's overloud chirps). But there was also the need to get out of Hollywood, with its emphasis on hedonism— even out of L.A. itself, where the palm fronds and sun beating on my father's study's glass door accentuated the dissonance between the difficult internal realms—the ventricles of the brain, the operating theater—of his vocation and the ease of the external world. That dissonance reflected his own contradictory yearnings. "Your father loved knowledge and he loved mischief," said Zeke. "He could be formal and diffident one minute; then he would talk slang and call the tools in his surgeon's bag 'my nutcrackers.' "

Those contradictions were not lost on us who lived with him. A blend of liberal and conservative, my father was in favor of social-ized medicine (which was adamantly opposed by the American Medical Association) and an activist in efforts to get the boxing commission to make headgear mandatory (a lost cause in those days of zero consumer protection and seat belt–free cars); but he also believed in what he darkly called "the bad seed": a neurological basis for character pathology. Like most neurosurgeons, he disdained the semiscience of psychiatry and considered psychoanalysts "quacks." Similar was the ethnic conflict. Though a Waspophile— insisting that Lizzie and I dress in tailored navy blue jumpers; cultivating a friendship with our neighbor Ralph Edwards—he had also begun studying the Talmud, and sometimes he would take me on his knee and sing a nonsense song, "Hidey-Didey-Didey-Diiii," so cornily ethnic it embarrassed me (which seemed his intention).

In 1952, hoping to reconnect with the serious, idealistic young surgeon-in-the-making he had been when he lived and worked in Boston, my father flew there to meet with his mentor Poppen and several other of his Lahey alums. The trip was a kind of pilgrimage, the paired institutions—Lahey and Mass General—his Mecca and Medina. Situating himself among people for whom movie stars, press agents, and studio czars meant nothing, in that old, tradition-rich city so teeming with research physicians, my father felt appreciated. He felt his better self was validated and encouraged by the lack of a dazzling competing ethos—and he told people so. Dr. Jean Hawkes said her husband Doug reported that "Danny Weller felt his work was being compromised, or his concentration was distracted, by being in Los Angeles. It seemed to have had something to do with a brother-in-law who—I believe— owned a distillery." It was exactly this crowd's ethereal remove from show business, evident in Hawkes's last phrase, that my father relished.

At the dinner the group discussed the grim success rate for ruptured-aneurysm operations. Swedish neurosurgeon Herbert Olivecrona (who was ligating aneurysms' necks with linen thread) had the best results—which didn't help American patients, since flying to Europe in the midst of a rupture was not an option. Some forthright souls, like Denny-Brown and Falconer, were even suggesting, in journal articles, giving up on postrupture intervention altogether. Poppen had some words of optimism. The patients on whom he had performed carotid ligation at Lahey (with my father assisting on some procedures) were showing a good survival rate. (Eventually that rate would be fixed at 79 percent). A new aneurysm clip was being developed by Frank Mayfield (one of Cushing's second-generation disciples) and a medical artist named George Kees, and up and down the East Coast neurosurgeons were experimenting with others, cutting rectangles out of sterile sheets of tantalum and bending them into U shapes over Kelly forceps, like Wright brothers and Edisons on a microscopic scale. (Eventually a series of increasingly perfected aneurysm clips—by Mayfield, Kees, Drake, Heifetz, Lougheed-Kerr, and Sundt—were developed, some of which my father used, some coming after his time.) Over at Mass General, Poppen noted, my father's first mentor, William Sweet, had grown fascinated by Canadian William Lougheed's hypothermia experiments on animal brains. Cardiac surgeons were lowering the heart's temperature to gain better control of blood flow during surgery. Lougheed's research had convinced Sweet and others that, once the right technique was found, hypothermia would prove just as useful in brain surgery.

The evening with Poppen left my father hungry and melancholy for the life he had savored during his residency, within a community of surgeon-scholars at an Eastern medical school. When he returned home he was a quietly—secretly—changed man: Over the next few years he became obsessed with returning to the East. Coupled with this was, apparently, an almost ruthless desperation, a desire to be

almost airlifted out of his life in California, his life in Hollywood—
his life with us. Ruth Page—a striking Big Blonde type, married to
my mother's cousin George Frankel—told me, "Your father would
tell me many times, 'I hate it here. I hate having these movie people
around. *Run away with me!*' "

Ruth's disclosure caught me by surprise. I had no idea my father
had ever flirted with Ruth, much less proposed such a thing to her. I
tried to disguise my shock and humiliation by playing the objective
journalist as I absorbed what she said next. "I told your father I had
no intention of leaving George or the children. Since I knew he was
talking out of his hat, I said, 'And you wouldn't leave Helen or your
children.' " Then she fell silent. I took this as a warning to go no
further. Nonetheless, I pressed on, "What did he say to *that?*"

She drew a breath. "He said he wanted to leave everything."

Twice a year, my father would travel to Mexico to perform free surgeries with an organization that was a precursor to Doctors Without
Borders. (He told us about the impoverished mothers who slept
beneath their children's hospital beds in the crowded wards, emerging from under the bedsprings with bowls of rice when the nun went
around ringing the mealtime bell.) It was during one such trip, just
before Christmas 1953, that the phone rang early in the morning.

I listened with alarm as my mother shouted into the receiver,
"What? *What?*! Speak louder! Speak English! Put someone on who
can speak English!"

Again, the warm air and clear sunlight streaming in the windows
mocked the anxiety-making news that was crawling through the
staticky phone wire.

"*How* bad?!" my mother screamed impatiently.

It had finally happened. My father had had a heart attack.

My mother flew down to Mexico, while Lizzie and I stayed with the housekeeper. A few days later a paler, unsmiling version of our father walked through the door, looking shamed as he was bolstered by my worry-faced mother. A few steps behind were the Abbey Rents men with the hospital bed and the oxygen tank.

Because he couldn't climb stairs for several weeks, the hospital bed was set up in his downstairs study, and when he wasn't in bed with the tube and mask to his mouth he was sitting at his desk, dictating all his cases for entrance into those organizations whose validation he craved. He worked with quiet urgency.

"Come here, Shelka," he said one day when he caught me watching him reading. The oxygen tube was looped over his shoulder, and a vital-signs monitor was clipped to his arm.

His use of my Hebrew name—which we never used (I had been a renegade from Sunday school)—scared me. (Was he dying?) Today I realize that his appropriation of Hebrew may have been an offshoot of his study of the Talmud, or part of an attempt to emotionally return East: back to not only the seat of neurosurgical scholarship but to the seat of American Jewishness.

He smiled when he saw my fear.

Embarrassed to be caught alarmed but too alarmed to care, I rushed over, careful not to disturb the tubes and wires.

"They think I'm a telephone," he said, of the various devices attached to him. "Tell me, Brooksie, do I look like a telephone?"

"No," I thought. "You look like the funniest, bravest daddy in the world, and I don't want you to be sick anymore!" My unbidden tears made that comment for me. "Psst," he said as they sprayed his face, "There's a wonderful new invention. Called the Kleenex."

I pulled the tissue from the box, and laughed as I cried and wiped both our faces.

. . .

My father made a complete enough recovery to continue working. He had to give up playing the trumpet; the physical exertion of blowing that horn would drain the stamina he needed to operate. He replaced the horn blowing with whistling, and another musical anthem came into his life: Mitch Miller's hit remake of the 1836 slave song "The Yellow Rose of Texas." The minute my father heard that song, one day in 1955, he adopted it as his.

On Saturday mornings he would walk around, whistling, as if leading a marching band. I would follow that jaunty, Old West martial cadence—"There's a yellow rose of Texas that I am goin' to see . . ."—into his minuscule bathroom, wallpapered in little tin soldiers. I'd sit on the closed toilet lid, the shower steam that moistened his skin moistening mine as well.

Holding his shaving mug while he pulled at the flesh of his Adam's apple, I would supply the lyrics, "Nobody else does love her, not half as much as me . . ." as he plowed the razor over the massed white foam, its ebb tide giving way to viscous, rubbed-raw pink. His whistling slowed the tune to an eerie poignancy as he carefully shaved; it became minor mode and cantorial: the cowboy prairie by way of Eastern Europe, just like his father's life.

Then—the shaving finished; medicinal astringence perfusing the air by way of the opened Mennen bottle—he picked up the tempo, and I sang along, "You can talk about your Clementine, and sing of Rosalie . . ."—but I was watching tiny red pinpricks flower on his fragile cheeks. "Daddy! Blood!" I would exclaim. "There's a wonderful new invention . . ." he started, and I picked up, ". . . called the Kleenex." Plucking the tissue from the box and dabbing protectively at his pencil-point wounds, I felt as happy as I'd ever felt in my life.

· · ·

That moment of validating intimacy with my father was a tiny reprieve from the overestrangement that had started the prior year.

One scorching day in July 1954, after Lizzie and I returned from a friend's house, she became ill with, as she recalls it, "a terrible headache and fever. I remember lumbering up those steep stairs to bed." Over the course of several days, I tried to divine the meaning of the frightening developments: She stayed in bed, where adults and doctors hovered over her, and where I was not allowed to go. The adults were secretive; the import of her severe fever was not explained, not even to her. At one point, she recalls, there was Grandma (the indomitable Celia Hover) propping her up and helping her into the bathroom.

That is how she realized she could not walk.

Enter Abbey Rents—again. Lizzie's hospital bed was assembled in our bedroom. I was to sleep downstairs, to keep my body free of the germs that were paralyzing hers.

My sister remembers, "There were several doctors' visits. Then, one day, the men in the ambulance came. I cried and held on to the bars of the bed. It was a horrible indignity, being transported in the ambulance down Beverly Boulevard. I remember cars pulling alongside and peering through the small crevice between the sides of the window curtains. I felt so humiliated."

My sister had contracted one of the almost thirty-nine thousand new polio cases diagnosed in 1954. (That particular epidemic had burst upon the scene in 1952—in that year alone, fifty-eight thousand cases were reported in the United States. The next year, there were thirty-five thousand new cases.) Ironically, the Salk vaccine, which fostered the beginning of the eradication of the disease, was developed less than a year after her diagnosis.

My sister recalls, "The first night at Children's Hospital I screamed and cried all night, until a mean nurse came in the middle of the night and chastised me for waking everyone up. That shut me up. The next day I was transferred to Ward B—we called it Bedpan Alley—where they wrapped us in scalding hot packs, from head to toe, put us all on wooden stretchers, and lowered us into a therapeutic swimming pool where the water was probably one hundred degrees, and we got massive physical therapy. They forced enemas and suppositories on us if we weren't regular—it was awfully humiliating."

Her illness was grave. Much later my mother said, "Liz came an inch away from having to be in an iron lung" (the automatic-breathing machines that constituted the permanent fate of the most severely afflicted patients). At the time, "Nobody ever told me how sick I was," Liz said, resenting the burden of that evasion even years later. "I was left to guess it on my own."

Our mother was beside herself. Nothing in her repertoire of loved ones' sudden tragedies—Sadie's death, Lenny's death, Danny's heart attack—had prepared her for the unique tragedy of her child's serious, crippling illness. She virtually moved into the hospital, joining a group of mothers who camped out there, memorizing their childrens' doctors' footfalls so they could accost them when they alighted from the elevator and ingratiating themselves with the nurses. Herman sent lavish presents, including a TV for the ward, but both our uncle's grandiosity and our mother's worried, noisy presence embarrassed Liz, who, with her calm, understated nature, had always felt temperamentally estranged from the Hovers.

It was our father who was Lizzie's lifeline, and her use of him in that regard was poignant. "I only remember one visit from Daddy, and I was so excited," she says. "When he came I 'convinced' him that I could walk. He made the nurse let me try. But I fell, right away. And my mantra to the nurses who brought me those awful dinners was this, 'My daddy's Dr. Weller. You don't need to give me dinner tonight because he is coming to take me home.' I said that night after night. I believed he was coming. He never did."

My mother told me several times, "Your father came to visit Liz exactly twice, and he worked in the hospital right across the street." She would whisper that sentence, in a tone more vulnerable and stunned than angry or judgmental. She identified deeply with her sick daughter during that time, and her husband's seemingly inhuman detachment hurt her as much as it did Lizzie. Perhaps it even hurt my mother more, for Lizzie's imagination had gone into protective overdrive. Over the years, whenever my sister was reminded of this paucity of paternal visits, she would wax perplexed—it *seemed* he had visited her often. Even today she is not sure whether he visited her without telling our mother (thereby avoiding our mother's neurotic, pumping questions) or whether "I imagined him there. I *willed* him there"—in her deepest crisis, transforming her desired, *needed* version of him into the truth.

It is possible that beneath my father's failure to visit his hospitalized daughter more than twice—if my mother's version is true—lay simple terror. Especially after his heart attack, confronting his sick daughter might have been more than he was able to bear and still remain in emotional fighting shape to perform his surgeries. Like his idol Harvey Cushing, who performed a complex tumor surgery hours after his favorite son was killed in a car accident, my father had internalized the neurosurgeon's defense mechanisms and personality: slash-and-burn compartmentalization, egomaniacal coldness, prima donna vanity intercut with flashes of room-rocking temper, and scholar's depth and piety.

According to Fran Douglas, the man who rarely showed overt vulnerability to us was, secretly, completely broken up by his daughter's illness. Fran startled me by saying, "Your father was obsessed with Lizzie's polio. He worried terribly about her. He talked often about how afraid he was that the polio would affect her adult life."

Just as his own childhood disease had affected his. Certainly their shared experience of childhood invalidism became a bond. "I became special to Daddy because of that illness," my sister remembered. "I was his Lizzie." She was his touchstone, his proxy within our family. "We became a team."

Shut out more than ever, I became the angry, self-absorbed big sister, hiding her confusion over her sister's calamity behind a scrim of jealousy at the attention she was receiving. I remember with hideous clarity going to Rexall Drugs with our mother to select ten comic books to be taken to Lizzie in the hospital. Before they were taken to her (never to return from the infected hospital ward to uninfected me), I sat on the bottom step of the stairs, savoring every single ballooned caption in every frame. I delayed my mother's leave-taking (she was standing in the living room with the car keys in her hand) and I was determined to wrest every bit of benefit I could from my sick little sister's windfall of stapled, colored newsprint funnies.

I was a bad sister! The polio had skipped over healthy me and had preyed on weak little her, and now I was monopolizing her comics! I was taking my own sweet time and making her wait, and wait, in her hospital bed for a little bit of relieving humor.

To punish myself for my bad character, and to even the score after having hogged our shared sibling's pot of health, I got rid of the one thing I knew I had: my prettiness. I cut my hair off and wore it in unattractive Dutch Girl style. I got chubby. I picked a fat, unpopular girl for my best friend, and the two of us became Girl Scouts—an extremely unhip thing in Beverly Hills. I flapped my hands from my wrists all the more. When Lizzie came home from the hospital, balloons and teddy bears filled the house, and construction on our swimming pool commenced (in order to help her recover). When my sister's physical therapist (who virtually lived with us) spoke in awed terms of her high threshold for pain, my new self-loathing was spiked with an even darker envy.

I was losing something more: my precious advantage in the family, my status as Mommy's Favorite. Also, I was losing it with no recompense: the seesaw of our two-adult, two-child family didn't tip to reward me for the loss of one parent with the gain of the other. My father had already decamped. The elusive ability I craved—to charm and elicit love and respect from him—which was always challenging, finally seemed impossible. My mother grew completely preoccupied with Lizzie.

I had to do something to remedy things. To get their attention and steal a little martyrdom off my sister's full plate, I embroidered the conviction that I wasn't even my parents' child. "I'm adopted! I *know* I'm adopted!" I'd stomp around the house, crying.

"Sheila, you're *not* adopted!" My mother, swallowing my gambit, pleaded heartfully. "I'll get your birth certificate . . . !"

My father saw that I was fishing for reassurance with my temper tantrum. "Don't encourage her, Helen—she's feeling sorry for herself," he would say. To me he would order, "Cut it out. Stop that business with your hands. Get control of yourself."

During the first months of my sister's at-home recovery—during which her hospital bed was in the brand-new lanai, and her physical therapy sessions were daily—my father fell ill yet again. It wasn't a heart attack this time; it was a bleeding ulcer. Another ambulance was called to the house. I remember its revolving red light and the men coming in with the stretcher. My father refused the stretcher. He limped down the flagstone path, book-ended by the hovering paramedics, whom he kept pushing away. From her own hospital bed in the lanai in the back of the house, Lizzie saw the red light and his vanishing back. She felt helpless; she felt aligned with him; she felt angry that our mother didn't tell her what had happened. With her illness-bred clairvoyance, she knew, from that moment, that he would walk out that door—*really* walk out that door. "I started preparing myself for our daddy's leaving, which I knew would be the most unimaginable tragedy in the world for me."

While Lizzie was quietly steeling herself against her premonition that our father might one day leave us, I was responding to my own anxiety about my father's illnesses (which had made him frequently sad and distant) in my characteristic noisier way: by fomenting activities that would make all of us one big, happy family. By all of us I included my uncle and aunt, and Lizzie's and my new young cousins.

Yvonne and Herman had two children—a girl, Ellen Jane, born in 1953, and a boy, Loring Ian, in 1955. I adored my little cousin Ellen, a sweet little girl (dressed to the nines by her mother), and I made it my business to give her a fantasy world: once planting fairy figurines in the backyard high grass for her to happen upon as we strolled. I also created for her a six-page, yarn-bound monthly magazine named *Magazette*. I typed it on my mother's typewriter, illustrated it with crayon drawings and cutouts from real magazines, and filled it with stories, columns, contests, and poems that I wrote just for her.

No one, of course, was more charmed by this gesture than my mother (who, with Lizzie's recovery, had now bounced back to her old pattern of indulging me). I was becoming a magazine writer—just like her in one more way. It was not that I had chosen to parrot my mother; I was already so much like her, the similarity just seemed fated. Sometimes it felt more like conflation. When my father screamed (which he did more often now), "Helen, you're being neurotic!" I felt as attacked and defensive as she did. A blow lobbed at her was a wound felt by me, and a blow lobbed by *him* felt to her like a blow meant for both of us. Separating from my mother seemed an impossible task, and bonding with her had an effortless, automatic—and illicit—comfort.

Less charmed by my efforts toward my little cousin Ellen was Ellen's mother, my aunt Yvonne. Our relationship had solidified along the lines of our first encounter in her boudoir several years earlier. She sensed I was overingratiating; befriending her husband's slightly cloying and overwrought niece was not on her agenda, so she responded with clipped distance. Since I was then both chubbier and older, I was more aware of the disparity that existed between our placement on the continuum of ideal femininity. (Sometimes it seemed that her very existence was a rebuke to me.) Since I was spending more time at their house, her vague annoyance at me was more apparent. I would watch her poring over fleur-de-lis swatch samples for the Louis XIV chairs Ciro s decorator Jamie Ballard had found for her, or dressing in such casual elegance for Miko's nursery school events that she rivaled the beauty of her co–class mother, Linda Christian, whose daughters by husband Tyrone Power— Taryn and Romina—were Ellen's classmates. She was competing within the thin-aired world of Hollywood trophy-wife moms, her iciness softened by maternal gentleness. She was like the woman in the Breck shampoo ad, like Jennifer Jones in some movie with picket fences, martinis, and horses.

The whole package was discomfiting to me. After all, my own mother was not the picture of maternal femininity (hers was the more addled, work-driven model). So Yvonne was trumping her in two ways: first with her aloof, gentile beauty and second with her more conventional embodiment of motherhood. As my mother's proxy, I resented my aunt even while I was in awe of her, even as I curried her favor. Why did that one chilly woman in the family have so many bases covered?

Lizzie had overcome polio enough to walk, although she had a limp and a thinned, slightly shortened leg, and her permanent exemption from phys-ed made her miserably self-conscious. To try to match my sister's Tiny Tim–like virtue, I beefed up the Girl Scout goody-goodiness. One day I saw Aunt Yvonne swatting a fly. "Don't!" I called out. "Never kill a living thing."

Aunt Yvonne turned and looked at me for one long, bemused moment. Then she said, "That is the stupidest thing I ever heard."

Later, driving me home, my mother asked me why I was so silent in the backseat.

"I'm just thinking," I said.

"Well," my mother said, happily accepting my daydreaming, "whatever it is, it sure must be interesting."

The emotion that had taken hold was so novel and heady and adrenalizing—like falling in love, I imagined; like having a baby, or getting shot in a war, or seeing God in a desert—that the rest of my body and mind seemed to shut down in observance.

There was someone in this world that I hated. I hated Aunt Yvonne.

Chapter Eleven

BEVERLY HILLS AND HOLLYWOOD:1955–1958

After having endured a heart attack and a bleeding ulcer, my father made a compensatory mad dash for the two-fisted outdoorsman's life. He seemed to think he could *will* his physical being into the same robust fearlessness he had fashioned for his psyche. First he took up hunting. Poppen, who had acquired the hobby of big-game hunting in Africa, was his role model, though my father pursued the sport in a much more local and humble way—buying a rifle and going on weekend bear hunts at Lake Arrowhead. Then he gave triumphant substance to the persona he'd been borrowing when he wore his gold-braided captain's cap on his weekend hospital rounds.

"Every time proud Danny Weller tells another doctor about the sailing sloop he just purchased, the *Manuiwa* (it won the Balboa-to-Honolulu race three years ago), he adds a few more inches to his length." That was Cholly Angelo's *L.A. Times* column item in 1956.

The *Manuiwa* (man-you-WE-vuh) was a beauty: all burnished, aged wood, and tall sails. Indeed, just looking at a Kodachrome of my father at the helm—his one hand slapped on his thigh, the other gripping the knobby spokes of the old wooden wheel, in that obligatory gold-braided cap, his zippered denim over his navy blue

Lacoste-style shirt—brings back a moment that was both the pinnacle of his life and, though we didn't know it yet, the beginning of the end. Over the decades, I've marveled at how that particular photograph has remained so vivid while other old photos have faded. (I can still see the white peaks in the blue-black ebb tide; I can trace the intricate braiding in each hanging rope.) It's almost as if the crystallineness of the print reflects the moment's larger meaning, for those days were, for our family, a period of last utter clarity before the destruction started.

We would drive down to the slip early on Sunday morning, and, while the crew got things ready, my father would walk over and talk to Roy Rogers, who had the slip next to ours. We would go out for all-day cruises—Daddy propping Lizzie and me, alternately, at the wheel. "Port! Starboard!" he would call out, and we'd pull the lines and duck our heads. Sometimes the *Manuiwa* careened so far over on a tack, we were almost *in* the ocean until the crew righted her back up and, usually, turned on the engine. Once we got entangled in some vegetation, and spunky Laura Budwill, actor Jeff Chandler's personal secretary and our family friend, climbed to the top of the mast in her T-shirt and cutoffs, propped a knife between her teeth, dived in, and cut the growth away.

Frequently Herman, Yvonne, Ellen, and Loring would come onboard. During one such family sail, our mother anxiously hustled all the children downstairs and fretted and scolded her brother and husband for the activity they had planned, but they weren't daunted. They climbed up the mast, tossed a bag of empty beer cans up in the air, and shot them with my father's rifle, which they passed from one to the other. *Pop! Pop!* You could hear the rifle shots from the cramped bunks.

This sport shooting was supposed to be all in good masculine fun, but it felt ominous to me. The contest—the combat—seemed an uncomfortably close symbol of a real joust. I knew that my father did not like my uncle (and I assumed that my uncle was too self-absorbed and unreflective to give his feelings about his sister's proud, slightly bitter-seeming husband much thought). They seemed to be forcing each other into outer-limit camaraderie on a dare.

Pop! Pop! Pop!? Didn't some shtetl *bulabusta* come storming out of some Swiss cuckoo clock in my father's and uncle's psyches, pull these soft-bellied *luftmenschen* by their pink ears, and scold, "You think because you come out to the edge of the world and make good, you can act this way that only the goyim know how to pull off?"

Back up on the deck, we smelled acrid cordite in the salty air. I ran to the edge of the boat, gripped the rope, leaned over, and upchucked my turkey sandwich. As the gulls scoured the swells for chunks of my bready vomit, I thought, "Please God, let it always stay like this." But by then I was worried it wouldn't.

When we weren't on the *Manuiwa* we were poolside at home. Lizzie and I twirled our hula hoops (she, while playing her violin—no mean trick). People came over—some doctors and their wives, my mother's burgeoning collection of Hollywood riffraff buddies, as well as my parent's couple friends: the Mannerses and the Newmans; Irving and Sylvia Wallace (he, finishing the novel that preceded his *Chapman Report* triumph; she, still writing for the fan books) with their kids, David (with whom I used to watch *Kukla, Fran and Ollie* under a tented card table when we were younger) and Amy; and Abe and Muriel Lipsey. (Abe was so quintessentially *the* furrier of that time and place, Joan Didion used his salon to characterize her neurasthenic *Play It As It Lays* heroine the way someone would use Prada to characterize the same kind of decadent young woman today.) Herman and Yvonne did not come to many of these pool parties; ostensibly they had their own—but I wonder now if

their absence was the result of a decision by my father to make events at 520 North Elm Drive a Herman—and Ciro's—free zone.

Ralph Edwards dropped by a couple of times; so did the comedienne Joan Davis, who, at one of our earliest pool parties, brought her plain-Jane daughter Beverly and Beverly's beautiful, strange, semiarticulate boyfriend, whose name was Jimmy Dean. Joan's dirty jokes always drew a circle of guffawing men. Also there would be my father's brother Alex, whose several years of residence with his family in Westwood constituted a kind of psychic life raft for my father. Not that the Alex Wellers liked L.A. any more than my father did—Alex's insufferably affected wife, Annette, disdained the city frequently and provocatively. (At least once my mother, who detested Annette, got the better of her: When Annette wrinkled her nose and asked, "Tell me . . . who is that . . . *Dabbie* Reynolds?" my mother replied, "Oh, Dabbie Reynolds! *Don't* you *know?* She's an opera singer.") With them would be their daughter Mary Lou, with whom Lizzie and I performed home-grown versions of Broadway shows. (A harbinger of Mary Lou's male-hormone-stoking role in *Animal House* may have been the time we affixed her padded bra to our housekeeper Virgie's broomstick and flew it as the American flag in our very own *South Pacific*).

The high point of these parties for me was perching on the top of the backseat of Laura Budwill's MG, with my hair whipping in the wind as we chugged off to Troc Drugs on Sunset Boulevard for more soda and ice. My mother's five-dollar bill was clamped in my retainer case, which I'd tucked in the elastic leg band of my bathing suit.

People would start arriving at noon. There were the glass doors sliding back and forth, and back and forth, wet feet tracking the linoleum lanai tiles, the living room piano alternately giving forth an adult's melodic Gershwin and the kids' crashing "Heart and Soul" and "Chopsticks." My mother bore trays of sliced Nate 'n' Al's water bagels, tubs of whipped cream cheese, strips of lox and whitefish, all under sheets of waxed paper to keep the flies out.

Once, during one of these parties (I was ten) I dashed upstairs to get something out of my bedroom. Daddy was across the hall. He bid me sit on his lap. He clasped his hands around me—nothing unusual there, but then he reached *under* the top of my bathing suit and he started massaging my still-flat-chested body.

That did *not* feel right.

As many times as I'd sat by his bedside, or sat in his bathroom singing "The Yellow Rose of Texas" with him, and as subliminally aware as I'd been that the pleasure I was feeling then was almost on the line—nothing about those other mornings made me squirm—but *that* did.

"Dah-deee . . ." I protested, wiggling off his lap.

He kept tickling. "What?" he asked, chuckling at my inability to articulate (or even understand) my own discomfort.

He released me. Walking downstairs, my head spun. I was so confused (half embarrassed, half elated) by what had just happened, I had to clutch the banister. I was seeing stars, as if I had just been conked on the head by Nancy's chum Sluggo. I had thought my role in my father's life was to be the the pesty, foot-in-mouth daughter. What was he saying with this very different gesture?

Looking back on that incident, I cannot say that I think it met the criterion of sexual abuse (though it was close); rather, I think it was a sign—which my father himself should have had the sense to look at—that he was careening off on a desperate, selfish course, recklessly suspending judgment.

With my father away from early morning to late at night because of his operations, the house took on a darkness. Less and less the sunniness of the weekends on the boat and in the pool could lift what seemed, by 1957, a grayness, a sad tension. My mother's phobia against seeing light under doors across halls (an unextinguished vestige of the toll Sadie's death had taken on her psyche) surely contributed to that atmosphere. Yet the darkness ran deeper than my mother's quirk, unliftable even with the sun making stripes on the pool water in the backyard and dappling the elm leaves in the front. Perhaps the internal grayness was a kind of psychic colorization at the hands of our forebears, warning my parents that they'd wandered too far off the spot on the ground painted for them, that they ought to sail back to safe harbor.

To Lizzie, whose sensors had been fine-tuned by those months in the hospital and whose adoration of our father constituted her salvation, these gray days foreshadowed our father's leaving. She knew that our life would come to that. She saw it like a death on the horizon. The domestic landscape seemed funereal to her. There was our mother, always on the phone with Herman, lumbering home from Ciro's in her pedal pushers, her arms full of food, writing her silly articles in that gray room, with that distracted, pencil-behind-the-ear air of hers.

Lizzie wanted a mother like many of her friends had: pretty, fashionable, social, a woman who knew how to charm and flirt with her husband. Her months in the hospital had steeled her. It was as if, in that most vulnerable state, she made a decision never to be vulnerable. She determined that, despite the physical handicap she would endure for the rest of her life, she would be beautiful, confident, and charismatic: She would *make* herself thus. She would be on the side of the winners. The winners were our father and the kind of women her friends had as mothers: serene and confidently feminine. The losers were the Hovers.

I, on the other hand, wanted to protect our mother. I could sense our father recoiling from her. His illnesses had made him graver and harder to read, leaving her disoriented. She compensated in the Hover way—by leaning in as he leaned back, by projecting anxiety, and by obsessive behavior: My parents had invested heavily in a stock called Cuban-American Oil, and she was so rattled by fear of its devaluation she would call the stock brokerage five, ten, finally fifteen times a day for an update. "You're neurotic, Helen! *Neurotic!*" my father would scream at her.

I sensed that her repetitive calls were to take the temperature of more than just the stock. The calls evinced a deeper desperation. She was trying to wrestle her marriage back to health, trying to figure out why her husband had become so distant and angry. She was also anxious about Ciro's. I deduced, by the way she sometimes talked to Herman, that he was having financial problems. (In fact, the IRS was claiming Herman owed considerable back taxes on revenues from his rear Ciroette Room.)

I read the sorrow and anxiety on my mother's face as if it were a map of my own future face. I knew Lizzie's illness had knocked the wind out of her, had used up what emotional resilience remained after Lenny's death. I'd huddle in her office to console her, but I was being consoled at the same time. The Hawthorne School playground was a daily guerrilla battlefield in which I (as socially off the mark as my mother was) weathered poorly. The right cinch belt, the right charm bracelet, the right zippered clutch purse, the right pageboy or flip, the right "chop" (insult), the right gossip plucked from Sunday night dinner at Hillcrest or Brentwood (the country clubs my parents eschewed) put you among the elect, and failure on these counts was cause for banishment and ridicule. ("Everybody! Throw the ball at Sheila's *face!* Her mother buys her clothes at *Lerner's!*" Vicki Rothberg once shouted to the girls during volleyball.) Huddling with my mother, I was retreating from the fray, overbonding with her (fragile and needy in her own right) to take surcease from the frightening peer world, in which my lack of success flowed more or less directly from my lack of success with my father.

The secret my mother and I carried was this: No one would ever love either of us as much as we loved each other.

Increasingly, I would notice that my mother seemed unfocused, slow talking. Sometimes her words seemed blurry. She had begun taking Miltown to get through the day, and Seconal and Nembutal to sleep. I knew that the druggedness, the sadness, the repetitive phone calls were pieces of a story surrounded by ellipses and left-out passages. I knew there was a part of the narrative of my parents'

marriage that I wasn't getting. Much later, when we talked as two adult women, she would say, biting off each word, "Oh, your father could be so cruel! So cold!" I learned how far his cruelty had driven her. Once she took a trip by herself to Palm Springs. I found out later it was to have an abortion. She had been ready to file for divorce; another baby was out of the question. Another time she took a trip to Laguna Beach. She stayed in a motel on the beach and walked on the sand, trying to figure out if her marriage was worth saving. She came home, of course.

She increased her dosage of tranquilizers. Later she would tell me, "Yvonne would see me in that stuporous state, and she would say, 'Why don't you take a drive through the canyons to clear your mind.' A drive through the canyons, in the state I was in? Can you imagine?"

. . .

Even the culture of the late fifties exuded a grayness, an edgy fore-
boding, as it was reflected in the black-rimmed glasses and pebbly
tweed suits of Charles Van Doren, Steve Allen, and Edward R.
Murrow (vapory smoke from his cigarette dancing over his fur-
rowed brow) on black-and-white television; the A-bomb drills we
had at school, the scrapbook of black-and-white newspaper clip-
pings of narcotics arrests that was our mandatory seventh-grade science project; the subversive humor of Lenny Bruce; the neurotic
humor of Mort Sahl; and the anxiety-music sound tracks of movies
like *The Man with the Golden Arm*. In the girded grimness of this
era, a death knell was tolling over the Sunset Strip. This crowning
moment and resplendent patch of real estate that so much of the
history of American popular entertainment had led to; this culmi-
nation of vaudeville, the Americanized Folies Bergères via Ziegfeld
and Carroll, and the Jazz Age speakeasies and race rooms; this after-
hours release valve for the movie industry, which was tweaked by
studio heads' motives, press agents' skills, and the synthesizing
genius of Billy Wilkerson: all of this was now about to tumble. As
one observing participant, Andy Williams, put it, "There was a
feeling of death on the Strip. Its shining moment was over. In retrospect, those years of the glamorous Sunset Strip nightclubs were like
a supernova."

Herman's friendly rival Charlie Morrison had died, and that
was sad enough. (Everyone was upset that Frank Sinatra gave a
benefit at the Mocambo for Charlie's wife's bills only *after* it was
too late for Charlie to have appreciated the boost. "Why didn't
Sinatra, that big 'humanitarian,' do it when Charlie was *alive*?" my
mother demanded.) That one key loss aside, there were financial

factors: Las Vegas had set a fee standard for name talent that the nightclubs could not match. Then, too, the culture had changed. "Rock 'n' roll was coming in big," Williams said. "It was the end of the era of the small, intimate clubs. Things had changed to people performing in large palaces or in very small rooms or doing dinner theater."

The jovial, under-the-table ethos—the knockabout bonhomie—of the nightclub business was gone. The IRS's sternness with Herman augured a new professionalism. (Just a few years earlier, when Charlie Morrison had lost a year's worth of receipts, he had offered to give the IRS a verbal audit; the agency had accepted.) Suddenly those old days on the Strip—when boxes of money were delivered to mobster Mickey Cohen; when publicists' tips led undersheriffs to send armed men to handcuff strippers; and when cops, gangsters, taxmen, club owners, columnists, stars, patrons, and staff mixed it all up—they were over.

Herman was billed for an enormous sum for back taxes and was given a deadline to deliver the money to the IRS officers.

The new circumstance did not bode well for his marriage. Aunt Yvonne left Uncle Herman—and Herman responded with violence. A series of articles in the Los Angeles papers in October 1957 tell the story.

According to a long October 5 *Examiner* account (which included a photo, captioned "Reconciliation Try That Failed," of a puffy-looking Herman, fifty-one, and a stunning, diffident-seeming Yvonne, twenty-nine, meeting with a judge), Yvonne moved out of the house and into an apartment on September 5 and filed for divorce less than a month later, charging "mental cruelty." They fought over alimony and child support, with Herman claiming that he was worth only half the $600,000 Yvonne claimed were his assets. More darkly, the article disclosed, "In her divorce petition, Yvonne complained Herman had harassed her with repeated phone calls, asked the court for relief from his 'telephone tyranny' and asked for a restraining order."

The restraining order only made my uncle more desperate—and more dangerous.

On October 18, the *Los Angeles Times* ran a story with the headline, "Ciro's Owner Seized at Mother-in-Law's Home," bearing the subhead, "Estranged Wife's Parent in Citizen's Arrest, Charges Disturbing the Peace."

As the paper described the incident:

According to [Yvonne's mother] Mrs. Goff, Hover drove to her home and began ringing the doorbell. She said she knew "he was coming to argue about the children" and she refused to answer the ring.

He kept screaming: "Let me in! I want to see my children!" Mrs. Goff said.

He ran around the house, trying other doors. Then he returned to the front, pulled the screen door off its hook and broke two panes of glass in the front door, she said. He was very profane, she added.

Meanwhile [Yvonne] called the police. . . . When police arrived, Hover was at the front door. Officers escorted him to the West Los Angeles jail where he later was released on his own recognizance. . . .

Hover told reporters, "I've only seen my kids nine days in the last 45. Most of them time I can't find them. She keeps threatening to take 'em back to Illinois where I'll never see 'em again."

A few days later, the *Herald Express* ran a story headlined "Hover's Wife Shuns 'Come Home' Plea," which disclosed that Yvonne was in court to ask for "'reasonable' alimony . . . She listed her needs at $1100 per month."

My aunt was slamming the door on her marriage to my uncle. "Yvonne was adamant, insisting there were obstacles to a reconciliation that could not be overcome."

Throughout the last six years—despite the setbacks to his health, the distractions of the nights at Ciro's, and the weekends on the boat or by the pool—my father's reputation within the neurosurgical community was increasing. In part, he was drinking from a trough of shared success—the patient mortality rate in his field was improving. Technology had advanced; powerful loupes made it easier to see an aneurysm. Bill Sweet was successfuly using the hypothermia he'd adapted from Lougheed on his patients. Beyond the benefit he accrued from his mentors' and academic peers' breakthroughs, my father's own body of surgeries was being recognized. With his serious "Eastern" nose to the grindstone, he'd gained entrance into professional associations. He was admitted to the American College of Surgeons in 1956 and the Los Angeles Society of Neurology and Psychiatry that same year. In 1957, he was inducted into the American Academy of Neurology and into the Pan-American Medical Association, becoming assistant treasurer of the latter's Southern California chapter.

Yet he still put off taking the examination for the all-important American Board of Neurological Surgery. In November 1956, he wrote away for the three-page-long application, but he didn't fill it out and send it in until September 1957. Two months months later, in a letter dated November 16, 1957, Dr. Leonard Furlow, secretary of the American Board of Neurological Surgery, told him that his application had been approved "for examination for certification." Furlow had even pretty much secured a date for him to take the highly selective boards. Furlow wrote:

> I will try, if possible, to include you in the group of candidates to be examined in St. Louis next spring, but I cannot make a definite promise at this time. You should send in to me within the next few months your check for $125, the examination fee, and you should also have submitted to me letters from two physicians who have known you during your period of practice testifying to your medical ethics, your moral character, and the fact that you limit your practice to neurological surgery.

Something else that my father was doing during those months of preparing himself for the professional validation of his lifetime was startlingly destructive. He was actually operating on two tracks: the earnest track, fueled by three decades of hard work and study and deferred gratification . . . and the nihilistic track, fueled by his desperation, anger, and terror at his shortened life. So, at the very same time he was reading the long-solicited instructions of Furlow's, he was also engaged in a penultimately transgressive activity that threatened to undercut, if not destroy, every good thing he had accomplished.

Manuel Reyes started noticing something at Ciro's that was making him very uncomfortable. He had certainly seen a lot of things at the club, in his years as head busboy, waiter, and headwaiter, to which he had turned a blind eye. Events he did not judge—not openly, at least. But this hit close to home.

Years later, with that gentle voice of his, which had been so effec-

tive in placating Howard Hughes and Sammy Davis Jr., Manuel told
me about it. "Back then, at the end, in November 1957, your mom
used to come with you girls early for dinner," he said, remembering
for both of us. "And then you left. But that wasn't all I saw of your
family. An hour or two later your dad would come in by himself."

By *himself?* (My father had always acted so superior to Ciro's, as
if that world kept him from his important work.)

My surprise must have radiated through the phone wire, because
Manuel paused before saying, "That was the time when Herman
was always upstairs in the office."

Apparently my father would go straight from the hospital to
Ciro's. No wonder he seemed never to be home in those dark days of
late fall 1957—those days when my mother was taking more and
more pills, when Ciro's fortunes were slipping, when Herman's
humiliatingly public and violent efforts to get his wife back were so
upsetting her, still viewing, as she did, her brother as the family hero.

"Your father and Yvonne would sit at a table together, right by
the entrance on the left side," Manuel continued. "They would hold
hands. Many times. Soon, almost every night. They tried to do it
when I was not around, but I could see it. A lot of employees—the
waiters, the bartenders—we all noticed. It was very noticeable. We
didn't pay too much attention, but we knew something was going
on, something very strong."

Why on earth would Yvonne and my father choose Ciro's of all
places to carry on in? She had gotten a restraining order against Herman—yet she was sitting in the nightclub? I asked Manuel if he was
certain about the timing of these events (not to mention their substance) and he said yes, he was certain. I can only conclude that my
father's long-bottled rage against Herman and the escalation of his
risk-taking alter ego led him to make such a move, and that Yvonne's

contempt for her husband and her confidence in her own charm with the staff at Ciro's led her to join him in it.

Then, too, they may have been unconsciously following a pattern of high-risk romantic behavior in the place. The aura, the ethos of the Strip and of Ciro's simply drew them in and made them suspend their judgment enough to add their illicit romance to a string of others activated in the hushed, glamorous room's banquettes.

Yvonne's view of her power over the Ciro's staff led her to try to make Manuel her confidant. "I was outside, and Yvonne saw me," Manuel said. She tried to talk to me about it. She said she was going out with your dad. She looked very happy. She wanted me to help her in some way, having to do with her fight with Herman for the kids. I said that I wouldn't help—I wouldn't be on her side. She seemed surprised that I wouldn't."

While this family high-risk drama was being played out in Ciro's booths in the early evening, a far bigger, more potentially explosive and more socially resonant drama was being played out in Ciro's dressing room later in the evening.

This involved the club's favorite-son headliner, Sammy Davis Jr. In a very real sense, it also represented a last gasp of the old system in which studio bosses held power over stars and in which the entertainment industry was in the grip of a segregation mentality.

Sammy—opening his holiday engagement—had been in the midst of a serious love affair with Kim Novak. For both stars, speculated Burt Boyar, Davis's good friend and *Yes I Can* coauthor, the romance was all the more passionate for its being inflammatory ("he, a black man, and she, the whitest of white women") and forbidden. "Sammy," Boyar said, "was being driven to Kim's house in Malibu; he'd duck in the backseat of the car so the *Confidential* 'reporters,' who'd gotten wind of the romance, wouldn't see him."

The Ciro's staff had seen Sammy through other love affairs with white women; they had cheered him on and had attended the mixed after-hours parties he hosted or invited them to. Now they were worried about him. Now something wasn't going well. "Sammy was angry and crying in his dressing room during rehearsals," Ciro's maître d' Johnny Oldrate told me the last time I spoke to him in 1997. "And before the first show of that engagement, he was crumpled up in a ball in the corner."

Burt Boyar gave me what I believe is the most authoritative account of the myth-and-misinformation-shrouded events that had led to his friend's preshow breakdown: Davis had been about to propose to Novak, and it was expected that she would accept his proposal. Word got out among studio insiders that their engagement was imminent. Harry Cohn, the head of Columbia Pictures, with whom Novak had a contract, did not want his cool blond movie goddess to marry a Negro. It was out of the question.

Just before starting the Ciro's rehearsals, Davis had been visited, in Las Vegas, by a man he was friendly with who had a message for him from Cohn: There was a contract out to break Sammy's legs if the romance with Kim Novak continued. "Cohn was behind it," Boyar said. "Definitely."

So the holiday season at Ciro's was shaping up as a tense one. The staff seemed to realize that this booking was make or break. (As it turned out, that would be the last holiday season in the club's history. Its doors would soon be forced closed.) Would Sammy—angry, preoccupied, and caught in this romantic tragedy—be able to hold it together and burst onto the stage with that cover-charge-worthy smile on his face, that amazing staccato tap dancing, that hilarious shtick?

Would Herman come down from the office and see his freshly estranged wife romancing his sister's husband?

"One day Herman did come downstairs," Manuel told me. "I

saw him standing in the back, in the hallway, from the side of the bar, in the dark, watching them. Just watching."

Manuel drew a breath. "He saw everything," he said. "I was afraid something was going to happen."

Ciro's got through Christmas and New Year's 1957–58 by the skin of its teeth. Sammy lived up to his billing—no one in the audience knew he had almost had a breakdown. (Shortly afterward, Davis contacted a black showgirl he knew, Loray White, and, according to Boyar, paid her $25,000 to marry him.)

As for the other drama: My uncle had apparently taken in the scene, at the table in the main room, between Danny and Yvonne with something less than equanimity. He began to plan its final chapter. A few days after New Year's he casually elicited from my mother the fact that Danny was taking the girls out to dinner the next Wednesday, at 6 P.M. January 8. She never knew why he was asking.

Drenched in Sunset Strip melodrama, intending to avenge his fall from professional, financial, and marital grace with one grand gesture that unsolicitedly stretched to include his sister's honor, my uncle drove his car from 606 North Bedford to 520 North Elm at 6:45 on January 8. He parked under the elm trees across the street.

He waited for my father.

Part IV

Chapter Twelve

BEVERLY HILLS: 1958–1959

My mother was in the process of selling back her full-length mink coat to Abe Lipsey's salon when Herman attacked my father. In preparation for the privation she feared after her divorce (which Lizzie and I had known nothing about), she was going to cash in her assets. She had left for Lipsey's showroom shortly after Lizzie and I had left with our father for Ah Fong's.

When she drove up and saw the street half closed off while detectives were still milling around, she got out of the car without turning off the lights or the engine and ran up the center of the asphalt, terrified that Lizzie or I had been in an accident. After the officers disabused her of that awful belief, they walked her into the house and told her what had happened.

She fainted.

As it turns out, Lizzie and I had been taken to the Lipseys' Benedict Canyon home. Our mother drove up the canyon to get us. Her head shaking, her mouth open so that puffs of steamy air issued forth with each of her grunting sobs, she stood with her arms extended like a scarecrow. I had never seen her so beside herself.

Muriel Lipsey held her on one side, their butler held her on the other, and they hobbled with her into the next room like nurses walking a stroke victim. "I didn't know. I *didn't* know," she kept repeating. "Good God—you must believe me!" That plea was occasioned by the fact that our father, from his hospital bed, was accusing our mother of ordering a hit on him.

The next day, when Lizzie and I went to visit our father in the hospital, he would not let our mother come in—he had turned her into the Enemy, along with the obvious enemy, Herman. In the rearview mirror her barbituate-reddened eyes reflected the disbelief, the pleading, and the blackmailed servitude of the egregiously falsely accused, stuck in the middle of a nightmare.

Leaving our mother waiting in the car, Lizzie and I entered Cedars of Lebanon and were led by solicitous nurses deeper and deeper into the hospital. We had been in that hospital dozens of times before, but always *with* Daddy, never to visit him as a patient. That role change, too, was disorienting. We'd also never been in the cardiac intensive care unit. The huge chamber—with beds around the edges, with a city's worth of buttons and blinkers and cords and tubes; the intimidatingly numerous nurses whipping around without stopping for breath—projected a dire sickness that sent a jolt to my temple, as if I'd just swallowed, too fast, a too-cold piece of Fudgsicle.

Our father was in a corner bed, separated from an old woman by curtains as flimsy as those in the Livingston's dressing room. I bristled on behalf of his dignity. He was under a beachball-taut oxygen tent, his face all scratched. He looked ten years older and ten pounds thinner than he had looked the day before. His eyes were watery. His arms were loosely straight by his sides, jutted out a bit at the elbows, like dolls' arms in doll-box packaging. Both hands were fisted.

"Now, I'll just stand right here, Doctor," the nurse sang, helpfully, "while your daughters talk to you."

"The hell you will," he shot back. "I'll have a moment with each of my daughters *alone*, god*dam*mit."

Flustered, she raised her hand to her face, as if to demur—then caught herself. She exited.

I smiled at my indomitable father, but clearly, that performance had taxed him. He was too weak to smile. Hot tears grooved my cheeks, tickling the side of my nose annoyingly. I sniffled.

A generic hospital-supply tissue box sat on the slideable metal tray that also contained a meal card, a rabbi's name, and his University of Louisville ring (the only one he wore), which had been sawed off his swollen finger. I nodded at the tissue vaporing up from the corrugated slot, silently referring to our Kleenex joke He nodded back, appreciating my subtlety. I plucked the tissue, wiped my tears, the gooey feel of which I suddenly couldn't have cared less about.

"*I* love you," I said, plaintive despite myself. Even under normal circumstances he hated it when I was too emotional; now it seemed that too much emotion blown his way could actually be dangerous.

He nodded as if to say, I love you back.

The tissue bit, the nodding—why had it taken *this* for me to finally key in to the graceful understatement that was the best way to have a relationship with him?

He closed his eyes, wearily. I'd seen that gesture before; it always meant he was thinking, and he was a little sad. Now I felt he also had something to tell me. (The reason for Herman's attack, after all, had not been explained to either me or Lizzie.) He seemed in no hurry to do so—also very in-character.

I assumed (as Lizzie must have, too) that what he had to tell us was the bombshell news that Lizzie and I had been told, earlier that morning, by our mother: They were getting divorced. That was enough to swallow. Herman's attack on him, we were given to believe, had to do with bad blood between the two men (I had cer-

tainly glimpsed it, at least from my father), probably now exacer-
bated by a brother's macho protectiveness of his sister.

I blew him a kiss, and gave Lizzie her turn to sit with him. She
got no more information than I did.

In school the next day, it became excruciatingly apparent to me that
my family's ears were burning. My classmates' parents had obviously talked about what had happened at the breakfast table. The
boys I didn't worry about—they didn't care. It was the raptorlike
girls who caused me terror.

In Home Ec—where we were graded, by prim and dandruff-
afflicted Miss Burditt ("Miss Birdshit" behind her back), on the
neatness of our three by five cards, and on our correct abbreviations
(c., tsp., T., lb.) in recipes for things like Apple Betty—every set of
eyes was on me.

At recess, a bunch of girls stood in a knot, flamboyantly whispering, "*Pss pss pss pss.*"

"Did you *hear*?" The gleeful bellicosity of the whisper tripped an
all-points alarm inside my head. It warned, "Don't listen!" But the
words were already snaking into my eardrums, "Her father was *living* with her aunt. Isn't that dis*gusting*? Hillbillies do that."

I think I'd be capable of replaying every contemptuous sneer,
pause, syllable, and hiss in that sentence in my ears, in my heart,
and in my brain on my deathbed.

So *that* is why Herman had come and done that.

That night I sat in my bedroom, staring at a shoe box in the
closet. *I want to be dead*, I thought. *I want to be dead and in that shoe
box.* That's how I would pay my parents and uncle for this!

It was my mother who struggled with the lion's share of the pain.
Over the next weeks and months she descended into a spiral of

hell. Her mind was simply broken by Herman's attack on Danny—
and the reason that lay behind it. Her thinking had no clarity. She
virtually stopped functioning. She fought an obsessive-compulsive
spiral unstoppable by medication. "No one knows what a nervous
breakdown is until you've experienced one," she said at the end of
her life. "It's not like depression; it's like a raging cancer. It completely takes over and destroys your mind."

She rarely left the bedroom. In the morning I'd wake, hear the
faint hum of her zombielike words—"Why did it happen? Why . . . ?
Why . . . ?"—issuing from the telephone receiver that had been
pressed to her ear since 5 A.M. Little by little, her regular friends were
begging off listening to her; she found replacements to take her calls,
to be her horse whisperer. I'd walk to her bedroom door, my ears
helplessly perked despite myself. I'd stand there, as frozenly avid and
scared as a mother trying to divine from her teenager's mutterings if
his deep, dark secret is kleptomania, arson, or homosexuality.

She had become *her* mother, my grandma Celia (who had
promptly had a stroke, from all that had happened, and had to be
taken from her apartment to a nursing home), wallowing in grief
over Sadie's death on Arlington Avenue. And I had become her
keeper.

Lizzie and I would make ourselves breakfast. We huddled
together during that period like animals in a storm, and we never
talked about the horrible events. We were simply too embarrassed
to acknowledge verbally that our parents' lives, *our* lives, had come
to such a disaster. She looked fragile and solemn across the breakfast
table. A prosecutor and our father's attorney had come to interview
her several times; each of them took copious notes as she sat,
shaken, recounting events. "You are the only eyewitness," both men
had told her. They told her there would be a trial—but there was no
trial. My sister believes that our mother's tremendous worry about

her welfare (she would have to sit on the witness stand and testify) was somehow behind the trial's mysterious cancellation. Herman pleaded guilty to a charge of aggravated menacing and did no jail time.

Despite our shared vulnerability and our love, I felt a distancing in Lizzie—even from me. She had always been our father's ally; at that point she had become his stand-in. Our mother (and Herman, mainly, of course)—was the Enemy—and I was the proxy for them.

Lizzie and I did not know it at the time, but this is what happened to my father: After he was released from Cedars he moved to a house in the Hollywood Hills, which he had rented as a trysting place for himself and Yvonne months beforehand. Ellen and Loring lived with them. Herman was barred. My father became my first cousins' stepfather-to-be. My aunt would soon become my stepmother. My cousins would become my step siblings.

He recuperated in that house slowly. He was bedridden, unable to work or drive. Operating was out of the question. While Herman endured the disgrace of conviction on a criminal charge, a closed and shuttered nightclub, and an imminent bankruptcy, my father also seemed to have lost the career he had so earnestly fought for.

Two invented lives—destroyed and broken.

In mid-March this letter arrived at my father's—abandoned— office:

March 11, 1958

Dear Dr. Weller:
    You are scheduled for examination by the American Board

of Neurological Surgery on Sunday, May 25, 1958 [in] St. Louis, Missouri.

> Very truly yours,
> Leonard T. Furlow, M.D.
> Secretary

On March 21 he wrote back:

> Dear Doctor Furlow:
>   In reply to your letter of March 11th which was just forwarded to me, I am convalescing from a recent illness and will not be able to take the examination on May 25, 1958.
>   Would greatly appreciate having my name placed on the list for the next coming examination.
>   Thanking you in advance for your cooperation, I am,
> > Yours very truly,
> > Daniel Weller, M.D., F.A.C.S.

His new letterhead also bore the engraved letters of his new status as a Fellow in the American College of Surgeons, for all the good that hard-fought distinction would have done him then.

A small article in the *New York Times*, datelined Las Vegas, April 16, read:

> Herman Hover, former proprietor of Ciro's on the Sunset Strip in Los Angeles, which is now out of business, was divorced here today by by his wife, Yvonne.
>   Mrs. Hover—who also won restoration of her maiden name, Yvonne Ealy—was awarded custody of the couple's two children. . . .

The last line announced that:

Mrs. Hover—or Miss Ealy—is now a hostess on the Hollywood TV show, *Queen for a Day*.

We suddenly had no money. My father still accused my mother of having Herman try to kill him and had frozen our accounts. We gave up the pool man. Debris and leaves floated on top of the water, despite my mother's attempts to use the long-handled cleaning net. The house was a mess; it wasn't that we didn't try to clean it— Lizzie and I immediately drew up chores, and we performed them, but our mother's chaotic state of mind defeated our best-laid plans. Ruth Page remembers walking into our house in early summer 1958—"and it was like a storm hit—bedding, stuff all over the floor. It looked like it could never be cleaned up, even with an army of help. She had come apart, your mother. Her whole world was disrupted. The house looked like what Helen felt like."

Once when my sister was in Ralph's Market with our mother she saw our mother try on a pair of sunglasses. Then she took the price sticker off the lens and affixed it to the bottom of a cake box she was holding and kept the glasses on. My sister was quietly terror stricken. "Aren't you going to pay for those, Mom?" she asked. Our mother was silent. She had shoplifted! Another time, when Lizzie came home with a purchase she had just made—the popular Purple People Eater doll (named for the novelty hit song)—my mother barked at her angrily in front of others, "We can't afford that! Return it!" She made her eleven-year-old daughter go back to the store and get her money back. My mother's outburst was her response to Lizzie's quiescence, her diffidence, and especially to her being Danny's favorite daughter.

One day our mother announced, with forced ceremony, "Lizzie

just got her period!"—as if she were welcoming a new sorority pledge to the ranks of the two already menstruating females in the household. My sister's face was white with contempt. She wasn't just angry that her privacy had been violated. *I don't want to be in this club of pathetic women,* her face said.

While Lizzie dreamed of joining our father, I had struck on a novel way to short-circuit our mother's obsessive morning keenings. I'd set my alarm clock for 4:45, go downstairs, lift the downstairs phone off the hook, dial one digit (to clear the phone of a dial tone), put the receiver right by the revolving spindle plate of the record player, and load a bunch of LPs on the notched silver pole. Then I'd flip the knob so the first would plop down and start sending loud, happy music—Sinatra's "Come Fly with Me," Dean Martin's "That's Amore," and my personal favorite, Frankie Avalon's "Dede Dinah"—into her ear the minute she woke up, grabbed the phone, and tried to start her morning's baleful litany.

On the last day of seventh grade I brought a friend home from school, Sharon Weisman. She wasn't really a friend, she was a Popular Girl I wanted to make into one, and her attitude was cool and superior. My mother and Lizzie were both out. The house was so quiet and dark, I walked around turning lights on all over and chattering away to pretend we still lived like Sharon and her family.

We began some project, and I went up to my mother's office to get a stapler. As I pulled open the narrow secretary drawer, instead of the flat, bare, felt-lined drawer bottom, I beheld instead a sheet of her HELEN HOVER WELLER stationery with her newly messy, shaky handwriting all over it.

The letter began, "To whomever finds me."

"*Whom*ever"—that *m* made it serious.

"To whomever finds me . . ."—that's as far as I got. I couldn't make out the words in the first paragraph because my heart was pounding like a log being rammed by police at a door, and the lines on the paper were jumping too much for me to focus.

The second paragraph started, "Weller."

She was calling my father by his last name. She sounded like an army sergeant barking orders to his troops.

"Weller," she wrote, "if you find the gun . . ."

If you find the gun?!

I stopped reading. I started concentrating, instead, on *not* having that bowel movement in my new, cute, plaid bermudas.

Did I telephone one of my mother's friends? I don't remember, but I don't think so. The surrealism of the nightmare we were in, the pieces of the story that I did not know, my overwhelming embarrassment and shame at the events that were slapping us in the face, the lack of anyone's concerted attempts to help Lizzie and me through it: All of that militated against my doing anything other than simply pretending it wasn't happening. To this day I don't know how I got through the next two hours, acting as if it were an uneventful day, trying to pretend I was every bit as blasé and coolly sarcastic as my guest was.

My mother came home. She hadn't committed suicide, after all. Well, hallelujah. For the moment, at least.

"Hello, Sheila, this is Roberta Lee Gill." This was my mother's new friend, whose librarianish voice streamed through the receiver. She drove a brown and beige Dodge, carried a sensible pocketbook, and lived in some part of L.A. (which she pronounced *law-SANG-luss*) I'd never heard of. She not only probably made but also *ate* the food Miss Burditt made us write recipes for—Apple Betty, Swiss chard, and hanger steak.

"Let me come by tomorrow and take you to lunch at Van De Kamp's," she said.

Uh-oh. What was that all about?

"Go with Lee; let Lee Gill take you to lunch; Lee is *such* a lovely person." My mother's Seconaled voice floated up from her pillows as if she were a woman dying of childbirth in the back of a covered wagon.

Slowly, a new cadre of strange people were replacing my mother's friends. Beadie Manners listened to her as much as she could while still raising a family. Ruth Page, too, was sympathetic. So was Laura Budwill. (I remember overhearing Laura making a phone call from our lanai, saying, "It isn't the same here without Danny.") But my mother tested the limits of all of them; she had gotten profoundly demanding. Her mind had been invaded by demons; her mouth ran a tape of misery, terror, and regret ("Why did it happen?" "What will I do?" "I want to die!"), and that called for a replenishment of troops.

A few she found at the Hollywood Women's Press Club meetings. Some were people—publicists, Ciro's staff—whom she had let come over and use our swimming pool and who were now returning the favor. Finally, others were just decent souls recruited as emergency stand-ins by her exasperated friends. Like brain-damaged children who need round-the-clock volunteers for "patterning" therapy, my mother now required round-the-clock voices on the other end of the telephone.

There was fervent right-winger Lee, administrative assistant to the president of the Fluor Corporation, who was a leader of the John Birch Society. There was kindly Bess Soloway, whose cotton housedresses and naive wide-eyedness gave no hint of the fact that she was Bugsy Siegel's sister. There was a mother–son German combo, Erica and Hans Rusche. Hans could have been crowned Mr.

Bavaria—you could hear the oompah accordion in his voice and see the bibbed lederhosen in his dopey, handsome countenance. Erica was a hardy, six-foot-tall Teuton whose husband had been a major in the German army (since she was willing to take care of stroke victim Grandma, my mother let that little background detail pass) and who smilingly exclaimed, "Ach, shit!" so often that Lizzie and I refered to her as Erica-Shit. The queen of the heap—my mother's savior—was a stooped, homely, saintly little woman named Dora Albert. Despite an unfortunate persona (she had a voice like a loud, raspy Minnie Mouse and she practically invented the concept of eating with your mouth open) and a level of naïveté and literalness that made Edith Bunker look like Kathleen Turner in *Body Heat*, Dora was an ace Hollywood reporter. Since my mother was by then non compos mentis as well as broke, Dora would accompany her to her interviews and then come home with her and write the stories with (or *for*) her, line by line. Chauffeuring them was Dora's jovial simpleton husband, TV repairman Sam Heend, who—while Dora and my mother were upstairs arguing over quotes in their Russ Tamblyn opus—would sit in the lanai, smiling his half-toothless smile, cracking his knuckles, wiggling his eyebrows, and asking Lizzie and me, "What's new in your zoo?" Dora and Sam always kissed on the lips when she descended from those sessions.

Right after the waitress clomped off in her wooden shoes with our menus, Lee Gill cut to the chase. "Boarding school. It's time for you and Elizabeth to go to boarding school."

"*What?*" I was taken aback. Even in those living-nightmare days I had never thought of *that* solution. Kids in L.A. didn't go to boarding schools. Only the poor, pathetic movie stars' kids were meted out such a dreary fate. Or kids like Michael DeToth, who was a movie star's kid *and* a troublemaker, so he'd had two reasons to be shipped off to some military academy. *"Why?"*

"Because," her hands were clasped on the doily place mat, as if over a hymnal, "your mother cannot take care of you."

"Yes, she can! Yes, she can!"

"She cannot." Those hands were so tightly knuckled that I was afraid they'd emit the Whoopee Cushion sound. "She cannot even take care of herself."

"No, no, no!" I shouted.

The waitresses at the condiments island turned around and stared at me, their lacy-bonneted heads like a row of ducklings.

"Sheila—" Lee Gill had ungripped her hands and was clutching the ends of the table. "Look the truth in the eye." (This was a line from her pamphlet, "Eisenhower the Communist.") "You and Elizabeth cannot stay with your mother, in that condition, in that house. It is dangerous."

Lee had been the one to come up with boarding school, having realized that all the other options were not good ones. (Living with our infirm father, enraged as he was at our mother and nurturing his romance with the cold and by-me-detested Yvonne in a secret love nest, was out of the question. Herman was a pariah, and Liz and I thought him an attempted murderer. There were no other relatives with whom we felt close.)

"But I'm scared to go to boarding school," I squeaked. "I've only been to sleepaway camp for two weeks. Ever."

She graced me with the indulgent smile of one explaining the realities of life to someone who didn't know that the Los Angeles Department of Water and Power was under the direct control of Khruschchev. "Boarding school," she said, "is character building."

When Lee dropped me off I ran up into my mother's bedroom.

She was, of course, on the phone, raspingly unloading that unceasing lament that had caused her to lose all her real friends.

"*What* boarding school are you talking about?" I demanded.

She raised her head like a person coming out of heavy anesthesia.

"Lizzie and I are *not* going to boarding school!" I insisted.

Her head wafted softly. She looked vaguely past me, as if she were trying to pick out a face in a crowd. "Borden's . . . Ice Cream?" she inquired.

It was hopeless. She was hopeless. I couldn't leave her, and we both knew it. I collapsed on her and held her like a baby.

To hold your mother like a baby—how nauseating.

"Girls, we are going to have an adventure," our mother announced one day toward the end of the summer. Even though she would rally enough, now and then, to put on a brave face, she didn't sound adventurous. She sounded, as usual, drugged. We were sitting under a purloined umbrella on purloined deck chairs at Ocean House, eating her homemade, hand-packed lunch of . . . hard-boiled eggs. A Chordettes song was on somebody's transistor radio. Young Jewish Adonises bounced up and down at the volleyball net, little white zinc-oxide triangles on their noses. Instead of being on the *Manuiwa* (sold, at a boat auction), or in our (by then thistle-, pollen-bud-, and banana-frond-clogged) swimming pool, we parked in a lot at the adjacent public beach, shlepped with our beach bags from its dirty sand across the Maginot Line to the impeccably manicured sand of members-only Ocean House (on the other side of which stood the anti-Semitic Jonathan Club), and squatted.

I was too busy praying to God that none of the Popular Girls (who were leaning back on their elbows with their legs out, flirting with the zinc-oxided volleyball gods) would recognize me, to hear much of what she was jabbering about. Through my fog of social ter-

ror I made out these snippets of phony gaiety: "... visitors ...!"
"... guests ...!" "... like one of those little New England inns
your father and I used to stay at. ...." "It will be *fun!*"

Oh, no. Did she mean we were going to take in boarders?

Yes, indeed.

The day Erica-Shit and Hans came over to pack up whatever my
father's movers hadn't carted away from his study and scrub the
room to a Third-Reich high gloss was the saddest, angriest day of
my life. What were these people doing picking through this sacred
lair where he'd dictated his cases, where he'd pored over the words
of Cushing and Dandy and Poppen—and the Talmud!? Out went
what office furniture was left. In went a metal cot and a cheap knotty
pine dresser.

More to the point: In came Marjorie the secretary, courtesy of a
Room to Let ad my mother had placed in the Beverly Hills *Citizen.*

Marjorie was a staid, unhappy woman of modest means and a
certain age. Her emptied Cutty Sark bottles gave the butler's pantry
a Listerine-ish smell, and a semicircle of her drying girdles lay
draped like nautical flags over the towels in the powder room. Sometimes I noticed Marjorie looking at me—when she rinsed out her
Ciro's tumbler in the sink while I was doing my homework, or when
she peeled back the thin tin foil cover of her Swanson's turkey dinner. Once she offered to take Lizzie and me to an art museum. Why,
how marvelous! our mother thought.

Lizzie had something else to do that day, so it was I, alone, who
trundled forth in Marjorie's dilapidated car. As we drove down
Wilshire I gazed longingly at the LaBrea Tar Pits. I would rather be
stuck in the black guck with those ancient reptiles than living the life
that our life had unaccountably turned into.

As we walked among the paintings and sculptures, I grew dis-
tinctly uncomfortable. The museum rooms were huge, but every-

where I turned, Marjorie was right on top of me. I walked left, she was right in my face. I walked right, same thing. I could count the moles on her cheek and smell her Clove gum.

"I feel good, being here with you," she said. "Do you feel that way, too?"

I have no idea what I said. The room spun.

Coming home, we hit every red light in the history of the traffic system of Los Angeles County. I bolted out the passenger-side door before Marjorie put her foot on the brake pedal. "Mommy! Mom! We're back!" I yelled, as I frantically depressed the front door latch.

Never had that dark, disheveled, dust-ball-filled house looked so good.

She was sitting in the lanai, staring at the TV screen, her eyes wide and sorrowful. The cigarette pincered in her fingers had sprouted a two-inch-long hot grey ash. It plopped in the crotch of her Capri pants. The red sparks leapt like fireflies.

"Mo-om! You're on fire!" I rushed to the bar, ran water into a pitcher.

I hurled the water in her lap. It must have been freezing cold. She bounced. Then tears streamed.

At first I thought she was crying because she'd set herself on fire and didn't know it. Then I thought she was crying because I had done her the indignity of throwing ice water on her, as if she were a house plant. I started sobbing lightly in apology. Then I saw what she was staring at on TV—why she was *really* crying.

"And for *this* Queen for a Day," the announcer's voice boomed, "a Norge refrigerator and a Longine-Wittnauer watch."

There she was: Aunt Yvonne, twirling around, looking calm and beautiful, just divorced from Uncle Herman—and Daddy's fiancée. "A dinner for four at the Pig-and-Whistle . . . a selection of lovely Coro jewelry . . . and . . . a Hotpoint electronic range!"

We had studied in U.S. history how John Adams and John Quincy Adams were the only father-and-son presidents. However, where else but in this dark house of shame could one study the one and only simultaneously ditched brother–sister combination? What kind of an award—what gold stars on your record as attractive people—do a brother and sister get when both their spouses bolt on them, violently and contemptuously and totally, for one another?

My mother and I fell into each other's arms, both crying big, hoarse, orgiastic, ugly tears. I couldn't look at her face—I was too humiliated for both of us.

Many years later I saw the documentary on Big and Little Edie, Jackie Kennedy Onassis's aunt and cousin, who lived together in an East Hampton estate called Grey Gardens and dressed as twins, cohabiting in a state of bizarre, eccentric mother-daughter symbiosis and deshabille. I immediately cringed and thought: *But for the mercies of sanity, that could have been me and my mother.*

Finally, as the embarrassing crying petered out to awkward simpers, I detached from her, bolted upright, and straightened my wrinkled dress. "Let's not watch this anymore!" I said, snapping off the TV. My fury at Aunt Yvonne, my repulsion at Marjorie the secretary, and my humiliation at such a scene with my mother were battling for ownership of the knot in my stomach.

I turned the knob to what I usually watched at that hour: *American Bandstand.* How did Justine and Frank manage to keep their stiff, mountainous hair and the expressions on their untouching, talking-but-unsmiling faces so immobile as they dipped and swooped to the Platters, the Chimes, and Connie Francis? That retrograde world beckoned like a gleaming oasis in the desert of my misery in that modern, sunny, privileged life of mine.

. . .

I told my mother that Marjorie was making me feel uncomfortable, and quickly she was asked to leave. But we got two more boarders—a mother-daughter team, Corita and Marcia Humeston.

Corita came first. She was a nudist, sun worshipper, and health food aficionado. She had the face of Dorothea Lange's Dust Bowl woman. Her skin was so leathery and black, and so bereft of adipose, her torso resembled a bag of Death Valley bones. Her gait was wide pelvised and stick-figure-like, as if she didn't dare let the insides of her thighs meet, lest the fried-wonton-like-consistency skin of the one thigh should damage the similarly parched skin of the other.

Corita wore the same dress every day—a see-through tan shirtwaist, with not a stitch of underwear beneath it. It wasn't really a dress, it was a wrap she threw on when she wasn't baking herself by the (leaf- and twig-shrouded) pool or hobbling along with a wooden pole—like some wizened Donner party refugee, with a dowsing rod—rustling the dirt in that little garden of sprouts and legumes she'd planted by Lizzie's and my hopscotch court. Through her gauzy wrap, her raisinlike nipples and her pubic mound glowed through the glass lanai doors like beacons from a lighthouse. Lizzie and I could not fail to see them as we spooned cornflakes into our mouths in the morning—and as we settled in with *77 Sunset Strip* at night after doing our homework. In these seminude backyard walkabouts Corita was accompanied by her weimeraner. The dog had the discomfiting habit of nuzzling up to her private parts. He slept in my father's study along with Corita. None of us asked any questions.

Corita was a frugal soul. She took all her—home-grown—meals

in a constantly rewashed pickle jar. I don't know what rent my mother charged Corita, but they often argued over it.

To get more revenue, my mother rented her office, upstairs, to Corita's daughter, Marcia. Marcia Humeston was that most exciting thing to me: a beatnik. She used a hair iron. (After using it—the upstairs had that great fried-hair smell—she would walk out on the front balcony and brush it until it fanned out in the moonlight.) She listened to Chet Baker. She bought her clothes at Jax (but, unlike the Popular Girls who also did so, she looked like you were supposed to look in them: as if she had just tumbled off the back of an existentialist's motorcycle). She was dating actor John Ireland (who was Corita's age), and they would drive off in his sports car to the Aware Inn or down to Synanon at the beach, where people talked about their heroin addiction and played bongo drums.

Corita and Marcia fought like barn animals. Upstairs, downstairs, upstairs, downstairs, we always heard their screaming matches: Corita's Okie accent, Marcia's Actor's Studio growl, Corita, Marcia, Corita, Marcia—in escalating pitch and timbre. Once bony, knobby, blackened, naked old Corita threw something at her daughter—maybe it was her cleaned-out pickle jar. Whatever it was, Marcia then descended on her mother like a gutter hawk on carrion. Shortly after that my mother kicked them both out, forgoing the extra income.

Having recuperated enough to drive, our father would come and take us out on Sundays. He would drive down from the hills where he lived with Yvonne and idle his Cadillac on Elm Drive and Lomitas, facing south; our mother would drive us *up* Elm Drive, to across the street from where he parked.

They never looked at each other.

Daddy was always angry. He would take us to Canter's. The ease, the loveliness, the dailiness of being in a family with him—it was all gone. He and Lizzie had their own sweet language, but for me there was such a crashing distance I would almost have preferred not to go with him at all.

Once we were sitting at a booth in the busy restaurant, Lizzie and I next to each other, facing our father. Lizzie and I noticed something, in unison.

I don't know whose sandalled foot first kicked the other's under the table, but we didn't dare look in each other's eyes. That's how much we feared *he* would notice *we* had noticed something.

There, in a booth not fifteen feet across the restaurant, right in our line of vision, sat Uncle Herman.

We both hated Uncle Herman with a vengeance. Whenever we caught our mother speaking to her brother (her voice larded with anxiety and disappointment—he had gone, overnight, from her hero to her millstone), we'd run into the room and disconnect the call. We *hated* Herman.

We ached to send our detested uncle a message: Hide! Duck! Get down on your fat body, like the weasel you are, and *crawl* out! We knew if our father saw him, he would lunge at him in fury and beat the shit out of him. He'd have another heart attack. He'd die on the restaurant floor.

Our mental telepathy must have been received. When we next dared to move our eyes in his direction, we saw that Herman was holding a menu up against his face. It was a very unsubtle gesture. How long could he keep it there? Had he told the person he was dining with, whoever it was, why he was doing something as absurd as holding a menu against his right cheek, like a geisha's fan?

The menu stayed up until we finished our meal and got up and left. Our father walked right past him without seeing him.

In the back of the car, when we pulled out of the parking lot, I could feel my sister's labored, relieved, almost doglike breath in my lungs. And she could feel mine in hers.

My mother had a new friend, Zeke Manners's sister, who had just moved into the neighborhood with her two daughters. As "Vicki Joyce," she had been a band singer (and, from her pictures, an absolute beauty) in the late thirties. Much later, during her divorce, her experience with the bad antidepressants then on the market had made her only more depressed. She understood the despair and disorientation my mother was feeling.

On January 10, 1959, Lizzie and I gave our mother a surprise forty-ninth birthday party. We baked a Betty Crocker cake. We bought streamers at Newberry's and laced them over all the Degas lithographs and fake Utrillos. We invited all her weird new friends, the people who took her twenty-five daily phone calls (each!) and who drove over in their old Dodges and Plymouths when she cried out in the night and threatened to kill herself.

Dora and Sam took her out on some ruse while the assemblage came over—Lee Gill with her John Birch Society tracts, Hans and Erica bearing bratwurst, sweet little gossipy Bess Soloway, a few old Ciro's hands who had kept in touch, Laura Budwill, Beadie Manners, and Beadie's sister-in-law Vicki. When our mother walked in the door everyone shouted, "Surprise! Happy birthday!"

As the photographs show, she looked like a ghoul that night. Her eyes were watery, and she had lost thirty pounds but in the wrong part of her body. With the strongest effort, she had managed to slap a faraway half smile on her face, like a hostage in a ransom picture taken by kidnappers. It was one year and two days since her world had crashed. She had wanted to jump out of her skin for that long. She told me later, "I just kept thinking, 'The girls will be better off without me. I've made a mess of my life. I don't deserve them.'"

A few days later she walked out the front door with a suitcase. She checked into a motel on Doheny and Santa Monica. The suitcase was full of sleeping pills. She guzzled them, and guzzled them, and guzzled them. She called friends from her past—Charlotte Simensky in New York and Edith Weiss from her old Fawcett days. In a shaky voice ("a whispery, Baby Snooks voice," Edith Weiss told me), she told them to "please take the girls, please take care of my children." As she weakened and her voice grew fainter, it occurred to her, with a panic that worked its way through her stupor, that these people she was calling were laughing at her. They didn't believe her! (Edith Weiss strongly denies she was laughing. She says she was very concerned.) Even half comatose, that alarmed her. She *had* to find a guardian to place us with before she laid her head on that pillow.

At the very end, when she couldn't sit up, she called Vicki Heller. Of all those she'd called, only Vicki understood the seriousness in my mother's voice.

"Helen, where *are* you?! Tell me where you are!" Vicki demanded as she jumped up in her breakfast room on Foothill Road.

My mother said nothing. She had passed out.

In the Hellers' bedroom, Vicki's fourteen-year-old daughter Peggy grabbed the phone and jiggled the button, SOS-style. Miraculously, the motel operator got on the line and identified the motel's location. The Hellers called an ambulance.

The paramedics got there in time—barely. My mother was transferred, comatose, to Edgecombe Sanitarium. Lizzie and I were hustled over to the Hellers' house, with a day's change of clothes, our cats, and our homework. Our mother's stomach was pumped out, but still she did not recover. Vicki Heller told Lizzie and me, "Your mother is getting help. She's in a sanitarium. You'll stay here with us until she's received her medicine and is ready to come home again." She then sent her housekeeper back to our house to get more clothes for us.

Vicki worried. So did my mother's other friends. All that whispery talk of hers—"Lee, take the girls . . ."; "Ruth, take the girls . . ." Would one of them now *have* to take us?

From Edgecombe, our mother was transferred to Cedars. She was hooked up to tubes, just as my father had been, but for a different though related reason. "I was unconscious for three days," she told me, just before she died. "From Sunday to Tuesday."

How Lizzie and I managed *not* to figure out what was happening during those three days is a tribute to defense mechanisms.

Our mother was released into the care of a psychiatrist my father knew, Benny Finesilver. The morning after she came home, Lizzie and I tried not to notice how swollen her arms were. As she opened the newspaper wide across the breakfast table we saw one Band-Aid in each elbow crook. Lizzie and I shot looks at each other. We could believe that "getting help" involved intravenous medication, but was she *really* getting help—or crying out for it?

"Benny says they're safe enough. I trust him." I had my right ear pressed to my mother's closed bedroom door the next morning. "He said, 'No one should suffer like this.' " I leaned in closer, cupped my right ear, stuck my second finger sharply in my left eardrum so I could hear through the wooden door more purely—I had gotten good at this. "No, they *don't know* how they work, but they seem to work. I don't care about my memory. Who needs a memory? I *want* them!" She was talking about electroshock treatments.

Later that week (she never told us where she was going), she lay strapped on a table at a psychiatric clinic. A paddle was attached to each side of her head. An IV drip was injected into the back of her hand, sedating her for the procedure. Then an electric current was shot through the paddles into her brain; she jolted in seizure for forty seconds. It was a primitive process, like kicking a TV to get it going again or hitting the reset button on a computer. After a quiescent period came another spasmic jolt, then another, and another. My mother flapped on that table like a netted tuna for twenty minutes. She hyperventilated extensively. She was wheeled into the recovery room, where she slept for an hour.

Dora and Sam brought her home. One of those Popular Girls I was still trying to make friends with was over. (In my mother's secretiveness about the treatments, she had neglected to tell me that it might be better for me not to have a friend over that day.) Pinioned between weird, homely Dora and dopey, toothless Sam, my mother was stuporous and giddy, stumbling around like a merry drunk, as they anchored and steadied and guided her like two furniture movers on a sloping ocean-liner deck trying to control a heavy, wheeled grand piano.

Dora shot me a most unsubtle wink; she kept her eye clamped closed for two minutes. "Your mother's . . . *cold* . . . is all better!" she gaily shouted. Her acting was as bad as her winking. "She had a bad *cold*, you know. We just have to take her upstairs and lie her down, and then when she wakes up she won't have her . . . *cold* . . . anymore!"

I didn't give a damn what my guest thought. I didn't care that I should be embarrassed at the spectacle. I was so relieved, I wanted to run up and kiss Dora and Sam. I wanted to grab them and do the Calypso! "She doesn't have her cold anymore!" The shock treatments had worked! They had *worked*!

Lizzie and I were getting our mother back.

Chapter Thirteen

BEVERLY HILLS; THE HIGH SEAS;
GREAT NECK, NEW YORK: 1959–1962

W hen one door closes, another door opens." This comfort verse that the Hovers had adopted after Sadie's death became my mother's motto. Snapping her fingers in the air like a band leader, she said it all the time. "When one door closes, another door opens." It was her rallying cry for a life beyond marriage, beyond Ciro's, beyond the two men who had tried to kill each other, and who, in the process, had nearly destroyed her.

After a series of four electroshock sessions, she had sprung, phoenixlike, from the ash heap of suicidal depression. Her recovery was, at least in the short and middle term, nothing less than amazing. Over the years there would be other depressions, including one that was almost as debilitating in terms of her daily life, although without the same suicide risk. Her habit of calling people early in the morning never exactly abated, and the tragedy of Ciro's and her marriage's simultaneous ends haunted her until her death in 1993. But the shock therapies had somehow jerked her back to her "Nancy Goes Shopping" self, and she approached her next three decades of life with an almost infectious appetite for the joy of work.

In the spring of 1958 she got a job, working from home, as West Coast editor of Dell Publications' *Modern Screen* and *Screen Stories*, and several other magazines. She had helped Joan Davis's daughter Beverly write a remembrance of her dead boyfriend James Dean, and David Myers, an edgy young writer who had unaccountably been brought on to edit *Modern Screen*, loved the story so much his acceptance letter consisted of one sentence, "Where have you been all my life?"

My mother and Myers were a great pair. They had the same sense of humor. Their cross-country telephone editorial sessions were full of quips and sarcasm. It was great to hear her laughing again.

She became a kind of den mother to the Schwab's crowd. The hell she had just climbed out of gave her a lode of empathy for the younger person's version of hell that a number of them—such as Nick Adams, the pack leader—were going through. One day I came home from school to find Adams and about six of his friends—Sal Mineo, Natalie Wood, and Connie Stevens among them—gathered on my front lawn, holding up a big ELVIS, WE MISS YOU! sign, on the occasion of their friend's induction into the army, as the *Modern Screen* photographer snapped their picture. A Paul Anka photo shoot required me to assemble a group of girls for a faux pajama party. (Anka, not quite evolved into the well-married lord of the manor he's been for most of the ensuing decades, was obstreperous; he pushed me into the pool clothed, and I reciprocated, unintentionally damaging his watch, which played "Diana" on the hour.) My mother's early help of Philadelphia pop manager Bob Marcucci rated me a meeting with my heartthrob Frankie Avalon and Marcucci's new "next thing," Fabian Forte.

My mother developed other male friends, some straight, like fan magazine and later TV writer Ed DeBlasio, but more often tortured homosexuals, like gravelly-voiced Hollywood *Reporter* columnist Mike Connelly, the "Rambling Reporter." Using her own recent recovery as an example, she rallied a maudlin Mike through many a bender and wee-small-hours depression, and she counseled him through heart disease. (He eventually died in the middle of open-heart surgery.)

Her persona as the compassionate dame and bustling writer-editor set her apart from the slowly increasing ranks of divorced matrons of Beverly Hills. Their tropism was to redecorate their houses or check the Saks sales; hers was to sleuth out Marilyn Monroe's mother in the Riverside sanitarium (I went along for the ride, doing my homework by flashlight in the backseat), pry an interview out of Susan Hayward's skid row–dwelling sister (I eavesdropped from the other room and provided the glazed mug I'd made in art class as a down-and-out-looking photo prop), and debrief Erol Flynn's sixteen-year-old girlfriend Beverly Aadland (I ate a Blum's almondette sundae as she recounted the bearskin-rug seduction). Those other divorcees' agenda was to remarry. It was not my mother's. She was both work motivated *and* vulnerable, independent *and* controlling, but also easily intimidated by men's cool and domineering nature. It was easier for her to be manless. Besides, she'd never find another Danny Weller. Her merry, tragic, soulful neurosurgeon was one of a kind. Other doctors were boring and smug, and either they were married or dating younger women. The men she met—publicists and producers—were fine to flirt, and even have liaisons, with (she discreetly had a few, of various lengths), but she judged them beneath her standards. She turned out to be surprisingly old-fashioned: a one-man woman.

So I went through adolescence with a mother who—depending on the mood I was in when I thought about it—was either a Fabulous Character and a feminist role model before her time or a Dumped Dame and a template for feminine failure. By either definition, the tragedy had neutered her.

. . .

Our Sundays with our father seemed to taper off. Lizzie and I rarely saw him. The loss was most painful to me on Sunday night, when the three of us Weller women would go to Hamburger Hamlet on Bedford Drive, like all the other families. From our booth I would watch daughters and fathers, and study them. Those girls were my age. They were not prettier than I, but they felt entitled. They pouted, cutely, and it didn't backfire on them. They tossed their hair. They speared food off their fathers' plates, tasted it, and wrinkled their noses disdainfully. They "expected things." Their fathers called them "sweetie" or "baby" or "princess," and hooked their large arms around their daughters' heads like football coach to captain after a game. They strolled slowly in tandem to the cashier stand, the father looking well fed and raffishly proud, his face announcing to the boys seated with their own parents, "You just *wish*, buddy."

My heart ached.

My father attended my Hawthorne School graduation. Avoiding the courtyard seats where the families sat, he stood diffidently under the Alhambran arch, as if to say he was just passing through; his purchase on me was remote and tentative. After the ceremony I went home with my mother, but he approached Lizzie. "I'm taking you to a secret place," he told her. (She only recently disclosed this to me.) They drove to a house on Vista del Mar Drive in the Hollywood hills. "I want you to meet my fiancée," he said, and there was—Aunt Yvonne! He reiterated that Lizzie had to keep the meeting secret from me and from our mother.

My sister took in stride our father's springing this by-any-measure startling news that Herman's wife was suddenly his fiancée. She was hungry for this version of a family, a fact he probably intuited. "Yvonne was on best behavior with me," she said. "And I was happy because she was feminine and beautiful and Daddy seemed happy. It seemed so much more normal than life at our house."

Even today, I can barely type these words without feeling anger for my father's cruel use of my graduation to cement a bond with Liz that was explicitly contrary to my feelings. Mostly I feel anger at the sadism he exhibited by shocking my little sister—sweet, still-limping, in-the-palm-of-his hand Lizzie—with that "my fiancée" business. Though she was happy to see Yvonne in that context, the context itself was provocatively jarring. Shame on him.

There may have been a reason he behaved with such poor judg-ment—he was unraveling. Although I had no idea at the time, six months earlier he had gone through the disappointment of his life.

Shortly before our mother's suicide attempt, my father had jour-neyed to New Haven, Connecticut. A portable oxygen tank and tent went along on the trip, which had been made against his doctor's advice. "Danny's cardiac guy told him he shouldn't fly, he couldn't go, he was much too weak for travel," Zeke Manners told me. "They fought about it. Your father got on the plane anyway. Rosie called me from Brooklyn—he'd passed out after getting off the plane. They admitted him to Kings County.

"Your father was hopping mad," Zeke continued. "He had an appointment, and he wasn't going to be sitting in some hospital. He got himself discharged and paid someone—an orderly, I think—to drive him to New Haven in time for his appointment."

The appointment—Tuesday, November 11, 1958, at 1:30 P.M.—was for (at long last) his oral examination for the American Board of Neurological Surgery. After nearly thirteen years of putting the exam off despite requesting applications, he was determined not to miss another opportunity to take this test. On September 10 he had written Leonard Furlow yet again, reiterating the fact that illness had kept him from the last session. Two more letters passed between him and Furlow to confirm this new appointment.

Did he arrive at the examination half blue in the face? Had the questioner noticed his destabilized physical state? Nine days after the exam, this letter was written:

November 20, 1958

Dear Dr. Weller:

I am very sorry to have to tell you officially that you failed to pass the examination recently by the American Board of Neurological Surgery. As I told you, you may repeat the examination upon payment of a $50.00 reexamination fee at any time within the next three years, except that the Board requires a waiting period of one year in order to allow you some time for study.

As I told you, you failed the examination in neurological surgery and in organic neurology, and you were very weak in general surgery. You should certainly put in some time in study on these subjects.

I hope you will be more successful next time.

Sincerely yours,
Leonard T. Furlow, M.D.
Secretary

It is Dr. Furlow's solicitude and his repeated "As I told you" that are most striking and poignant to me. My father was not a man to have anything told to him twice; betraying anxiety or lack of applomb was antithetical to his personality. Obviously, his miserable failure at the orals (a lifetime's work and a career-long emotional investment, and now, this!) had so shocked him that it had forced out his earnest streak; he had committed the uncharacteristic heresy of tugging on Furlow's shirtsleeves.

My father's messy personal life was the buzz of the small, proper Los Angeles neurosurgical world. Even if he was healthy enough to work in L.A. just then, would he be accepted by his peers? Did he even want to stay in the city he told everyone he hated?

On July 16, 1959, Dr. Furlow's replacement at the board, Donald D. Matson, M.D., wrote my father, inviting him for reexamination in November. For the first time ever in his otherwise eager and respectful correspondence with the neurosurgical establishment, my father did not reply.

Clearly, my mother could not financially keep up a large house and swimming pool. We pleaded with her to take no more boarders; the "adventure" had been bizarre and humiliating. So we embarked upon what, among the kids I went to school with, was a dreaded geographical demotion: We moved south of Wilshire. Our mother sold the house on Elm Drive (it was hers in the divorce) and bought a duplex unit consisting of two three-bedroom apartments, one on top of the other, a half block down the street from Beverly Hills High School, where I would enroll. We rented the upstairs to another family and took the downstairs. Though the apartments were homelike, they were just that—apartments. In the Hawthorne School world "apartment" meant disgrace. I had graduated from Hawthorne, of course, and was about to enter Beverly Hills High School, but all those status-conscious Hawthorne girls (as well as students from the more socioeconomically diverse other three elementary schools) were going to Beverly High with me. Liz would attend seventh and eighth grade at Hawthorne, even though we were technically out of its district.

Our mother tried to make the move to Durant Drive a fun event, a next chapter in our life. Indeed, it had its pluses—the configuration of the large apartment was such that Lizzie and I each got our own bedroom, and we were right across the railroad tracks from the brand-new Beverly Hilton Hotel, occasioning all kinds of potential (eventually consummated) adventures, such as hiding in the linen closets and crashing banquets. Mostly our minds were elsewhere: I dreaded high school, and Lizzie longed to go and live with our father.

From late summer through the fall of 1959, my father seemed to have vanished. His lease on the Vista Del Mar house had lapsed. Private investigators determined that he was not in Los Angeles.

"Where *is* he?" I would hear my mother shouting—pleading—on the phone from her bed every morning. (I was back to my habit of pressing my cupped ear to her bedroom door, listening anxiously.) She would ask the question of my father's brother Alex, his divorce lawyer, Leonard Horwin (the father of Lizzie's classmate and, later, cabaret singer, Lee Horwin), and several doctor friends. My father apparently intentionally kept Zeke in the dark, whether to protect his decent, soft-touch friend, whose wife and sister were my mother's two best friends, from a conflict of loyalty, or to protect himself from detection, I can only guess.

The men with whom my mother pleaded refused to give her answers. My father's contention was that my mother had conspired with Herman to kill him, and she was trying to finish the job with her divorce lawyer's "harrassment," as he and his lawyer put it, that took the form of attempts to locate him, extract alimony and child support, and attach any future income. Were such moves fair game from a "wronged wife" (as my mother, with uncharacteristic solemnity, called herself)? Or were they harrassment, given that the infirm recipient was attempting to pick up his life and career after a devastating heart attack? As in any divorce, it would depend on which side of the *v.* your name was on in the filed motion.

As summer turned to fall and there was still no word of him, our concern about his health and welfare turned to panic. There were other feelings, too. For Lizzie, it was pain at being separated from him, "her" parent, and disdain at being stuck in this pathetic, all-female life of ours. I felt a sting of familiar humiliation. I had already gotten used to a house without a father, a daily life without a father, and I had even tried to swallow the fact that my father had had a romance with the one woman who so obviously highlighted my failure as a female. Was the next step sheer evaporation? Were we—Danny's ex-wife and two daughters—now so off the affiliative charts that no one would even pay us the courtesy of informing us of what had happened to him?

Here is where my father was: on the high seas. He had joined the Coast Guard and signed on as a surgeon on a vessel circling the globe—from North America to the South Pacific, and then to the Asian mainland, the Middle East, and Europe. In our life of ironies here was the latest: My father was living out the plot of my mother's novel.

On August 11, 1959, in San Francisco, he was officially sworn in as a staff officer of the U.S. Coast Guard. Going to sea, of course, was what he had desperately wanted to do in 1941, losing the chance because of his heart condition. Back then, that closed door had opened the door to his neurosurgical residency. Now, in 1959, his dismay at his failure on his neurosurgical boards had led him to take another crack at it. He was months away from his fiftieth birthday, and his health was far worse than the first time he'd applied. Even his signature, shaky and broken on the documents I tracked down years later, evinced his phyiscal weakness. However, it was not wartime, and those old leftover warships' missions were civilian and meandering in nature, so the standards were lower. His application was boosted by his credentials as a certified civilian boat captain—of the *Manuiwa*. My father was persistent: He filed a lost document application so that his 1941 merchant marine application could be retrieved and credited; he used his brother Alex as a reference. He *wanted* to go to sea. It turned out that one workhorse vessel—the S.S. *President Polk*—needed a second surgeon, or, at any rate, did not turn down the offer of one. He was accepted. Like his father on the prairie, he had grabbed his little corner of the sky.

Setting off from San Francisco, Staff Officer Weller (in a white Coast Guard uniform) and his fellow officers and crewmates sailed a shipload of missionaries and some tourists, at seventeen to eighteen knots an hour, to Honolulu, then to Yokohama, and after that to Hong Kong, Singapore, Penang, Cochin, Bombay, Karachi, Suez, Port Said, Alexandria, Naples, Marseille, and Genoa. In India there was drama—the bursar had been found smuggling gold bars. My father later told Zeke this story—"Danny said it was like a movie"—which also shows up in the ship's logs.

Yvonne flew to Europe with Ellen and Loring and rendezvoused with my father in France. There they were married, by a local justice in a little village. After his tour of duty they resurfaced as a family in Great Neck, Long Island, the upper-middle-class Jewish suburb in which his friends Danny and Esther Kaufman were living.

My father rented a large modern house—179 Hillpark Avenue—and the Dr. Daniel Wellers joined the country club where the Kaufmans and my father's brother Milton were members. (Milton had married a Nazi-Germany-émigrée ballerina named Irene Sokolsky; they had a daughter, Mona, who, like Alex's Mary Lou, was born in 1946.) My father's health had declined during his tour of duty on the *Polk*. Unable to drive a car, he hired a chauffeur. Esther Kaufman told me, "Danny Weller arrived and said, 'I gave Helen every-thing.' And, 'I'm not worried about my kids—they're well cared for.' My Danny used to say, 'Only Danny Weller would cause a scandal in L.A., go on a ship around the world, get remarried in France, land in New York, sick, with no money, to try to start all over again—and believe he could do it.'"

He tried to set up a practice. He joined the staff of two hospi-tals—Mother Cabrini and Sydenham—that served the poor. "He was well thought of," neurosurgeon Leonard Essman, with whom he worked at Sydenham, told me. "But he was different than the rest. He had a sense of humor." He rented a medical office on East Thirty-sixth Street in Manhattan. Yvonne became his secretary—his new Della.

When I heard that my father had married Yvonne, I cried all night. To have a romance with his own sister-in-law was bad enough, but to marry her? I never believed something that grotesque and insult-ing could happen, that he would transfer the full dignity—the weight of years of my mother's relationship with him—onto her. Not only was there that unseemly familial connection (now mak-ing, perversely and hurtfully, my little cousins as much my father's children as I had been), but Yvonne was the woman who had intimidated and shamed me. What a nightmare this was.

The news of my father's remarriage unleashed rage in me. I stormed around the house like a massively overworked housewife on a night out with a bottle of tequilla. All the good-girl "managing" I had done over the last two years—taking care of my falling-apart mother, pretending to get as excited as she was about the move to this part of Beverly Hills ("more citylike, like Paris!") and this dreary apartment, spending too much time phonily cheering her on as the Plucky Rebounding Careerist in order to forestall my own social failure—fell away, consumed by my humiliated anger.

One day in the fall of 1960 I was huffing around my bedroom in that then familiar state. I was hyperventilating. I was talking to myself. I couldn't hold in my hurt, anger, and humiliation any longer. I sat down and, breathing deeply like a person possessed, I wrote Yvonne a letter. I told her I wanted to run my fingernails down her face until I drew blood, that I wanted to hurt her. I wanted to watch her suffer. I told her I hated her. (Did I tell her I wanted to kill her? No. I was too much the good girl to go *that* far.) I ended my letter with a sad, transparently Elektra-complexed line, "And I am more beautiful than you."

"And I am more beautiful than you!" Wouldn't *any* father have to be just a little flattered by his daughter's throwing her hat in the ring that way? Wouldn't that line have revealed how childlike and in need of parenting I still was, since I was being so blatantly competitive in an adult game?

I addressed the envelope to the Great Neck house and put an airmail stamp on it. I marched to the corner, and, as I slid the letter down the mailbox chute, I realized I had just bet the house, but that it was a principled bet, a wager of conscience. Even before the days when feelings ruled, there was enough in the popular media, and in the cultural air swirling around reasonable, upper-middle-class Jewish households, for me to feel that even this ungainly tantrum pointed to an emotional state caused by a wound inflicted by others that a parent would respond to. My pouts to my father ("Daddy, why can't *you* own a nightclub?") had been fake and ployish, but these emotions, though exaggerated and even ugly, were real. It had to count for something that this letter was a scream of pain to two people who should have expected to hear it.

Furthermore, I knew that, with this melodramatic action, I was sending my father a message: "HELP! Daddy, *love* me!"

My father called me four days later. I walked to the phone—the receiver of which my mother was holding in her outstretched hand, as if to make perfectly clear that she and her ex-husband were no longer speaking—feeling my oats simply at having gotten him to call me. I had read in the Emily Post Q-and-As in *This Week* magazine that it put a remarried parent "over a barrel" when his kid didn't like his new spouse. As I walked from my bedroom to the breakfast room I resisted picturing my father's body rounded over a barrel; it was Yvonne's I wanted there, in the barrel, preferably, going over Niagara Falls or some other dangerous place.

My cockiness quickly vanished.

"You have caused me great pain," my father said, more gravely and angrily than I had ever heard him. "That was an ugly, terrible letter." (Later I would learn that Yvonne didn't even see the letter; he'd intercepted it.) "I'm shocked and ashamed of you. I am very angry. You have caused great pain to someone I love."

I felt stunned and weak-kneed.

My father had one thing left to say, "I do not ever want to talk to you again."

"Ever"? "Again"? After he had disappeared on that ship, after we had feared that each ring of the phone would bring news of his death, after all that earnest grasping at evidence that he was alive, the blithe finality of those words was stunning.

It felt like it took several moments for the desired words to come up into my vocal cords, the way it feels when you are half asleep, slipping into a nightmare of being smothered and can only stop the smothering by screaming.

I said what I wanted to say, "I hate you, Daddy!"

The sound of the plastic receiver slamming down on its cradle was the sound of my heart falling out of my chest to the floor.

Within days I was sunk deep into remorse and regret. I had miscalculated. I realized I had killed my relationship with my father with a foolish diva gesture. Who did I think I was, doing that and expecting to get away with it? Once, many years later, I remembered Sholem Aleichem's Tevye stories. The scene of Tevye in his cart, almost running over his daughter Chaya (who had shamed him by marrying a gentile) as she begs for forgiveness—as she risks her life to plead with him to talk to her, to accept her as his daughter again—stopped me in my tracks. "Papa! May I hope to die if you drive away now!" Chaya pleaded. "Papa, listen to me first!" That is how I had felt.

My emotional banishment was not the end of my father's revenge. One day, soon afterward, I walked up the street to the Beverly Hills Medical Center pharmacy to pick up my prescription for my dermatologist's overpriced antiacne cream. Dr. Paul Levan fashioned his waiting room with a Polynesian theme that included birdsongs, a waterfall, and unending film clips of his family's last vacation to Hawaii. The cream was priced accordingly.

The lady behind the counter looked at my ten-dollar bill and said, "You don't have enough there, dear. It's $21.50."

"No, it's not," I said. "It's always $9.95 for two. Doctor's discount."

She smiled impatiently. "It's $21.50."

She turned and spoke to the pharmacist, who was standing in his raised, godlike lair, behind a row of pill-bottle-filled small paper bags affixed with stapled prescription labels. I watched this white-coated man pick up the phone and call my mother. He was placating her; she was evidently angry. Once, twice, three times, he put on his glasses and checked a piece of paper. This conversation was taking way too long for a simple tube of zit cream.

Finally, the pharmacist put his hand over the receiver and called to the woman who was waiting on me, "Give Sheila there her refills. We'll put it on Mrs. Weller's account."

When I tried to give the woman the ten-dollar bill she wouldn't take it. I walked home with my prescription *and* my ten-dollar bill, confused. Why wouldn't they just take my money? Why had they charged it when I had exactly the right amount?

The next morning, something told me to put my ear to my mother's closed bedroom door. As I had when she had been making her suicide attempts, I listened closely. I could always tell by the tone of her inaudible words if there was something bad-and-important coming—something I had better brace myself for. That day a fog of more than mere dismay—a fog of heartbreak—shrouded her whispers. This called for the special, shock-treatment-sussing-out form of eavesdropping. I cupped my right ear and stuck my finger in my left one. Then I heard it, "It doesn't cost a doctor anything! It's just a professional courtesy. How mean! How *cruel!* Yes: Pobirs, Levan . . . ! Of *course* I'm not going to tell her!"

Pobirs was my pediatrician. Eventually I got her to confirm what I had just deduced: Shortly after I had written that letter to Yvonne, my father had called all my doctors and all the local pharmacies—everyone who, according to the first principles of the Hippocratic Oath, gave my family the traditional medical services and products. With astonishing pettiness—the discount, after all, cost him nothing—he was calling them all to revoke this privilege from me.

My father was disowning me.

In his sick, frightened, angry, cornered state, he must have viewed my graphically threatening letter to Yvonne the same way he had viewed Herman's physical attack and the persistent calls and letters, threatening income attachment, of my mother's divorce lawyer: as another pair of beating fists on his body. That's the only way I can explain today why he did that to me.

Lizzie, too, was medically victimized by the divorce. In a stunningly unethical move, our orthodontist removed her braces months before he should have, leaving her with slightly crooked front teeth today, presumably because he thought my parents' divorce would leave my mother unable to pay for the treatment.

I am sure that my father's summary rejection of me after my epistolary outburst—his inability to see my letter to Yvonne as that of a child needing reassurance—has governed my life in countless ways, maybe even more than I know. In the short term—I was barely a teenager at the time, just coming into my sexual self—it created a black hole where my relationship with the opposite sex should have been. Having a boyfriend was for other girls; like albinos without pigment, I just didn't have the gene for it. So I avoided all contexts where this secret preordained failure of mine would be apparent. I went to noon study hall at school instead of facing the social battlefield on the front lawn or the English patio. I seized as best friends those libidoless, overly goody-good girls whose uncritical tolerance of me made them proxies for my mother. I always managed to be "somewhere else"—in the bathroom or leaving to go home to do my homework—when the cool boys came swaggering into Biff's after the football game or zoomed their T-Birds or Corvettes into a friend's circular driveway. Otherwise that scarlet *D* (Dumped Daughter, Disowned Daughter) on my forehead would light up like a streetlamp—but I couldn't hide out forever.

My mother went back to my bedroom to get me, one day in the summer of 1961. "Sheila, the new boys from across the street are sitting in the den, waiting for you." She seemed as surprised as I was.

There, like a couple of renegades from *Goodbye, Columbus* who had lost their way to Brenda Patimkin's house, were our two new neighbors, a handsome Jewish UCLA medical student and his brother, a rakish-looking artist undergrad. They had just moved in, with their widowed mother (destined to be my mother's friend) and their sister, Lizzie's age (destined to be a good friend of hers). They lived exactly across the street—our houses were like facing chess pieces on a small, otherwise-empty board, our windows in spitting distance of one another.

There was no way this family was not going to be in our face every day. The brothers—Gary, the older; Roger, the younger— looked at me in that cocky, cool-person-to-person way, and said, kidding on the square, that they had seen me on the street and they both had a crush on me.

What cruel God played this trick? I was a tone-deaf imposter who was not only ushered into the first violin chair at the Boston Symphony, but forced to stand up, every night, for a solo.

The nightmare played itself out according to my expectations over the summer. By August the once-smitten Gary was barely saying hello to me, but that was nothing; Roger had taken a nastier tack: He was making fun of me for being a cheerleader (a desperate overcompensation I attempted that year, not unlike my efforts to woo my father with my "cute girl" act). Every night Roger would bellow in a microphone from their balcony, entreating me to come outside and do a cartwheel. With the sigh of a fat person yielding after a grueling day to a nightly gallon of ice cream, I played right into his ridicule and occasionally came out and obliged him.

But this idiotic cheerleader isn't who I am! I thought, burrowing into my mother's office afterward to escape Roger's loud mockery. I knew I was being humiliated, but, as with my antics with my father, I couldn't stop myself from being a partner in the process; there simply seemed no other way to be. The office was still my haven. I would burrow in there, avoiding a social life, pretending to read my mother's articles on Edd "Kookie" Byrnes and Troy Donahue. However, I noticed with alarm, my cover was being blown—the Lennon Sisters were becoming *Modern Screen*'s cash cow. To pretend to be reading those articles would fool no one.

If this smiley, ridiculous cheerleader wasn't who I was, then who was I? That question became more fraught and confusing one night in February 1962, when I was ensconced in my mother's office. A neatly folded cut-out page of the *Los Angeles Times*'s society section caught my eye. My mother didn't usually save things from that page—it reminded her of the stuffy doctors—and she also hadn't circled anything in her familiar red pen. Whatever was important enough for her to have saved also filled her with a certain ambivalence.

My eyes scrolled down the various items. Then I came to "Happy news from New York: Dr. Daniel Weller and his wife, the former Yvonne Ealy, have just welcomed a daughter, Victoria Louise."

I felt like Snow White in the ancient Disney movie: misty, swoony, stuporous, and sleepy-walky. Well, there went my father—going, going, gone. "Movin' o-on down the line," as the Drifters would say. There he was with his new wife, his new baby girl (like I had once been), their backs to me, walking off to some future where I didn't I exist, where I had never existed in the first place.

I developed a gum disease; my gums were bleeding all the time now. "Your gums are crying," the dentist told me. With my new driver's license I got to drive to the dentist myself—he was in a bad part of town. Now that I had no doctor's discount, we got a cheap dentist. I thumbed the radio. What was I hearing? "Trouble in mind, I'm blue, but I won't be blue always . . ."

Trouble in mind: That is just how I felt.

"Trouble in mind. I'm blue . . .": The sound and the words sank into my agreeing bones. "Trouble in mind . . .": What an elegant way to put how I was feeling.

I had eagerly located the station, which broadcast largely from a mysterious place called Dolphin's of Hollywood, right after I got in the car by myself. Sliding the dial around and landing on it was my secret ritual. Then I made the big move from car to home—I set my own radio to it. Gone were the strident, echo-chambered white dee-jays; behind my closed door, day and night, an alternately mournful and elegiac sound now washed over my pink walls and vacuumed up my Daddy-dumped, selfish-healthy-big-sister-of-polio-victim, phony-school-spirited, taunted-by-the-boy-across-the-street-who-started-out-with-a-crush-on-me, tantrum-throwing self. I could start over! Whatever miserably pathetic person I was outside of the closed world of the car or my bedroom, when I listened to "Trouble in Mind" and all the other "trouble" songs ("bad luck and trouble," "livin' in a world of trouble," "lay my troubled head on the railroad tracks and sanctify my mind"), I was a person of worth and authenticity.

The station became my lifeline. One time, I got in the car at midnight, drove straight down Olympic Boulevard, and found it—the exotic Dolphin's of Hollywood—a tiny storefront off Central Avenue. My heart leaped. I savored Charles Brown's seasonal laments, so bathetic, they seemed sung from the jailhouse. I was entranced by the elegiac Reverend James Cleveland, who phlegmily growled, "The love of God . . ." as grandly as Moses with the tablets.

Then I took the next step: I started going down to the African Methodist Episcopal Church on Central Avenue on Sundays, just to be closer to the sound, to hear it live. The only white person there, I would stand shyly in the back, a sixteen-year-old Beverly High cheerleader: blond, Toni hairsprayed, with a teased-topped flip. I would take in Reverend Cleveland—and Lou Rawls, the Pilgrim Travelers, and Little Billy Preston, in his purple satin robe over shirt and tie, bobbing around on his feet with his fat-toothed smile, working those amazing chords out of that battered old organ. Once Reverend C. J. Franklin came all the way from Detroit with his daughters Carolyn, Irma, and Aretha. (Rushing in the back door afterward, "Mom," I said, to the old nightclub talent scout in her, "you would not *believe* this girl's voice!")

My favorite of all was Ray Charles. Blind drug-addict Ray, moaning, "Hard times. No one knows better than I." *Say it, Brother Ray,* I would hum under my breath, as I put on my short orange pleated skirt and my white sweater with the big orange B on it and headed out to the football game. *And can I get a witness?*

Maybe one day I would fall asleep doing my geometry homework and by some miracle I'd wake up in the morning not as myself but as Ray's Head Raelette Margie Hendricks.

Exempt from my father's embargo, Lizzie finally received a summons to visit him in New York. Neither of us had seen him since shortly after my Hawthorne graduation—a full four years earlier. So one day in June 1962 (the lawyers had worked things out so she could stay the summer) the three of us drove to the airport, suitcases packed. Lizzie got on a plane to New York, and my mother and I got on another plane. To avoid going straight home to the dark apartment, we had signed up for a press junket, sponsored by some movie studio for some long-forgotten film that was shooting in Lake Tahoe.

My sister was stunned at how weak our father was. Indeed, from photographs Esther Kaufman later showed me, he was almost corpselike in those months. His features were sunken and seemingly etched in black, as if the spirit of death was pushing through his pink skin and planting its stigmata on him.

He wasted no time telling Liz that he blamed our mother and her lawyer for his state—and he threw me into the bargain. "He would take me to his office," she said, "and, while he worked, he'd give me his Lord & Taylor credit card. Later he'd say [of the purchases made on the card], 'If I ever find out you let Sheila wear any of these clothes, I will not talk to you anymore.' "

Hearing my sister recount those words—sensing, even all these years later, his fury, like a heavy fish smacked across my face—I find myself feeling like the servant girl grown old in de Maupassant's *The Necklace.*

All these years I've felt horrible about that letter to Yvonne. As I revisited that incident from an older and older vantage point, I justified my father's rage at me this way: He was engaged in a love affair and marriage that, however much it hurt me and however sadistic-seeming was his choice of woman, was spontaneous and unbidden. In falling for Yvonne, he had reacted on blind passion. Blind passion sets the person off on a chain of responses to protect the original, passionate choice, and some of those responses (especially to the provocative outbursts of others) will inevitably be excessive. Cutting me off was such a reaction.

Over the decades, I've organized much of my personality around this justification. My outburst against Yvonne and my father's subsequent disowning of me were things I came to understand by seeing them through the lens of a man who was the impassioned protagonist of a drama he could not have predicted, and certainly hadn't willed, for himself. Flailing about wildly, feeling himself the injured innocent, he had lashed out. So it wasn't really, exactly, his fault alone. Therefore, it had to have been partly my fault.

Now, as a result of my research for this book, I know that his affair with his sister-in-law wasn't spontaneous at all. He had rehearsed his incest-tinged leave-taking by persistently imploring my mother's cousin's wife, Ruth Page, to leave her husband and run away with him. He had also (though less persistently and less dead-seriously) propositioned his nephew's wife, Fran Douglas, and my mother's cousin, Hilda Stone (Ruth Page's sister-in-law). *Three* other women within the family before Yvonne! (Were these women just a coincidental sample within a larger sample? If I had tracked down, say, a group of hospital nurses, would I have found that he had hit on them, too, thus making his imprecations to the family women less remarkable? Or was this something darker and more conscious? I will never know.) So, in a very real sense, my father had test-marketed the act of bolting into the arms of a family member. He had lived with, and revved up, this curious impulse of his before he acted on it. Taking up with the likes of Yvonne was almost pre-meditated.

In the de Maupassant story, the servant girl feels responsible for the loss of her mistress's diamond necklace, so, without the mistress knowing, she and her husband hock the rest of their breadwinning lives in order to buy, on credit, a new diamond necklace to replace the old one. Decades later, after they have paid off their debt, the servant and her husband find out that the original necklace hadn't been diamond but paste. They had spent their lives paying a debt they never owed.

My father's reaction to my outburst at Yvonne was the paste necklace, but I psychically paid, all these years, as if it were the diamond.

"You're killing him. You're killing Daddy with the way you have that lawyer call him, and he doesn't have any money," Lizzie stonily announced when we picked her up at the airport at summer's end. She was just fifteen, but she was somber beyond her years—and she was angry. Her face was enclosed by the little Jackie Kennedy–style white scarf she was wearing to go with her checked "shift" dress, and she wouldn't look at our mother or me.

We went to a coffee shop near the airport. Miserable from the tension, everyone made a big deal of looking at the menu.

"Oh, by the way," my sister loudly informed me, with a glower. "Vicki Lou—our baby sister—is beautiful."

I spat my Coke out all over the table. (Where, oh, where, was that sanctifying railroad track for me to lay my troubled head down on?)

Everyone was quiet during the car ride home on endless Sepulveda Boulevard. When we got inside, the dam broke. I can't remember how we ended up there, but Lizzie and I were in her bedroom closet, our hot, wet little teenage-girl bodies wrapped around each other, crying like there was no tomorrow.

"We can't *be* like this to each other!" I said to her.

"I *know!*" she said.

"I *love* you! I can't lose *you* in all this," I said.

"I love *you*, and I can't lose *you*," she said.

We walked out of the closet in our rumpled clothes and told our mother she had to call her lawyer and tell him to stop calling our father—not to ask for more money.

She broke down in tears at the simplicity of it all, at her two daughters' initiation of a peace treaty. Were we all caving in to our father? Probably, but it didn't seem to matter. We all still loved him, and Lizzie had convinced us how terribly sick he was. Our mother had jump-started a respectable career for herself, and we owned this new income-generating house, free and clear.

She called her lawyer and told him to stop all the calls and letters, to withdraw the motions, and to immediately inform our father's lawyer that she was letting up. She didn't want any more attachments. We didn't need any more money.

That evening I prepared to talk to my father for the first time in over a year. The news that my mother would leave him alone—and, possibly, the understanding that he had been terribly wrong to cut me off, to single me out as his enemy—had caused him to retreat from his vow never to speak to me again.

I was scared. What would it be like talking to him again, after the harsh fury of that last conversation? He got on the phone and invited me to come to New York over Thanksgiving. I accepted. It wasn't that easy to erase everything that had happened from my mind and my heart and my nervous system. My father was now this faraway-voiced man who was acting as father to my cousins and who was married to a woman who had always intimidated me, whom I hated, and against whom I had taken a preposterous stand . . . and lost, so badly. Was there still a father-daughter bond beneath all that bloodshed? Could we cut through the thicket of issues and slights that had existed even before any of this awful stuff happened and make a relationship?

Even after my mother bought my plane ticket, I never expected the trip to happen. By October, however, I had become sufficiently focused on seeing my father—on hugging him, on looking in his eyes, on sitting on his toilet-seat lid while he shaved—not to obsess about being in the house with Yvonne, witnessing the spectacle of him being married to Yvonne, and seeing Ellen and Loring in that context, as my stepsiblings. I talked to him once on the phone in preparation for the trip—it was too awkward to talk more than was necessary. I asked him what to bring, and at the end of the conversation he surprised me by saying, "The baby looks just like you, Sheila." Then he said, "She is beautiful, like you."

I hung up the phone and thought, "My father thinks I'm *beautiful?*"

Four days before my flight my father grew gravely ill and was hospitalized. "I want to come now, instead of next week! I'll get on a plane! I'll change my ticket!" I cried to Yvonne, through the long-distance phone wire.

"That won't be necessary," she said, evenly.

I wanted to scream, "Damn you, damn you, damn you to hell! If I don't get on the plane right now, I'll never see him!"

I said no such thing. I couldn't risk it.

He called me that night, from his hospital bed. His voice was so weak I could barely hear him.

"Oh, I've made mistakes," he said.

"No, you haven't!" I said, in a panic.

"Yes, I have."

"Oh, no, Daddy! Don't think like that! You haven't!"

He would not be appeased. After living all his life with bitter, blithe selfishness—with the solipsism of the self-invented man—he was now acquiring a conscience. "I have made mistakes. I have not been good," he said, his voice full of sorrow. "You don't see this now, Sheila, but one day you will."

That pointed prophecy set me to sobbing.

Then he said, "I'm so sorry, Sheila. Forgive me."

I lost control. "Of *course* I forgive you! I *love* you!" I wailed, blubbering through the phone wire. It was too late for the weak Kleenex joke. It was too late for humor.

Many years later, during the last segment of *The Mary Tyler*

Moore Show, I (along with the rest of America) watched Mary Richards depart her newsroom office, then walk back into it on an afterthought and turn a last, forgotten light off. I, unaccountably, burst into hysterical tears at that moment.

I was that last remaining light, and my father's apology to me was his last-minute return to the room, his finger on the light switch.

Early the next morning the phone rang. My mother picked it up and asked, loudly and harshly, "What is it, Esther?" She had never liked Esther Kaufman. Then she screamed, "*TELL* me!"

I didn't hear her hang up the phone. I only heard her crying.

"Dr. Daniel Weller, Neurosurgeon, 52," the *New York Times* obituary headline read. It was only three paragraphs long. "His widow Yvonne" and "a daughter, Victoria" were listed as his rightful survivors. The three of us were listed in the past tense. "His first marriage to the former Helen Hover of Los Angeles ended in divorce. They had two daughters, Elizabeth and Sheila, both of Los Angeles." *Had* two daughters: It was like a dismissal.

My father almost didn't have a funeral. He died penniless and his brothers threatened not to pay for it. We didn't go because it was far away—anyway, as my mother always said, you don't go from west to east: That's going backward.

Seventeen years later, on the way to reckoning with this whole story, I would make a pilgrimage. I would hunt out my father's grave (it was in an unkempt, low-rent corner of the cemetery, and it bore the cheapest and most indistinguishable of markers), and there I would lay a single yellow rose—for his favorite song, for our shaving duet.

For the funeral itself, on November 23, 1962, we sent three white roses. The three white roses lay on the pine box as it was lowered into the Brooklyn ground. It was the same Brooklyn ground that all of them, the three of them—my father, my mother, and my uncle—had run around upon as big-dreaming youngsters with nowhere to go but up and west, with all the world to conquer.

AFTERWORD

And so our lives continued. Lizzie (Liz, by now) and I both went to college at the University of California at Berkeley during the most exciting times there, and then moved to New York. We got caught up in the adventures of the 1960s. Then we battened down, applying the work ethic that coursed through both sides of our lineage, to get on with our lives: she as an entertainment industry attorney; I, as a journalist and author.

Back on Elm Drive, via *West Side Story* and Drifters' songs, I had fallen in love with New York. I went on to make my life there, living in Greenwich Village all these years. (That I chose to go "backward" and settle in the retrograde East never failed to amaze, and disturb, my mother.) Liz returned quickly to Los Angeles (many years later, she relocated to Atlanta). It was always easier for her, the less maternally enmeshed daughter, to live close to our mother, whose personality—like a fine cheddar—became stronger as she aged. Within her little world—of old movie stars, publicists, hairdressers, opportunists, tip merchants, and wealthy party-givers—she was iconic. I alternately embraced and fought my emotional dependence on this wise, loving, and sometimes maddening woman until she died, vir-

tually in the middle of an *Enquirer* deadline, at age eighty-one, in September 1993. She was my lifeline, and she was a force of nature.

Liz and I made solid marriages to good men—Jack Fiman and John Kelly, respectively. Liz has two beautiful, talented daughters, Rennie and Casey. John and I have a son, Jonathan, of whom we are almost inexpressably proud. Before Jack's tragic death in 1997 we would often vacation together, both families, at the Ritz Carlton Hotel in Laguna Niguel in early September. At day's end we would sit around the swimming pool. Waiters would bring drinks and a singer/pianist would fill the air with wistful songs. In that cusp-of-fall melancholy, the scene—pool, waiters, pianist, songs, and the fading sun—was hauntingly resonant of our childhood. Yet here Lizzie and I were, adults, with our wonderful families. We had carried on—and we had overcome.

If we flourished, it was not so for Herman's children. It was through them that the skein of our family's tragedy continued.

Herman himself gave up on life early on. He spent the last

(almost thirty) years of his life in a cluttered apartment on Hollywood Boulevard, typing his memoirs on the back of Ralph's Market
flyers. It anguished my mother to watch her once-idolized brother
sink into hasbeenhood so unresistingly, so wholly.

Much of his inertia came from heartache. On July 14, 1976, his
and Yvonne's twenty-three-year-old daughter Ellen—sweet, lovely,
"cautious and responsible" (as the newspapers would put it) and
(like our Aunt Sadie, whom none of us got to meet) a talented
pianist—disappeared from Manhattan. She had been living alone
after graduating from college with a degree in biology and a minor
in music. A notation in her calendar indicated that she had made a
date with a man who, it was later revealed (through a check of his
aliases) was a photographer with a record for rape. Ellen's bones
were eventually found in a wooded area in Westchester County, and
the photographer was convicted of abducting and murdering a
twelve-year-old girl in California. (He remains on death row in a
California prison.) An arrest was never made in Ellen's murder.

Yvonne married her third husband, garment-industry lawyer
Reuben Schwartz, shortly after my father died. She and Schwartz
had a daughter, Charlotte—Yvonne's fourth child. Like a character
in a soap opera, Yvonne hid the details of her life between her first
and third marriages from my half sister, Vicki. Vicki grew up thinking Reuben Schwartz was her biological father.

Yvonne Schwartz and her family made their home in a large
apartment in a prewar building in Gramercy Park, not a mile from
where I lived in Greenwich Village. My hidden little sister and I
were thus within bumping-into distance of one another in Manhattan. I knew this from Loring (who was now calling himself by his
middle name, Ian), who had been kicked out of that apartment and
had spent his adolescence living with Herman in L.A. Ian had been
a somewhat difficult boy, but he wasn't incorrigible. The real reason

he was made to leave his mother's home, Esther Kaufman told me, was that Yvonne's husband Reuben found him too hard to handle.

Ian worked as a messenger for a record company. He married a very nice young woman named Renee. They had a son named Nicholas. Nick was slightly younger than my son Jonathan. During one of my trips home to L.A., Ian and I got our toddlers together. "My mother doesn't want to meet her grandson," he told me, as our little boys played with Legos on my mother's floor. "It's her loss."

"What kind of woman doesn't even want to meet her grandson?" I asked my psychoanalyst, the late, eloquent Fred Wolkenfeld.

Fred was a somber man. The weight of the world always seemed on his shoulders. "A very unhappy woman," he answered.

The urge to find Vicki was always with me. Especially in my twenties and early thirties—when melodrama is one's middle name, and when I was dealing with the "issue" of my father in that raw, intense, and finally tedious way that is a jumble of youth, psychoanalysis, feminism, and solipsism—I kept imagining I would recognize her on the street or secretly sleuth out her life, in any case, bond with her. However, I did nothing. My half sister and I occupied the same wedge of Manhattan for thirteen years—between 1967, when I moved to New York, and 1980, when she went off to college—but we remained hidden from each other.

Then, in 1990, Liz and I decided it was time to try to meet her. She was twenty-eight, living away from her mother. We hired a private detective. It proved remarkably easy. The detective called the next day and said, "Turn on your fax. I am sending you your sister's married name, address, and phone number."

The unexpected surname, the 215 area code—the "thereness"—

radiated on the slick paper, blurry with significance. I sat down and, on behalf of Liz and me, typed a letter:

Dear Victoria:

After so many years of imagining this moment, we find ourselves a bit tongue-tied in beginning. Please bear with us. We feel great tenderness, hopefulness, and no small amount of awkwardness and presumptuousness in approaching you. The last thing we wish to do is to discomfit or startle you, or for you to think we are trying to intrude on your life. We deeply respect the wholeness and integrity of your life—a life we know nothing about—and the fixed completeness of your sense of family.

But how sad it would be for any more years to go by without reaching out and introducing ourselves to you—without getting a chance to finally know you, as we've always dreamed of doing.

We are your sisters.

I burst into tears as I read Liz that last sentence.

Vicki called Liz right after she received the letter. She told her that she had sent a copy to her mother, that she hadn't intended to reply, but her husband saw the trouble we went to and urged her to at least call us. "I can't meet with you," she told Liz. "My mother would think Herman put you up to it."

When Liz called me—after midnight, New York time—with this news, both of us were crestfallen—and astonished. To think that Herman, that sad deadweight of a man, had any pull on us was ludicrous, and that this young woman was still so obedient to her mother was breathtaking. Nevertheless, Vicki did call me, and I can't remember what I said, but that conversation turned things around. We planned a three-way meeting in Buck's County, Pennsylvania, near where Vicki lived with her husband, for a time a few months away, when Liz would be visiting New York with her family.

When we got to the appointed bed-and-breakfast on a warm May day in 1991, the innkeeper smiled and informed us, "Ah, 'Weller.' Your sister already checked in." "Your sister": Liz and I had smiled, touched that Vicki had chosen that designation.

We hugged right away. She had the fat Weller cheeks! She was adorable! We lined up for a picture, snapped by the innkeeper, who could tell this was a special reunion, and we laughed at how our heads lined up. We were all the same height, exactly!

Vicki told us that, all her life, she had secretly suspected that she had another father. "My sister Charlotte and I looked so different." She had those disembodied premonitions ("I dreamed of being a doctor"; "I thought I'd have twins") that pointed to hidden details in her geneology, but those doubts were private. Then one day when she was in her late teens, Ian had spat out the name "Daniel Weller." She went to the public library and looked up his obituary. There was her mother's name, "his wife, the former Yvonne Ealy," and hers, "a daughter, Victoria Louise." She confronted her parents, Yvonne and Reuben, and they told her the truth—at least some of it.

I had approached meeting Vicki with an emotional agenda. I wanted the writer in me—the lover of complex characters—to push the petulant daughter past her anger. I was a feminist—I believed that women were noble. I longed to see Yvonne, through Vicki's eyes, as a worthy soul. It was time to get past my crippling one-sided version of her. In the same way that parents of dead soldiers want to know their sons went down for something essential—not by accident, not in friendly fire—I needed to leave that weekend thinking, "So, my father's throwing away of his life, and his throwing away of me—it was worth it!"

But everything Vicki told me about Yvonne that weekend ("My mother loves it when I tell her she's pretty"; "I used to make her place cards for her dinner parties") only cemented my long-nurtured image of shallow vanity. Vicki opened her wedding scrapbook—and there was the deep-middle-aged Yvonne, stout and blond and toughly matronly looking. A line popped out of my memory's anguished deep storage and danced impishly around my consciousness. "And I am more beautiful than you!" Now it was true. I enjoyed that.

Vicki evaporated from our lives for a few years.

My mother had once said, with a rueful laugh, "God, I hope Herman dies before me—I need a little peace." He did not oblige her. She died in September 1993; he held on, in a nursing home, until April 1996. He was placed in the crypt, which she had paid for long in advance, next to hers. (My mother chose an above-ground burial. A friend suggested that was because she wanted "to stay a part of the action.") Liz and I were left to foot the bill for Herman's funeral, but, in a gesture of thrift (as well as, perhaps, of leftover anger for his attempt to kill our father, and for the grief he caused our mother), we declined to spring for a cryptstone right away.

I felt guilty visiting my mother's crypt and seeing Herman's conspicuously undemarcated adjacent one. "Help Herman out! Your uncle used to be so big in Hollywood!" I could hear her soul sputtering, plaintively.

About a year after his death, the accountant for the *National Enquirer* called, desperately trying to find a home for a stale-dated check that had been returned to them. The check was for $400, to my mother. I read the notation—Liz Taylor/Larry Fortensky—and smiled. My mother had supported herself (and helped us, whenever we needed it) by pounding out one tabloid story after another, working late at night, for years. God bless this plucky, most original woman.

Liz and I used the $400 to give Herman a proper headstone, with the etched saying "Through these portals . . ." that anyone viewing the words would take to mean the entrance to the afterlife. Liz and I knew better.

Vicki surprised me by calling, out of the blue, one day in 1999. She had read an article of mine that was the rudimentary beginning of this book in *Vanity Fair* magazine. She called to say she was so happy I had written it. Reading the story of the family had liberated her—and had almost changed her life. This was a different Vicki: gone was the uncritical obeisance to her mother. She had two children; she was interested in thinking for herself and openly exploring the truth about the past. She was tougher.

We spoke every few weeks for a while. We made those extravagant mutterings about getting together—after all, we only lived a few hours apart—but we could never seem to make a date and keep it. The melodrama of our siblinghood, so fraught all those years earlier, had faded to the busy women's dance of promises, then demurrals over crowded datebooks. Live long enough and all mysteries become routine, I began thinking.

Vicki had wanted to reconcile with Ian, whom she hadn't talked to since he had been kicked out of the family. By way of a tearful, four-hour phone conversation, they did so.

Ian, by then, was divorced from Renee, and Nick was living with his father. The two times I spoke to Nick on the phone (I had called his father in hopes of finding old photos for my *Vanity Fair* piece), he struck me as an unusually lovely and intelligent young man. He told me how much he wanted to be a writer. "You're so mature; you seem like such a fine young man," I said, unconsciously appropriating my deceased mother style of enthusiasm while feeling sorrow for the destroyed connections among the younger members of my bizarrely configured family.

What I did not know was that Nick—almost-brilliant, lovely Nick—was also a diagnosed schizophrenic. He had been in and out of psychiatric hospitals. Twice he escaped confinement. The second time Ian assisted Nick's escape. Perhaps he, who had been a shunted-off son, did not want his own son packed off or warehoused.

Vicki and Renee considered Ian's misguided championing of Nick—his refusal to accept Nick's illness—very dangerous; they vigorously opposed it and tried to have Nick rehospitalized.

In March 2001 Nicholas Hover, seventeen, threw himself off a tall building in L.A. and killed himself. Two months after that Ian Hover, guilt-wracked over his son's suicide, shot himself to death. Of that entire family—Herman, Yvonne, Ellen, Ian, and Nicholas—only Yvonne survived. When the coroner called Yvonne to ask her what her son's birthday was, she angrily said she didn't even remember it.

I had once wanted the writer in me to push the angry daughter toward some enlightened epiphany about this woman, my lifelong nemesis. I had needed that in order to make the risks and losses of our family saga seem like a worthwhile journey; but sometimes—in untidy true life—empathy and epiphany are not in the cards. Sometimes all you're allowed is to say, "Character is destiny," and then shrug, be happy you survived as you did, count your—many—blessings, and get on with it.

ACKNOWLEDGMENTS

When, after thirty years as a writer, you have finally gotten around to taking a deep breath and attacking the subject of your family (just as the memoir train has issued its final boarding call and is about to pull out of publishing's station), you are right to expect a difficult journey. Writing about other families—a neat, bordered enterprise where emotion is limited, signposts are plentiful, and ignorance is bliss—does not prepare you for diving into the murky narrative swamp of your own family's life. For their patience and faith while I tangled with the creatures in that swamp, I heartfully thank my editor, Diane Higgins, and my agent, Ellen Levine. For their great support during my dark moments I thank my husband, John Kelly, my son, Jonathan Kelly, and my sister, Elizabeth Weller. And for riding to my rescue, waving her magic pencil-wand, just when I had almost given up, there aren't words enough to thank Elisa Petrini, book doctor—and, now, friend—extraordinaire.

I thank all those who graciously consented to being interviewed for this book. Sharing their memories of the Sunset Strip during those great old days were: Army Archerd, Burt Boyar, Jim Bacon, Jim Byron, Reggie Drew, Irving Fein, Gerry Galian, Johnny Grant, Mary Scott Hardwicke, Frank Liberman, Johnny Oldrate Sr.,

Johnny Oldrate Jr., Manuel Reyes, George Schlatter, Nick Sevano, Sylvia Wallace, Edith Weiss, Mark Wanamaker, Willie Wilkerson, and Andy Williams. People who spoke honestly about members of my family were: Mona Birk, Vicki Heller, Esther Kaufman, Gloria Luchenbill, the late Zeke Manners, Ruth Page, Fran Douglas, Buna Rosenbloom, Hilda Stone, and, of course, my sister, Liz Weller. Years ago, before I had even conceived this book, Dr. Irving Newman did, too.

Helping me to understand neurosurgery then and now were Dr. Charles Fager, chairman emeritus of the department of neurosurgery of the Lahey Clinic (how honored was I to speak to someone who knew Poppen, Horrax—and Cushing) and Dr. Victor Ho, associate professor in the department of neurosurgery at New York University. These two gracious men took time out of their busy days to help me familiarize myself with this most difficult science that was my father's life's work. I am immensely grateful for their invaluable aid.

I would never have been able to reconstruct my mother's career as a movie magazine writer without the assistance of her dear friend Marvin Paige, whose archive of old movie magazines, studio press releases, and Hollywood memorabilia is a treasure trove of a glorious lost world. Lydia Boyle generously assisted me, in countless ways, from the very beginning. Her great affection for my mother, her former *Enquirer* comrade, informed the many small and large tasks she performed during those overwhelming first months: the clips she assembled, and the phone numbers and spot details she ceaselessly acquired. David Newman and Laurie Sarney of Research Unlimited Associates were trivia sleuths extraordinaire. The patchwork of arcana they dug up—on the 1920s treatment of rheumatic fever, the Jackson Whites, Gold Rush prospectors, Jews in Brooklyn, Stork Club debutantes—helped give texture and specificity to this story.

Reggie Drew: Thank you for your wonderful pictures of the nights at Ciro's, taken by Nancy Caporel, and by you. There are many more where these came from, and they're available to others by contacting: reggiesciros@aol.com.

Specialty archives and libraries, and the experts therein, were a godsend.

Dina Abramowicz of the Yivo Institute for Jewish Research generously led me to the congregation where my great-grandfather was cantor, and to the town in Lithuania from which the Wellers emigrated. Staffers at the New York Tenement Museum and the Henry Street Settlement patiently answered my additional questions.

The day that Michael P. Musick, reference archivist at the Old Military and Civil Records at the National Archives and Record Administration in Washington, D.C., called me to say he had located my grandfather Louis's cavalry enlistment papers in the *Index to Indian Wars Pension Files,* a lifetime of doubting that wonderful story went gloriously out the window. Sandy Cohen, archivist of the Jewish War Veterans of United States, directed me to Musick. Then (an embarrassment of riches!), I was lucky to have historian Guy Fringer—expert, enthusiast, and gentleman—agree to go to the archives and pore over the century-plus-old muster rolls, photocopy them, analyze them, and send them all to me. At the Oklahoma Historical Society, library technician Brian Basore and photo archivist Chester Cowan located and sent me images of my grandfather's days in the cavalry. Jack Reuter, tour guide and interpretor at the Fort Reno, Oklahoma, visitors center, authoritatively filled me in on the day-to-day life of Troop G of the Fifth U.S. Cavalry. Endless thanks to you all.

Gratitude to Jane Barger, of the board of directors of the Vandergrift, Pennsylvania Historical Society, and Beth Caporali, the society's museum director, for giving me a vivid image of my father's
birthplace; to Joy Holland, assistant division director of the Brooklyn Collection of the Brooklyn Public Library, for peeling back the
layers of time and reclaiming elegant Highland Park and Arlington
Avenue, as the neighborhood and street appeared during my
mother's girlhood; to the staff at Room 100 of the main Forty-
second-Street building of the New York Public Library, where I
spent weeks staring through the lens at the old newstype, turning
and turning the spool, plunged into the world of steerage-class
immigrants in the 1880s, the influenza epidemic of 1918, and the
cheeky pragmatism of women in the 1920s and 1930s, exemplified
by "Nancy Goes Shopping."

The Billy Rose Library of the Performing Arts at Lincoln Center
brought me my mother's *Click* and *Radio Guide* pieces and transported me into the dazzling world of Florenz Ziegfeld and Earl Carroll. In the Motion Picture Academy of Arts and Sciences Library
in Los Angeles and the Beverly Hills Public Library I found rare old
books on the history of Los Angeles and Hollywood.

In uncovering the details of my father's medical career, I was
reliant on the kindness of many. Bottomless thanks to Mary Louise
Sanderson, administrator at the American Board of Neurological
Surgery in Houston. I had called her early in my journey, identify-
ing myself only as Daniel Weller's daughter and asking if the board
still retained his records; she briefly looked, then said no. I did not
know that as soon as I hung up, something made her go look again.
She found the bulging file, but, to her distress, she had no way to
reach me: I had not left my number, or even the city I lived in.
(That's how emotionally gnarled starting a family memoir can be—
I had abandoned my usual journalistic thoroughness, without even

realizing it.) I called her a full year later, and she was so happy I did. I was sent the rich, invaluable file, with its heartbreaking final chapter, which did so much to solve the mystery of my father's tempestuous rebellion in the last few years of his life. All the details of my father's career—the names and dates of his publications, the letters of application and recommendation—that connected and provided context for the colorful stories he had told me about Alice, the Sylvius teenagers, Poppen, and Globus as I walked with him through Cedars of Lebanon and Queen of Angels hospitals and sat on his lap in his study. They were all here, enabling me to descend into the deep and bring up the lost continent of Atlantis of his life as a neurosurgeon.

Chris Phillips, archivist at the Congress of Neurological Surgeons (formerly the Harvey Cushing Society) was so welcoming and personable, and, through the Congress's cyber-museum of neurosurgery, supplied me with invaluable biographies of and speeches by the specialty's pioneers and giants. I was lucky to be able to speak to Dr. Jean Hawkes, Dr. Leonard Essman, and Dr. Aidan Raney and to draw on their memories of Daniel Weller, neurosurgeon. Appreciation to William Jacobs, cataloging librarian at Cedars-Sinai Medical Center; to archivist Barbara Niss at Mt. Sinai Medical School; to Robert K. Williamson III, records and archives administrator at the American Medical Association; to assistant dean for student affairs and registrar Sophie Christoforou, and archivist Jack Tremaine at the State University of New York Downstate Medical Center. Also helpful were the adminstrative staffers at the University of Missouri Medical School, Lenox Hill Hospital, Cabrini Medical Center, Kings County Hospital, and Southern California's City of Hope, and San Bernardino General, and Kern County General Hospitals. Thanks to all of you.

Finally, the library of the New York Academy of Medicine in

Manhattan is an extroardinary chamber. Sitting in that stately, tranquil room, under those high ceilings, the cares of the city disappear and the majesty of pure medical science is the air you breathe. The library is genteel—you turn in your request slip, sit at your appointed seat, look out the high windows at the Central Park trees and think of your life, and precious, musty old books are handed to you by polite helpers. Leafing through the crackling, yellowed pages—finding my father's papers—became a peace-making spiritual experience for me. Long decades after he, genuinely hurt, had accused me of not caring about his career, I was proving him wrong—I was coming full circle. The people who run that elegant library were accomplices in the healing of my soul as much in the advancement of my research.

Sleuthing out and tracing my father's desperate end-of-life caper—his running off to sea on the S.S. *President Polk* (as well as his much earlier attempt to join the merchant marine)—involved many helpers. Thank you to Daniel Nealand, director of the National Archives and Records Administration, Pacific Sierra Region, in San Bruno, California; to Don Gill at the Merchant Marine Academy on Long Island; to Bill Koyman at the J. Porter Shaw Library in San Francisco; and finally to Miss Celestine at the Coast Guard National Personnel Records Center in St. Louis. I called Miss Celestine on my cell phone during my grand jury duty, and when she said she had located the logs of my father's tour of duty on the high seas I yelped for joy in the middle of a drug indictment.

There is a sweet, ironic lesson in the fact that those who gave us life—those who loved us and raised us—can sometimes best be known, long after their deaths, through the stream of hidden records, the jottings of dreams, goals, desperations, even simple bureacratic notations, that have fallen into the keep of the vaults, archives, and libraries we never thought to look in while they were living or in the years just after they were taken from us. Thank you, all you helping strangers. With your innocent dispassion and your sheer incidentalness, you held a special flashlight on my beloved parents.